A Subsidiary of
Henry Holt and Co., Inc.

First Edition—1994

ISBN 1-55828-356-0

Printed in the United States of America.

10 9 8 7 6 5 4 3 2 1

Library of Congress Cataloging-in-Publication Data
Erdos, Dawn.
Fractal design painter / Dawn Erdos.
p. cm.
Includes index.
ISBN 1-55828-356-0 : $34.95
1. Computer graphics. 2. Fractal design painter. I. Title.
T385.E69 1994
006.6'869--dc20
94-21719
CIP

MIS:Press books are available at special discounts for bulk purchases for sales promotions, premiums, fund-raising, or educational use. Special editions or book excerpts can also be created to specification.

For details contact: Special Sales Director
MIS:Press
a subsidiary of Henry Holt and Company, Inc.
115 West 18th Street
New York, New York 10011

Book Design: Dawn Erdos

Cover Art: John Derry

Development Editor: Cary Sullivan

Production Editor: Patricia Wallenburg

To Michael Erdos

who introduced us to the worlds of fine and commercial arts while we were still young and impressionable, and provided us with the foundation we needed to get where we are today.

Acknowledgments

We would like to thank the many people who helped make this book possible:

Stephen Manousos, Mark Zimmer, Daryl Wise, and John Derry at Fractal Design Corporation for their valuable input and support. Steven Berkowitz, Publisher, and Cary Sullivan, Managing Editor, for continuing to provide us with an avenue to publish our books.

Patty Wallenburg for her superb production skills. Joanne Kelman for her technical assistance. Erika Putre for gracefully handling many details.

Dennis Orlando, John Derry, Gary Clark, and Richard Noble, as well as the many other talented artists in this book, for letting us pick their brains.

The Best family for providing us with a great environment during a time of transition.

Jeffrey and Ronni Erdos for the Ben & Jerry's connection.

CONTENTS

PREFACE

Hi! I'm Mark Zimmer, the original and still primary author of Painter. When I was little I was an incessant artist. I worked in pencil, ballpoint pen, and fine point felt marker, often in full color. By the time I was 18, I was drawing portraits and sketching landscapes. These early excursions into art and design were absolutely essential first steps on the path to Painter. But first technology had to catch up.

I have long considered tablets and paint programs to be very interesting. In 1975 I started working at Calma, a computer-aided design company in Silicon Valley, where I met Tom Hedges (another author of Painter). There we were introduced to digitizing tables (which were as big as battleships then) made by CalComp. In 1983, at Tricad, I worked with a digitizing tablet, the Summagraphics Bit Pad One, and built my first 8-bit paint system as a way to retouch images created in a 3D rendering environment I had written. In 1985, I started working on PatEdit, a program for latchhook rug design and pattern editing. That's when I first hit on the idea of simulating charcoal on a computer. Back then on the desktop there were only mice to draw with. Wacom's cordless pressure-sensitive tablets were introduced to the desktop two years later and it was only then when the concept of a natural-media paint program became feasible. By the way, PatEdit became GrayPaint which became ImageStudio finally in 1987. By then Tom Hedges and I had formed Fractal Software. To Tom's credit, he saw the advent of scanners to be a primary reason to develop image processing software. So Tom and I then developed ImageStudio and then ColorStudio for Letraset and we were plunged fully into the world of image processing, color separation, visual effects, and incidentally, pressure support for our paint brushes.

But it wasn't until 1990 that I began work on Painter. With all of this image processing work, I began to feel that I had lost the focus of my original work: to make the computer a valid medium for artists. I had been working on a model for the interaction between pencil and paper since 1987, so I began to implement some of that research using a pressure-sensitive tablet and a Mac II at home. This experimentation became Painter. Finally in 1991, we formed Fractal Design Corporation to market Painter.

So, I am especially pleased to see a book on our product. This book is beautifully illustrated and also features sections on artists who work with Painter to create works of wonder. As I read over the proofs for this book, I have concluded that these pages should be required reading for any serious artist who wants to use the computer as a medium.

Mark Zimmer

May 1994

Aptos, California

Section I

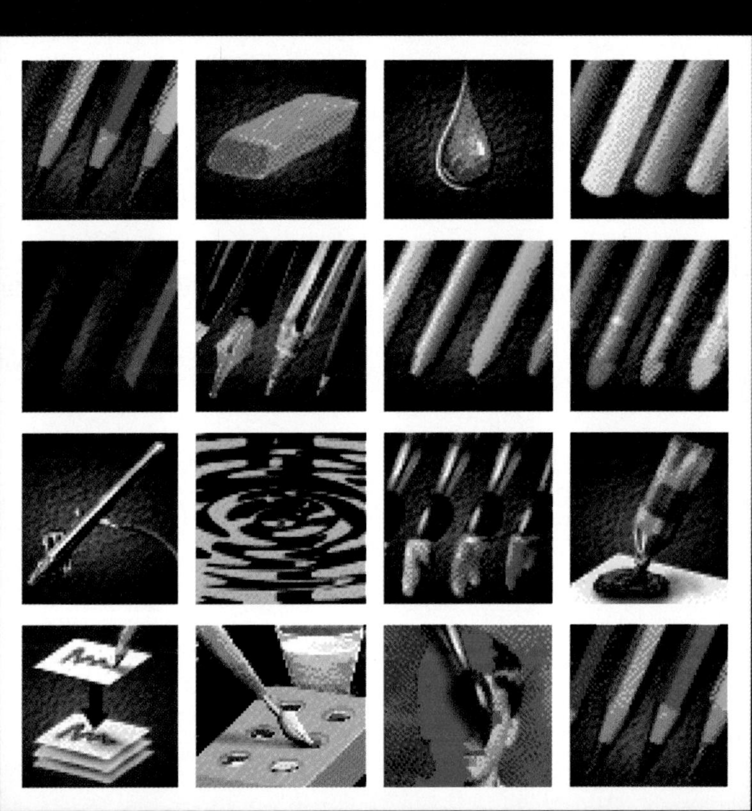

Getting Started in Your Electronic Studio

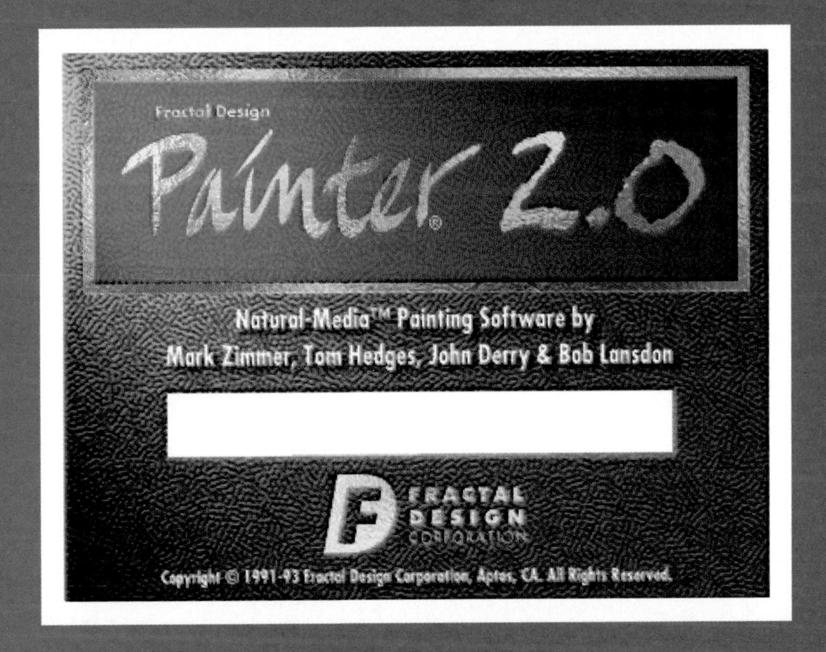

CHAPTER 1

INTRODUCTION

Welcome to Fractal Design Painter! With Painter you'll be able to work with all of the traditional art tools you're used to, as well as many new digital features. In addition to pen, pencil, chalk, pastels, oil paint, water colors, and friskets, you now have access to powerful image-editing options that let you work with scanned photographs or illustrations, add light sources, adjust contrast, change density, sharpen images, create marbled effects, rotate, distort, and many other digital options. Painter also provides you with choices for surface textures, including different types of water color paper, canvas, and Bainbridge board.

There are many advantages to working in Painter's electronic studio: You never run out of paint or canvases. You don't have to worry about destroying your brushes if you don't clean them properly. You don't have to worry about the limits of your studio space. You have a palette of 16 million colors—there aren't many traditional artists who have a palette like that! You can work dry mediums over wet mediums, for example pastels over oil paint, and other unusual combinations of mediums can be used in new ways. You can literally apply a medium to *thousands* of textures, and even select individual areas in a painting to emphasize, such as the dimples on an orange.

In an electronic studio you also have the ability to try a vast array of effects on a painting without ever changing the original. The tools available in Painter allow you to explore other options without ever damaging a painting—you can try something different without destroying the original work!

Painter also enables you to view detail and composition simply by clicking your mouse. You can zoom into the most minute detail, then zoom all the way back to view it as if you were 10 feet away.

We interviewed a lot of artists while creating this book. We kept hearing phrases such as "it's like magic" over and over again. As you'll read in Section II, many artists feel Painter has not only changed the way they work, but the attitude and enthusiasm with which they do that work.

TECHNICAL CONSIDERATIONS

One of the features of Painter that is so often highly praised is its natural, intuitive interface. First, however, we will address a few digital topics before jumping right into using Painter.

SYSTEM REQUIREMENTS

Painter runs on all Macintosh II, Performa, Centris, and Quadra series computers. While this is true, performance on 68020- and some 68030 based computers (most Macintosh II and Performa models) may be slower than you desire. The speed of any Macintosh will benefit from the installation of an accelerator board.

System Software

Painter needs 32-bit QuickDraw to operate, so you'll need Apple System 6.0.5 or later, and Painter supports System 7.0 or later.

Memory

Painter will run with 2.5Mb of RAM, although not terribly efficiently. Fractal Design Corporation recommends 4Mb. We recommend 12- to 16Mb, or more if you'll be working with more than one file at a time, or if you plan to run other programs (such as Photoshop) at the same time you are running Painter. You'll also need more RAM if you use a Power PC.

Painter takes up only about 3Mb on your hard drive, but your art files can get *very* large—some of the art files used in this book are well over 10Mb *each*. It may sound a bit flippant, but use the same rule of thumb for hard disk space as for RAM: as much as you can afford.

If you plan on sending large graphics files to a service bureau or printer for output, you may want to investigate the necessity of a high-volume transportable system, such as a cartridge drive (44Mb or 88Mb, by SyQuest), Bernoulli drive (44Mb or 90Mb, by Iomega), floptical drive (a high-capacity floppy disk using laser technology), or an optical drive. Before purchasing a transportable media drive, please check with your service bureau to make sure it supports the system you plan to purchase.

Display

A color monitor is recommended, but Painter also works well with a grayscale monitor. Painter is designed to run with a 24-bit color board (16 million colors), but an 8-bit board (256 colors) produces adequate results with some *dithering* (pixellation) of the image. If you are a perfectionist and want to see very accurate on-screen results, spring for the 24-bit board.

Input Devices

You can create wonderful art using your mouse or a standard tablet, but Painter supports the use of Wacom, CalComp, Summagraphics, or Kurta pressure-sensitive graphics tablets. If you shop around, you can find a tablet for less than $300 and we highly recommend using one. Although you can achieve most of the effects in this book using a standard tablet or a mouse, this book assumes the use of a pressure-sensitive graphics tablet.

Output Devices

There is a wide variety of output options for your Painter files, from simple black-and-white laser prints, to film output for process color printing and color prints on a color laser copier, or Iris printer. Some color printers even support diverse media, so your painting can be output directly onto water color paper or canvas. Some of these output options are addressed in Chapter 10.

INSTALLING PAINTER

Installing Painter is as easy as it gets. In fact, this type of installation is sometimes referred to as a "forehead" installation: You simply bang your forehead on the keyboard a couple of times, and you're up and running.

To install Painter, insert the floppy disk labeled **Install Disk 1** into your floppy disk drive. Double-click on the Painter **Installer** icon, then select the installation location. Click **Install**. Follow the prompts to insert the other floppy disks, and you're all done!

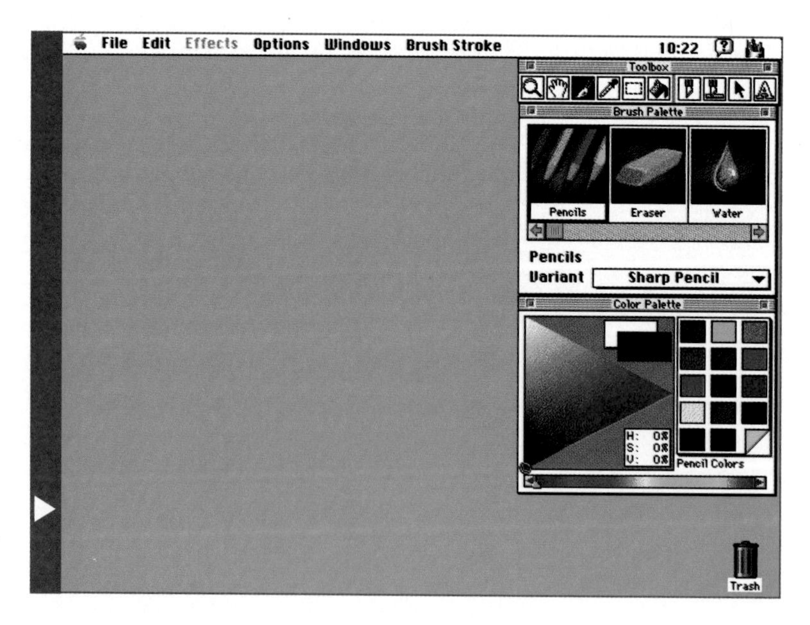

FIGURE 1.1

The Painter screen.

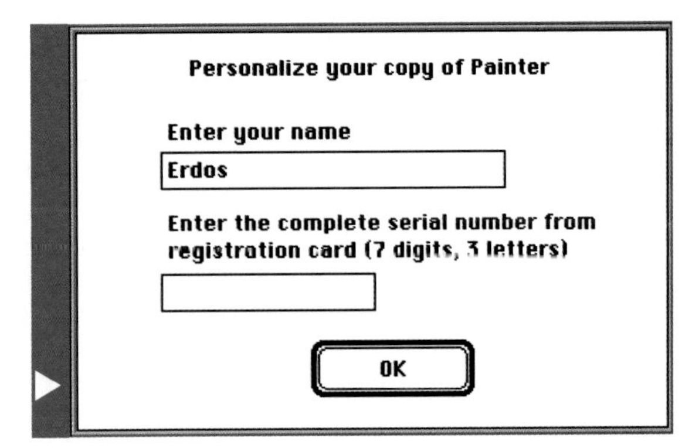

FIGURE 1.2

Personalizing your software.

LAUNCHING PAINTER

To launch Painter, simply double-click on the Painter application icon. You see the screen displayed in Figure 1.1.

LAUNCHING FOR THE FIRST TIME

If this is the first time you are launching Painter, you will be asked to personalize your software, as shown in Figure 1.2. Enter your name and the serial number printed on your registration card (the last page of the user's manual), and click **OK**.

The dialog box shown in Figure 1.3 is displayed for selection of third-party, Photoshop-compatible, plug-in modules. Plug-ins work with Photoshop to provide special effects and additional file formats. If you want to use any plug-ins with Painter, use this dialog box to

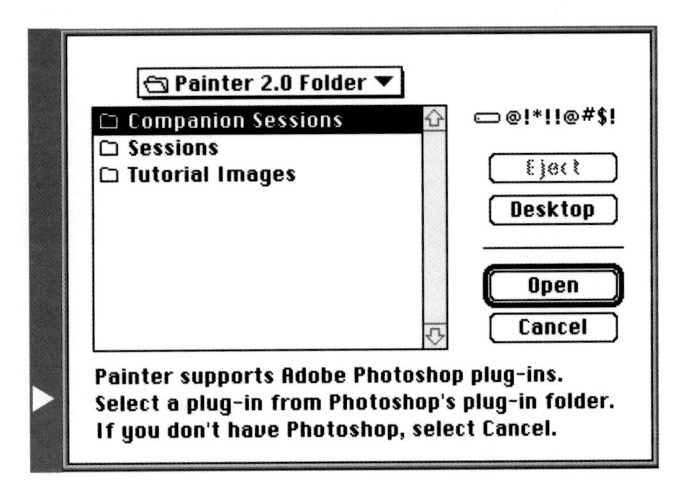

FIGURE 1.3

Selecting Photoshop-compatible plug-in modules.

locate them on your hard drive, and click **Open**. If you do not want to select any plug-ins right now, click **Cancel**.

To add plug-ins at a later date, hold down the **Command** key while double-clicking on the Painter application icon. Do not release the key until you see the plug-in dialog box.

After personalizing Painter and selecting plug-in modules, select **Quit** from the **File** menu, and relaunch the program.

TECHNICAL SUPPORT

Some older versions of INIT and DEV files can conflict with Painter. If you are experiencing trouble installing or launching Painter, call Painter's support line at (408) 688-8800 between 8 am and 5 pm Pacific time.

STARTING A WORK SESSION

Once Painter is launched, you can create a new file or work from an existing one. Painter uses many standard menu and dialog box options for opening and saving files.

To start a new file, select **New** from the **File** menu. The New Picture Size dialog box, shown in Figure 1.4, is displayed.

Enter the width and height for your image in the **Width** and **Height** fields and select the units of measurement from the pop-up menus. The default settings are for a standard 13-inch monitor.

Press **Tab** to move from one field to another. Click and hold on the pop-up menus to display your measurement choices, then drag to make a selection.

The resolution setting in this dialog box specifies pixels per inch displayed on your monitor, as well as the dots per inch (dpi) rendered by your printer. Many

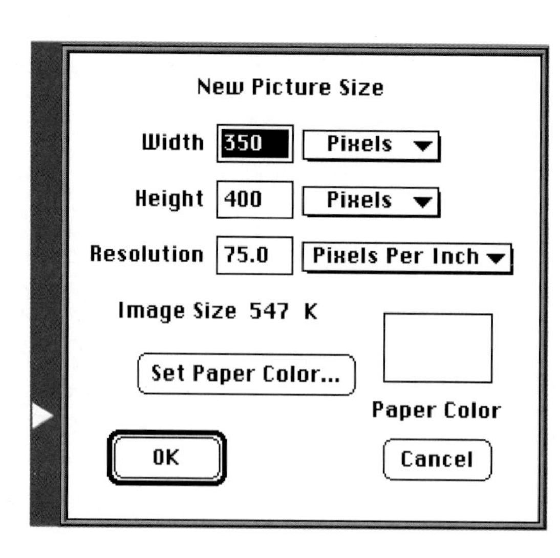

FIGURE 1.4
The New Picture Size dialog box.

artists work using 75 pixels per inch, then increase the size for output. This saves disk space while working—smaller files use less RAM and process faster.

The **Image Size** lets you know how much memory your file is using. Reducing the width, height, or resolution results in a smaller image size, increasing them results in a larger image size.

Click on **Set Paper Color...** to select the paper background color for your image. The standard Apple color selector, shown in Figure 1.5, is displayed.

Select your background color by entering values or clicking on the color wheel. Click **OK**. The background color is now displayed in the Paper Color window. Click **OK** and a new window is opened. Your canvas is ready and you're all set to paint.

SAVING A WORK SESSION

To save your work, select **Save** from the **File** menu. The Save dialog box, shown in Figure 1.6, is displayed.

Select the location for your art files and enter a file name in the **Save Image As** field.

This dialog box also gives you several file format options:

- **RIFF** (Raster image file format). This is the *default* option. Select the RIFF format to toggle the **Uncompressed** option. To save file space, always leave the **Uncompressed** option unchecked.

- **TIFF** (Tagged image file format). A versatile graphics format that stores a map specifying the location and

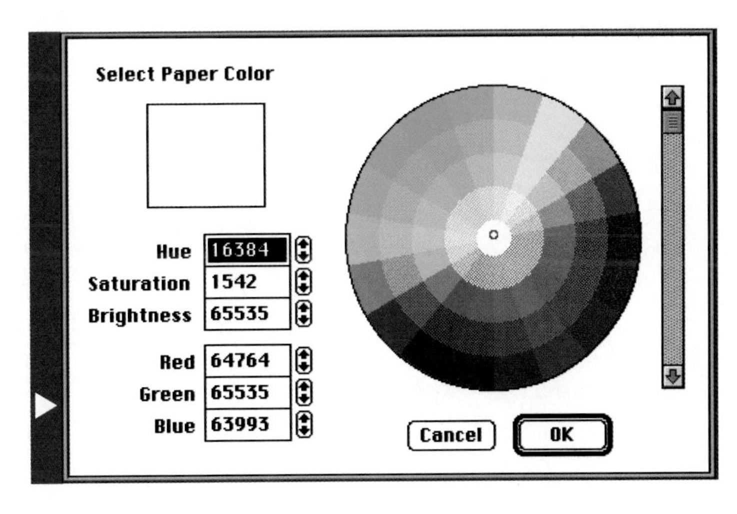

FIGURE 1.5
The standard Apple color selector.

color associated with each pixel. TIFF is supported by IBM-compatible and NeXT systems.

- **PICT.** Collections of QuickDraw routines needed to create an image. It is the main format used by the Macintosh clipboard.

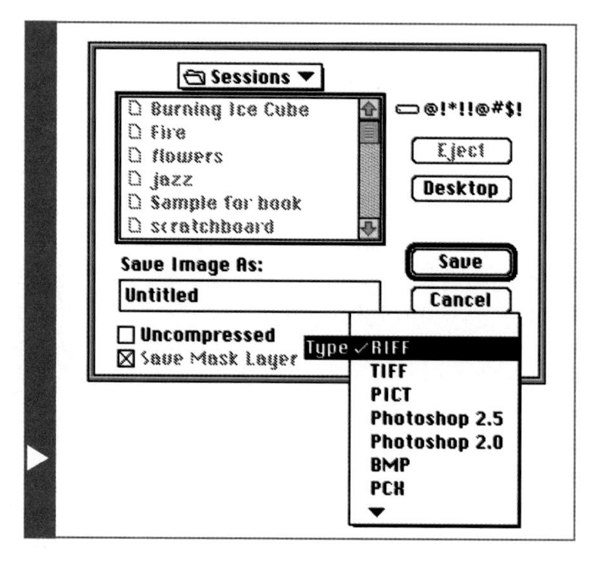

FIGURE 1.6
The Save dialog box.

- **Photoshop.** The native file format for Adobe Photoshop files. Photoshop files are always in 24-bit color.

- **BMP.** Bitmap files are the main format used by the Microsoft Windows (IBM-compatible computers) clipboard.

- **PCX** (Picture exchange). A PC format used by many scanners and paint-style programs.

- **Targa.** A file format used by high-end, PC-based paint programs. Targa files can have 8, 16, or 32 bits per pixel.

- **EPS** (Encapsulated PostScript). Painter's EPS files conform to the EPS-DCS 5 file format, used for desktop color separation. Please note that files saved in this format *cannot be reopened* by Painter. If you want to reopen a file saved in this format, save it in another format first (with another name) *before* saving it as an EPS file.

  Selecting **EPS** opens the EPS Save As Options dialog box, shown in Figure 1.7.

  - *Hex (ASCII) Picture Data.* Select this option for programs, such as PageMaker, that require it.

  - *Suppress Dot Gain.* This option enables Painter's dot gain adjustment.

- *Suppress Screen Angles*. This option disables Painter's screen angle adjustment.
- *Clip Path Frisket*. Select this option to save only the portion of an image inside a frisket. A frisket must be active for this option to be disabled.
- *Use Page Setup Settings*. This option enables Painter's default printer settings: 133 lpi, standard screen angles, and 16 percent dot gain.
- *Spot Type*. Select a dot, line, ellipse, or custom shape for your halftone screen grid. The **Custom** option lets you create your own shape using a PostScript command. You must know the PostScript programming language to do this.
- *Save PostScript data into main file*. This option saves a printable preview of your EPS document. When this option is selected, the radio buttons for color or black-and-white previews are enabled.

After mulling over this list and selecting your file format, click **OK** to save your work. If this file format list confuses you, don't worry; you can always select **Save As** to change your file type.

OPENING AN EXISTING WORK SESSION

You may open files saved in any of the formats listed previously (except EPS), which makes it easy to work with files that have been modified in other programs (such as Photoshop, Color-Studio, or Sketcher). Please note, however, that files must be saved in RGB color format in order to be opened in Painter.

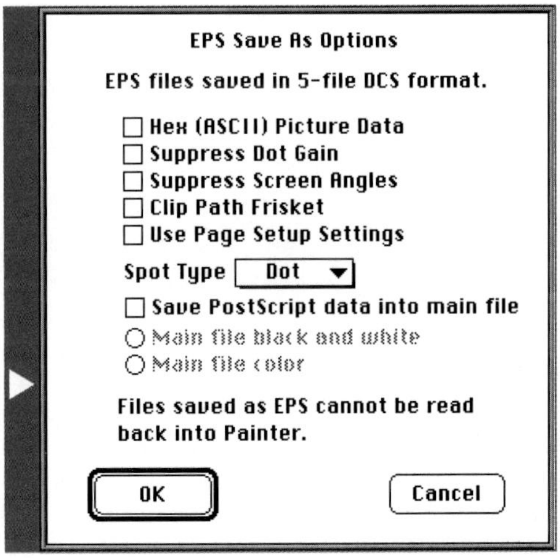

FIGURE 1.7 *The EPS Save As Options dialog box.*

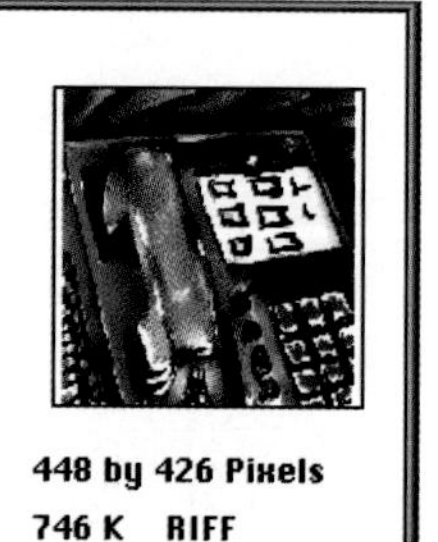

FIGURE 1.8
The File Open dialog box.

To open an existing file, select **Open** from the File menu. The dialog box shown in Figure 1.8 is displayed. Locate the file you want to open. If the file was saved using Painter or Sketcher, you'll see a thumbnail preview in the right side of this dialog box.

Below the preview window, you'll see file information for every document (even those not created in Painter): file dimensions in pixels, how much memory it takes up, and its file type.

Click on **Browse** to display thumbnails of all Painter and Sketcher files in the folder you currently have selected, as shown in Figure 1.9.

To open a file from the main File Open dialog box or from the Browse dialog box, select the file and click **Open** or double-click on your selection.

You're now ready to pick up your tools and start painting!

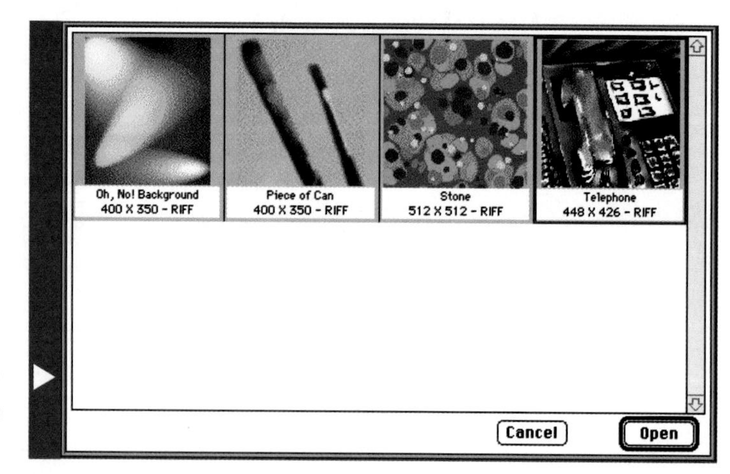

FIGURE 1.9
Browsing the contents of a folder.

Your Toolbox

CHAPTER 2

Painter is very simple and straightforward to use, yet it also has many complex and sophisticated features. Part of its ease of use lies in the simplicity of the Toolbox.

INTRODUCTION TO THE TOOLBOX

Painter's Toolbox should be displayed in the upper right of your screen when you launch the program. If it's not, select **Toolbox** from the Windows menu.

Clicking in the zoom box in the upper right of the Toolbox opens and closes the extended Toolbox, as shown in Figure 2.1.

To select any tool in the Toolbox, simply click on it once. Be careful not to double-click! If the tool has a palette associated with it, double-clicking not only selects the tool, but also toggles the palette open or closed.

Let's look at the Toolbox, starting from the first tool on the left.

MAGNIFIER TOOL

The **Magnifier** tool lets you zoom in on the tiniest detail of your painting, and with a few clicks of the mouse, you can zoom out to view your composition as if you were standing across the room—all while you're parked in your chair!

Click on the **Magnifier** tool to select it. Place your cursor over the area you want to zoom in on. Notice that your cursor changes to a magnifying glass with a plus sign (**+**) in the middle when you move it over your active window. Click once, and Painter magnifies the area. The magnification factors progress in the same increments as under the **Zoom Factor** option on the Windows menu (from 8.3 percent to 1,200 percent), as shown in Figure 2.2.

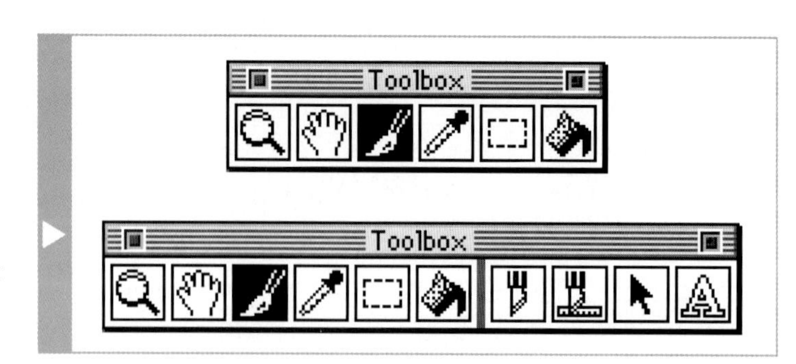

FIGURE 2.1
The standard Toolbox (top) and the extended Toolbox (bottom).

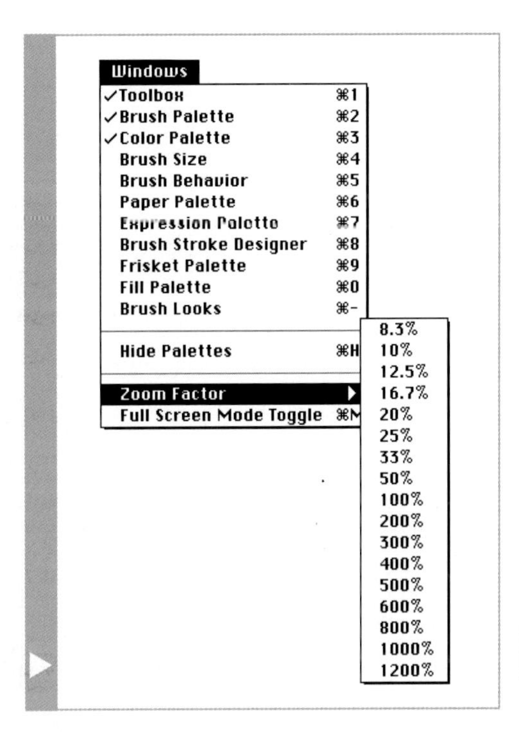

FIGURE 2.2

Painter's zoom factors.

The magnification factor is indicated in the title bar of your window; for example, it may say **Untitled @ 200%**.

To zoom out, place your cursor in the active window, and hold down the **Command** key. Notice the plus sign in the magnifying glass cursor changes to a minus sign (–). Click in the area you want to reduce. Your image zooms out in the same increments that it zoomed in.

To use the **Magnifier** tool while any other tool is selected, press **Command+Spacebar** to zoom in one increment, and **Option+Command+Spacebar** to zoom out one increment.

GRABBER TOOL

The **Grabber** tool is used to move your image around in a window—just grab it and move.

To use the **Grabber** tool, select it, then click and drag the cursor in your window. Release the mouse or stylus. Figure 2.3 shows the **Grabber** tool in action.

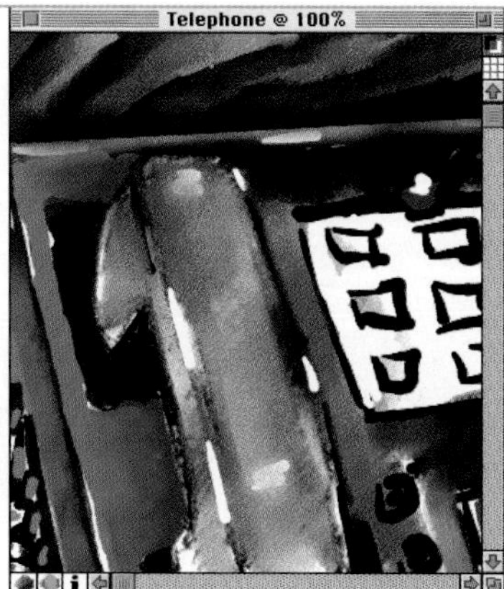

FIGURE 2.3
Using the Grabber tool.

If you have the **Paintbrush** tool selected, you can toggle the **Grabber** tool by pressing the **Spacebar**.

BRUSH TOOL

Here's where the action is. Select the **Brush** tool to access your painting and drawing tools. Please note that unlike most paint programs, this simply places you in painting mode; specific painting and drawing tools are selected from the Brush palette (coming up soon), not from the Toolbox.

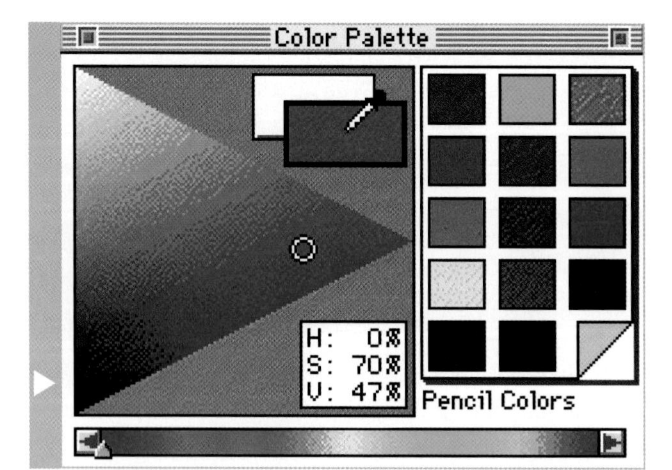

FIGURE 2.4
Activating the foreground color on the Color palette.

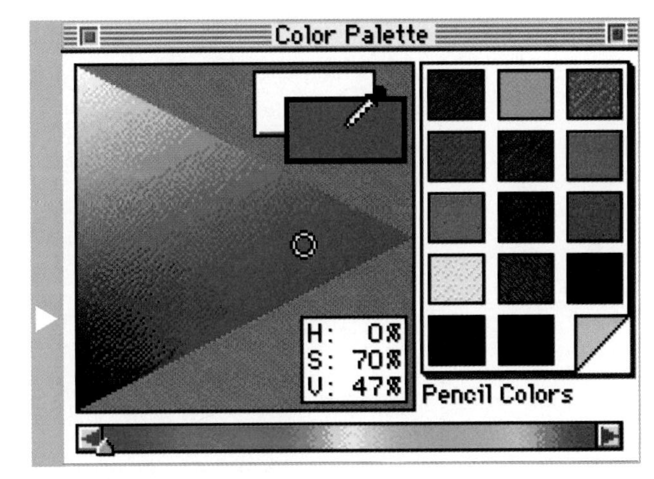

FIGURE 2.5
The color is picked up with the ***Eye Dropper*** *tool and shown in the Foreground indicator of the Color palette.*

EYE DROPPER TOOL

The **Eye Dropper** tool lets you select a color from a painted area to use on another area. You can even use it to get a color from another open file.

When you use the **Eye Dropper** tool, make sure your Color palette is open (it's the third item on the Windows menu). There are two rectangles on the palette—make sure the front one is selected, as in Figure 2.4.

Move your cursor, now shaped like an eye dropper, over the source area for your color, and click once. Your color is now shown in the foreground rectangle on your Color palette, as in Figure 2.5. Now you can select a brush and paint with the selected color.

To select the **Eye Dropper** tool when you're using the **Brush**, **Selection**, or **Fill** tool, hold down the **Command** key.

SELECTION TOOL

You guessed it—the **Selection** tool lets you select areas of your painting. However, it only lets you select rectangular areas. To select other shapes, see Chapter 7, *Using Friskets*.

Double-clicking on the **Selection** tool selects all of the image that is visible in your window. Choose **Select All** (**Command+A**) from the **Edit** menu to select the entire image.

Click and drag over the area you wish to select. To deselect an area, choose **Deselect** from the **Edit** menu,

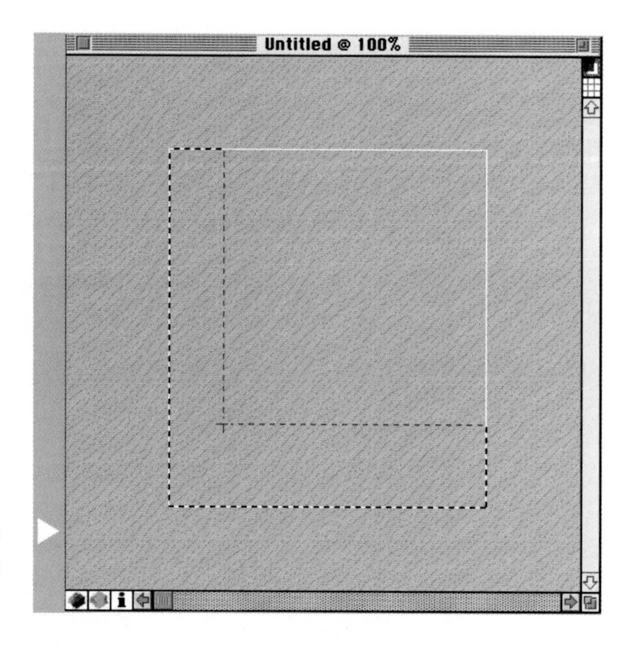

FIGURE 2.6
Adjusting the boundaries of a selected area.

or press **Command+D**. Double-clicking on the **Selection** tool also deselects any area.

To adjust the boundaries of a selected area, hold down the **Shift** key and click and drag on the selection marquee, as shown in Figure 2.6.

Chapter 7, *Using Friskets*, covers many of the options you can use on a selected area.

FILL TOOL

The **Fill** tool, often referred to as the **Bucket** tool, lets you apply color to a selected area. Double-clicking on this tool opens the Fill palette, which is covered in detail in Chapter 5, *Using Color*.

THE EXTENDED TOOLBOX

The extended Toolbox is comprised of the **Frisket Knife**, the **Frisket Line**, the **Frisket Selection**, and the **Frisket Text** tools. These are all covered in detail in Chapter 7, *Using Friskets*.

Brushes and Paint

CHAPTER 3

This chapter covers the fundamentals of Painter's Brush and Color palettes—the backbone of the program—and lets you get right into painting. After reading this chapter, you should be able to select colors, paint, and draw with any paintbrush or drawing tool.

THE BRUSH PALETTE

This is the part you've been waiting for! Get out an old art supplies catalogue, and look at all of the tools you can't afford to buy. Now sit down at your computer and blink your eyes like Barbara Eden in "I Dream of Jeannie"—they're all here...and then some.

To get started, make sure your Brush palette is displayed. If it's not, select **Brush Palette** from the Windows menu, or press **Command+2**. Select your **Brush** tool from the Toolbox, choose a brush from the Brush palette, shown in Figure 3.1, and you're ready to go.

Each major tool group (chalk, water colors, oil paints, pens, etc.), represented on the Brush palette by colorful icons, has choices of variants, such as brush sizes and types, available on the pop-up menu on the lower half of the palette. This section describes the major tool groups and their variants. You also have an enormous array of customization choices to apply to these tools. Since that's a more complex and advanced subject, we'll cover it in Chapter 4, *Customizing Your Brushes*.

To select a tool group, click on it once. To select a variant, click on the **Variant** pop-up menu, and drag to the selection you want, as shown in Figure 3.2. Release the mouse or stylus to

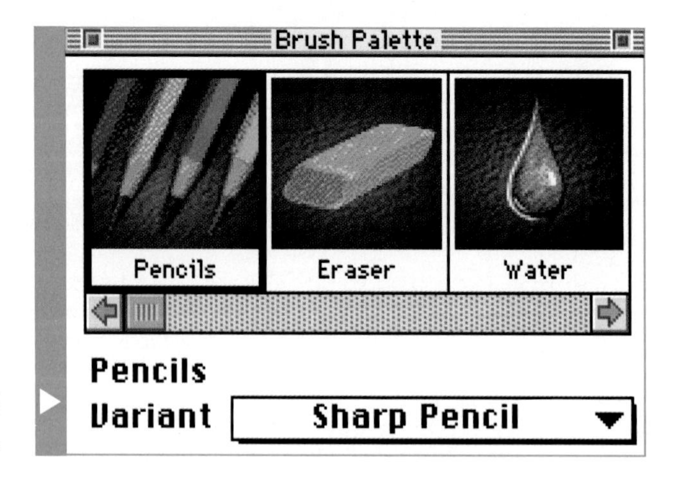

FIGURE 3.1
The Brush palette.

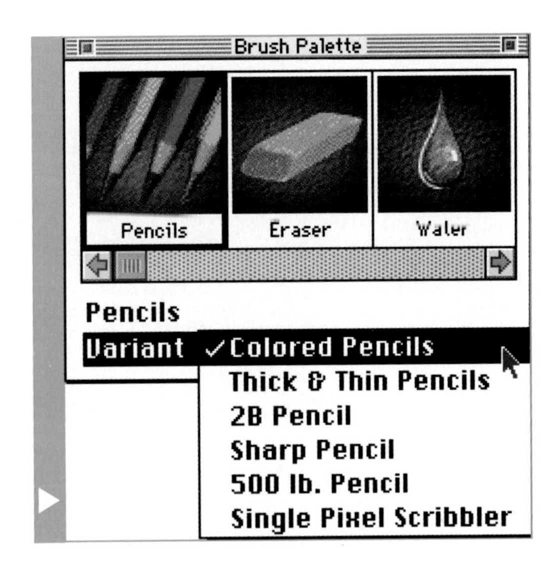

FIGURE 3.2

Selecting a variant on the Brush palette.

choose your variant. Slower computers may exhibit lag time for some tools.

One of the coolest features of the Brush palette is the ability to "tear off" variants. Very few artists will want to use only one variant of any given tool, so the folks at Fractal Design Corporation created tear-off variants, so you can have the variants you use most right at the tip of your stylus.

TEAR-OFF VARIANTS

To tear off a variant, first select the tool group, then the variant you want to use. Click on the tool's icon, drag it off the palette, and place it where it will be most convenient. Figure 3.3 shows several variants that have been torn off, and one being torn off. To clear a variant from your screen, click in the close box in the upper left of the variant window.

THE EXPANDED BRUSH PALETTE

Like the Toolbox, the Brush palette is also expandable. Click on the zoom box in the upper-right corner, and more (can you believe it!) options become available: Penetration, Concentration, Method, and Library. Figure 3.4 shows an expanded Brush palette.

- **Penetration.** This setting controls the amount of color that penetrates the paper when you use grainy method brushes. Move the **Penetration** slider left (less paper

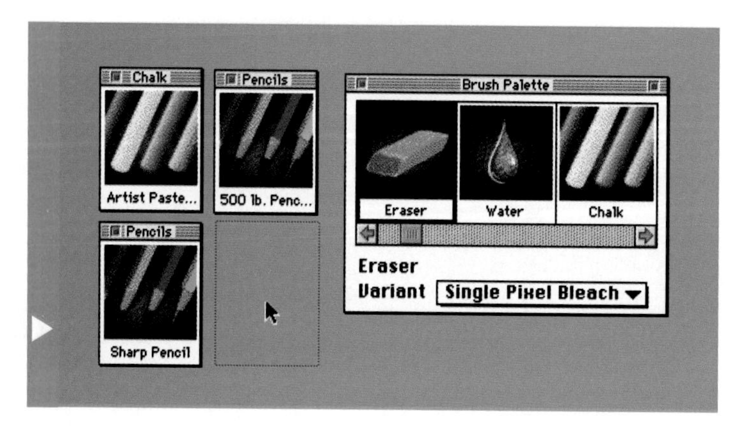

FIGURE 3.3
Using tear-off variants.

grain shows) or right (more paper grain shows) to adjust this setting.

- **Concentration.** This setting works in two ways:
  - *Buildup brushes.* Move this slider left to keep your colors truer to the color on your palette, or right to let them muddy up quicker.
  - *Cover brushes.* Move this slider left for more transparent coverage, or right for more opaque coverage.
- **Method.** This decides the nature of the brush stroke, and is probably the most important part of customizing your tools. If you click on the pop-up menu, it seems pretty

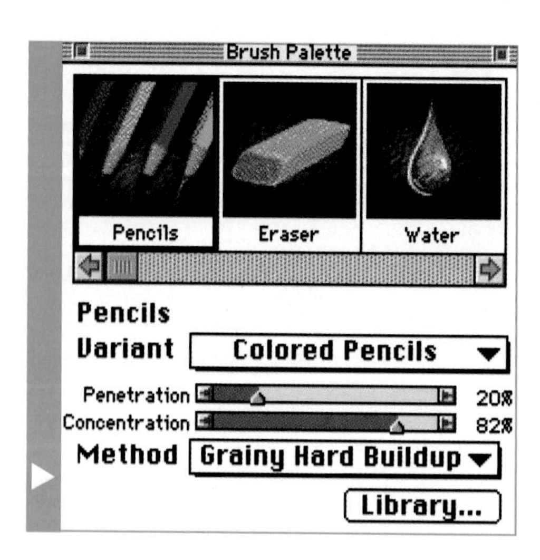

FIGURE 3.4
An expanded Brush palette.

intimidating, but it is really organized quite well, and is actually easy and fun to use. It is covered in detail in Chapter 4, *Customizing Your Brushes*.

- **Library.** When you create custom variants—also covered in Chapter 4, *Customizing Your Brushes*—you'll definitely want to save them (well, most of them). This feature lets you access saved custom brush variants.

Remember, like their traditional counterparts, these digital tools react to the surface to which you apply them. Chapter 5, *Creating Your Canvas*, dips further into this subject.

Unlike their traditional counterparts, you can combine mediums you never dreamed of, such as placing chalk over a layer of oil paints, erasing felt pens, or using friskets with any medium. Take your rule book, throw it out, and write your own.

Pencils

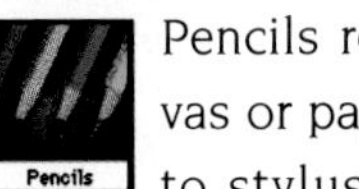

Pencils react very well to canvas or paper surface, as well as to stylus pressure. If you are using a mouse or standard stylus, you can adjust pencil pressure by moving the **Penetration** slider left (lighter), or right (darker) before stroking.

Colored Pencils. Produces the same effect as traditional colored pencils.

Thick & Thin Pencils. This has the same effect as drawing with both the sharpened tip and the flat edge of pencil lead. It creates lines that vary from thick to thin, depending on the direction you are drawing in.

2B Pencil. A thin, soft-lead pencil.

Sharp Pencil. A thin, hard-lead pencil.

500 lb. Pencil. This quarter-ton monster generates (boy, does it generate) fat lines. *Very* fat.

Single Pixel Scribbler. The antithesis of the **500 lb. Pencil**, this produces one-pixel lines—as thin as they get.

Eraser

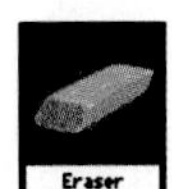

Oh %#@!!*&$!!! You just made a mistake. Not a big deal—just erase it. Painter offers three kinds of erasers, all pressure-sensitive:

Eraser Variants. These erase right down to the paper color chosen when the document was created. Eraser variants come in five flavors: **Flat**, **Ultrafine**, **Small**, **Medium**, and **Fat**.

Bleach Erasers. Just like Clorox, these variants erase to white, regardless of the paper color. It's available in **Single Pixel**, **Small**, **Medium**, and **Fat**.

Eraser Darkeners. There was a little bit of liberty taken when they named these variants erasers: **Darkeners** actually *increase* the density of the image. Choose from **Ultrafine**, **Small**, **Medium**, and **Fat**.

Water

Use the **Water** tools to smudge areas created by other tools, or to dilute strokes made by any other tool.

Just Add Water. This variant smudges with smooth, clean strokes. Be careful, though, because it removes paper grain while it smudges.

Grainy Water. Use this when you want to retain and work with paper texture. It is also useful for adding texture to smooth areas.

Frosty Water. Smears with a harder edge than **Just Add Water** while retaining some texture.

Tiny Frosty Water. Works like **Frosty Water,** at about half the width.

Big Frosty Water. Works like **Frosty Water**, at about two or three times the width

Single Pixel Water. An itsy-bitsy smear of water, this is like dragging a wet thread through your image.

Water Spray. Sprays water onto your image, as if you were using an aspirator.

Water Rake. Produces the effect of dragging a wet, hard-bristled brush through your image.

Chalk

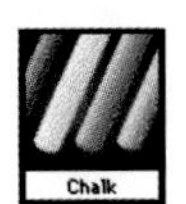

More like traditional pastels than chalk, these tools are the favorite choice of many artists. You can get some amazing effects when you use the **Chalk** tools with paper textures and the **Water** tools.

Artist Pastel Chalk. This variant creates an opaque chalk stroke.

Sharp Chalk. Works like **Artist Pastel Chalk**, at about half the width.

Large Chalk. Works like **Artist Pastel Chalk** at about twice the width.

Charcoal

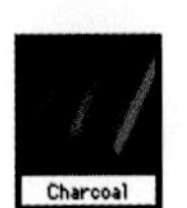

Like traditional charcoal, this tool is great for sketching out your composition, but here you get 16 million colors and no dust. Charcoal produces a more opaque stroke than chalk.

Gritty Charcoal. Produces a rich stroke that varies in width according to the direction of the stroke, as if you were alternating between the flat edge and the point of the charcoal.

Default. A more textured variant of this tool.

Soft Charcoal. A textured variant of this tool, using very soft strokes.

Pens

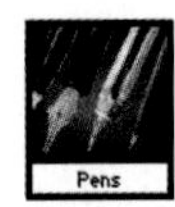

An incredible assortment of pens with no clogging, no ink jars, and no splattering (unless, of course, you *want* splattering).

Fine Point. This tool works just like a ball point pen.

Smooth Ink Pen. This variant works like a fountain pen, with greater pressure creating a thicker stroke, and less pressure creating a thinner stroke.

Calligraphy. Fine hand lettering is now a breeze! Select this option for incredible calligraphic strokes.

Pen and Ink. A very opaque, smooth stroke.

Flat Color. A cousin to the **500 lb. Pencil**, this lays down an oversized, opaque stroke.

Scratchboard Tool. Scraffito made fast and easy. For loads of fun, set your paper color to black, and scratch away.

Scratchboard Rake. We call this one sgraffito with a cat's claw.

Single Pixel. A single-pixel pen, unaffected by stylus pressure.

Leaky Pen. The longer you drag, the bigger the leak. Careful, you don't want to get this all over your shirt.

Pixel Dust. Not exactly like any pen we've ever used, this tool sprays fairy dust all over your image.

Felt Pens

No, these pressure-sensitive pens won't dry out if you leave the caps off. And they're great for comps, cartoons, and caricatures.

Fine Tip Felt Pens. Press as hard as you want, this narrow pen won't tear your paper.

Medium Tip Felt Pens. About twice the width of the **Fine Tip** pen, and very opaque.

Felt Marker. A much softer and transparent version of the **Felt Tip** variants. The nib of this pen is wider for horizontal strokes than for vertical strokes.

Dirty Marker. A much darker and muddier version of the **Felt Marker**. The nib of this pen is wider for horizontal strokes than for vertical strokes.

Single Pixel Marker. Finer than any pen we've ever used, this marker produces a *very* thin stroke.

Crayons

When you were little, did you ever beg your parents for one of those great big boxes of crayons—96 colors and a sharpener? Well, look what you've got now—Crayola eat your heart out!

Like their traditional counterparts, these strokes get darker as you layer them; in fact, they can get downright muddy. Press as hard as you want—they won't break.

Default. Plain and simple, this is a crayon.

Waxy Crayons. Did you ever put your crayons on the radiator, then try to draw with them? Well, now you can do it again, but without getting grounded for a week. Melt away.

Airbrush

This tool lays down gradual tones of color, with a very soft edge to your strokes, as if you were using a traditional airbrush or spray can, with none of those CFCs or fumes. As with most other tools, increasing stylus pressure or **Concentration** increases the opacity of your coverage.

Fat Stroke. A thick, soft, semi-transparent stroke, good for covering large areas.

Thin Stroke. Produces the same coverage as the **Fat Stroke**, at about one-quarter of the stroke width.

Feather Tip. Lays down soft, thin lines with greater opacity than the **Fat Stroke** or **Thin Stroke** variants.

Spatter Airbrush. A very textured, transparent, and thick-stroked variant that reacts well to paper texture.

Dodge. Dodge fades the color from an image. The color selected on your color palette does not affect the way **Dodge** fades an image.

Burn. The opposite of **Dodge**, this variant increases the color of the image to which you apply it. This tool increases the color of the image without being affected by the color selected on your color palette.

Single Pixel Air. A very fine **Airbrush** variant.

Liquid

Most **Liquid** variants smear more than they paint. You can get effects that range from using oil paints with a palette knife, to dragging a wet brush through your image, to good old fashioned finger painting. Use these variants both for applying new paint, and for adding effects to existing images. To move smear paint without adding color, reduce your **Concentration** slider to **0 percent**.

Smeary Bristles. A very texture-sensitive and pressure-sensitive tool that smears color from your color palette onto your image.

Total Oil Brush. Creates a thinner stroke than the **Smeary Bristles**.

Tiny Smudge. A small, textured smudging tool. The default setting has the **Concentration** set at **0 percent** so that no color is applied from the Color palette. To add color to this tool, move the **Concentration** slider to the right.

Smeary Mover. Basically the same tool as the **Smeary Bristles**, but with **Concentration** set to **0 percent** so that it moves existing paint around, rather than adding new paint.

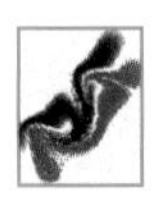

Coarse Smeary Mover. Moves existing paint around with a coarser texture than the **Smeary Mover**.

Distorto. A very wet, smooth tool that moves, more than smears, existing paint. Very cool.

Coarse Smeary Bristles. Like **Smeary Bristles**, but with a larger stroke and more texture.

Coarse Distorto. A more textured, less smooth version of the **Distorto** variant.

Thick Oil. A very thick, very opaque wet brush loaded with oily paint.

Brush

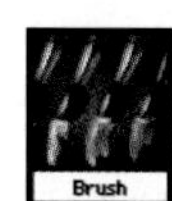

Although all of the tools on the Brush palette are called "brushes," this is where the more traditional brushes reside—oil and acrylic brushes.

Please note that these brushes always cover the paint they overlay, even if your **Concentration** is set to a lower percentage. Setting the **Concentration** of these brushes to 0 percent doesn't make the paint more translucent—it simply doesn't apply paint.

Hairy Brush. Your regular bristle brush. The stroke width and penetration of this oil-like variant is determined by the amount of pressure placed on your stylus—less pressure creates thinner strokes with less penetration, more pressure creates thicker strokes with greater penetration. Wait until each stroke is rendered by your computer, or else you'll end up with dots rather than strokes.

Graduated Brush. A thinner oil-type brush that uses two colors, depending on the amount of pressure on your stylus. The colors are taken from the two rectangles on your Color palette: the primary color is selected in the front rectangle, the secondary color is selected in the back rectangle. Greater pressure adds more of your primary color, while less pressure increases your secondary color.

Penetration Brush. This variant works like acrylics and reacts well to surface texture. Slower strokes give the effect of having your bristles closer together, faster strokes spread the bristles.

Oil Paint. Produces an oil-paint effect using a hard-bristled brush. This variant has very hard edges, and the width of your stroke is reduced with less stylus pressure or increased with greater stylus pressure. **Penetration** and **Concentration** are increased with greater stylus pressure.

Camel Hair Brush. A softer oil brush than the **Oil Paint** variant. Slower strokes give the effect of having your bristles closer together, faster strokes spread the bristles. The width of your stroke is reduced with less stylus pressure or increased with greater stylus pressure.

Rough Out. Named because it is a good brush to create rough, textured images, slower strokes with this dry brush variant increase the width of your stroke, while faster strokes decrease the width.

Big Rough Out. A larger, more textured version of the **Rough Out** variant.

Huge Rough Out. A larger, more textured version of the **Big Rough Out** variant.

Digital Sumi. A multiple-bristled sumi brush, with a rake-like effect. Increased stylus pressure increases stroke width.

Cover Brush. A soft, very slightly textured brush. Increased stylus pressure increases stroke width and concentration.

Artists

These variants give you the ability to paint using the brush types of the old masters. The Impressionist color palette gives you some great results. Increased stylus pressure increases concentration, and faster strokes produce thinner widths.

Van Gogh. If you use the Impressionist color palette, strokes from this brush give you the multi-colored effect used by Vincent Van Gogh. The **Van Gogh** tool hides underlying strokes, regardless of the **Concentration** setting. Short strokes work best with this variant. For each stroke, a dotted line is displayed while the image is being rendered. Wait for your computer to completely render the stroke before beginning your next stroke, or you'll end up with dots rather than lines.

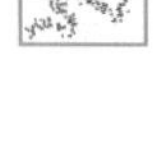

Seurat. This variant gives you the pointillist (dabs of pure color to produce intense color effects) technique developed by Georges Seurat.

Impressionist. It's easy to emulate the French Impressionists with this tool. Increased concentration adds more color, reduced concentration spreads existing paint.

Auto Van Gogh. This is another way to get Impressionistic results. The **Auto Van Gogh** variant works using a clone, and is explained in Chapter 9, *Cloning and Scanned Images*.

Flemish Rub. Another take on the **Impressionist** variant, **Flemish Rub** smears existing paint to produce an Impressionistic effect on an existing image.

Cloners

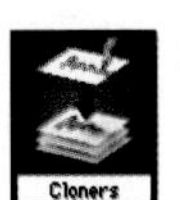

Cloner brushes let you take an existing image (usually a scanned photograph) and apply different types of media to them. You select a default clone setting, and Painter provides color information while you control how the brush strokes are applied. Cloners are covered in detail in Chapter 9, *Cloning and Scanned Images*, but we'll give you a brief overview of the variants here.

- **Pencil Sketch Cloner.** Lays down pencil strokes.
- **Felt Pen Cloner.** Adds strokes from a felt tip pen. The darkness (or "dirtiness") of the strokes increase as you lay more down.
- **Hairy Cloner.** Produces strokes that emulate the **Hairy Brush** variant of the brush.
- **Oil Brush Cloner.** Paints with oil-paint strokes that cover underlying paint.
- **Chalk Cloner.** Creates the effect of the **Artist Pastel Chalk** variant.
- **Hard Oil Cloner.** Lays down hard-edged oil-paint strokes that cover underlying paint.
- **Van Gogh Cloner.** Produces strokes that emulate the **Van Gogh** variant of the Artist brush.
- **Melt Cloner.** "Melts" an image by painting with strokes similar to the **Distorto** variant of the Liquid brush.
- **Driving Rain Cloner.** Creates an image that looks like it is being seen through a window in the rain.
- **Straight Cloner.** Re-creates the original image.
- **Soft Cloner.** Creates an image that is softer than the original.
- **Impressionist Cloner.** Paints with the short, multi-colored strokes found in the **Impressionist** variant of the Artist brush.

Water Color

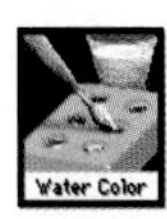

The **Water Color** variants produce beautiful, soft, translucent images. You'll get great results if you use the default Water Colors setting on the color palette. All of the **Water Color** variants react well to surface textures, except for the **Wet Eraser**.

You must select **Wet Paint** from the **Options** menu to use any of the

Water Color tools. When you do this, you are painting on a layer that "floats" above any existing image you may have on your canvas. When you are done using your water colors, select **Dry** from the **Options** menu. This "dries" your water color layer and sends it to the underlying image layer.

The **Selection** and **Frisket** tools do not work on a wet water color layer. To clear a wet layer, select **Dry** from the **Options** menu, then select **Undo** from the **Edit** menu. When you are all through using your **Water Color** variants, toggle off the **Wet Paint** selection on the **Options** menu.

Pure Water Brush. This brush adds water (with no color added) to your image.

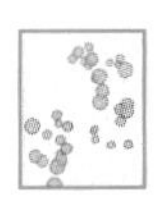

Spatter Water. This variant splatters colored drops of water onto your image, as if you were flicking your brush.

Simple Water. Your basic water color stroke, without bristles. Adding layers of colors using this variant produces a smooth, blended effect.

Broad Water Brush. Paints with a very wide, translucent stroke that shows some bristle marks.

Water Brush Stroke. Your basic water color stroke, showing bristle marks. Increased stylus pressure increases stroke width. Wait until each stroke is rendered before beginning another stroke.

Large Water. Lays down a very wide, lightly colored, translucent layer of paint.

Diffuse Water. Lays down a concentrated layer of paint with diffused edges. The edges diffuse after the color is laid down, as if it were being absorbed by the paper. Increased stylus pressure increases stroke width and concentration.

Wet Eraser. Use this variant to erase water color strokes on the "floating" layer of wet paint.

Large Simple Water. A larger version of the **Simple Water** variant.

Once you select the tool group and variant you want to paint with, paint. Really. That's it.

THE COLOR PALETTE

Sixteen million colors. We'll say it again: 16 *million colors*. And you'll never run out of them.

The Color palette is your main source for selecting, creating, and saving colors. Click on the zoom box in the upper right of the palette to display the extended Color palette, shown in Figure 3.5.

This section covers the basics of selecting and using colors. Chapter 6, *Using Color*, discusses more advanced color topics.

SELECTING COLORS

Use a combination of the spectrum slider and the triangular color picker to create your colors. The spectrum slider selects the dominant hue in the triangular color picker. The triangle exhibits the saturation and value of the hue selected on the spectrum slider. Use the color ring to select saturation and brightness by sliding it around in the triangle.

Or, choose from one of the existing default color squares. To change to a new set of color squares, click on the upturned corner of the page of squares. Clicking on the white area below the upturned corner lets you return to a previous page of squares. Then click on the square you want to use as your color source.

You may also select a color palette by clicking on **Palette...** and selecting from the choices in the User Color Palettes dialog box, shown in Figure 3.6. Click on the palette you want to use, then press **Return**.

Changing a Color Square

To edit the color in a color square, use the triangle or the **Eye Dropper** tool to

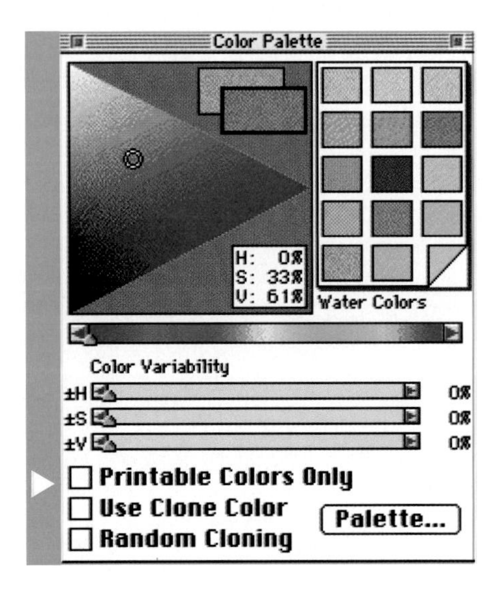

FIGURE 3.5
The extended Color palette.

select the new color for the square. Hold down the **Option** key while clicking on the square you want to change. Presto! A new color square. Unless you save the new square, it reverts to its old color as soon as you turn the page.

Saving Color Squares

The ability to create new pages of color squares gives you the flexibility to create custom palettes for projects, clients, and more.

To permanently save new color squares, you have to create a new page. Make sure the Color palette has been expanded, then edit an existing palette to suit your needs.

Click on the **Palette...** button to open the User Color Palettes dialog box. Click on **Save**, enter a name for your new palette in the Save Palette dialog box, and press **Return**.

Deleting Color Squares

To delete a page of color squares, open the User Color Palettes dialog box by clicking on the **Palette...** button. Select the name of the page you want to delete and click on **Delete**.

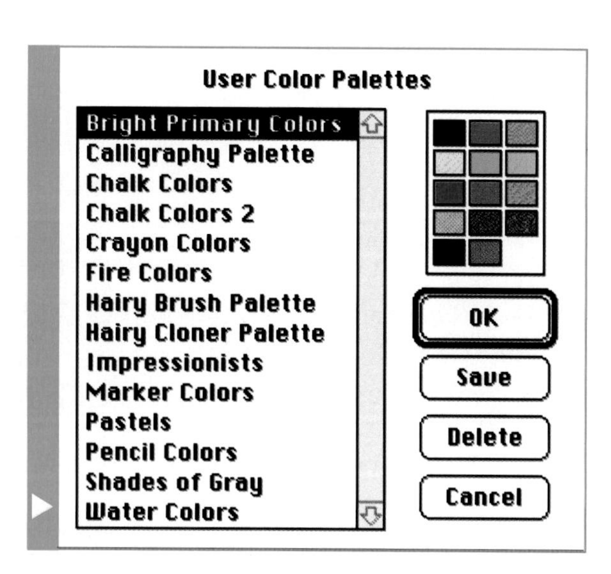

FIGURE 3.6

The User Color Palettes dialog box.

PRACTICE SESSION

1. All right. It's time to get down to work. Let's paint! Select **New** from the **File** menu. Select the default settings in the New Picture Size dialog box by pressing **Return**.

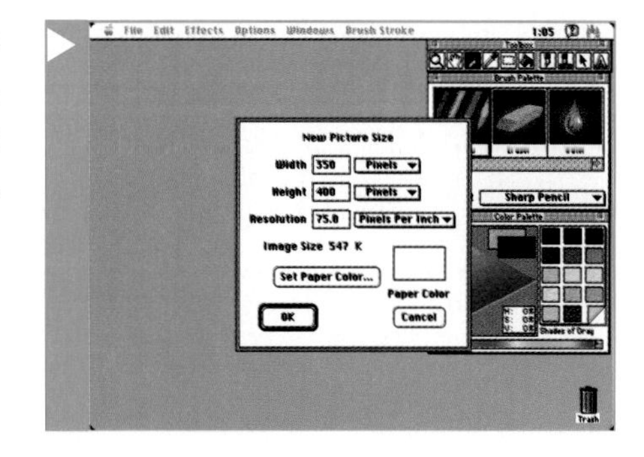

2. Select the **Sharp Pencil** variant from the Brush palette, and black from the Color Palette. Now sketch the outline of a cow.

3. Select the **Artist Pastel** variant of the Chalk brush. Flip to the Pastels page on your Color palette, and choose a pale color for the cow's body. Start filling in your outline. Then select a darker color for shadowed areas, and apply that to the undersides of the cow.

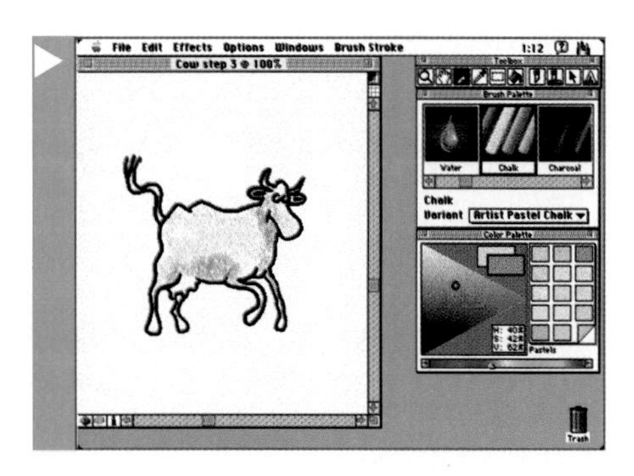

PRACTICE SESSION CONTINUED

4. Use the **Feather Tip Airbrush** variant to add some pink to the muzzle, udder, and ears. Add some tan to the horns and the tip of the tail.

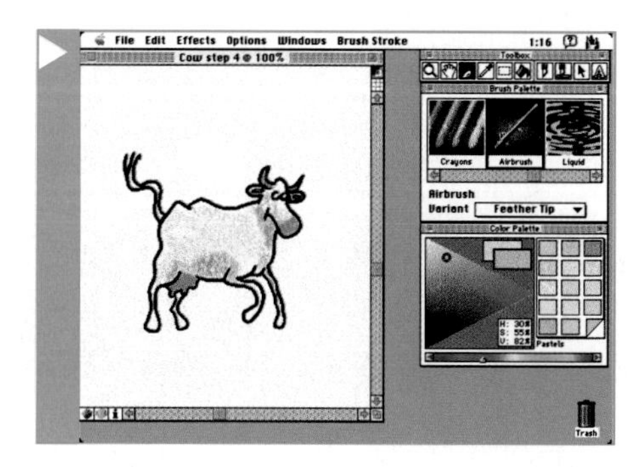

5. Airbrush some black spots on the cow, then add details to the eyes, nose, and hooves using the **Single Pixel Pen** tool. A bit rough, but it's a good start.

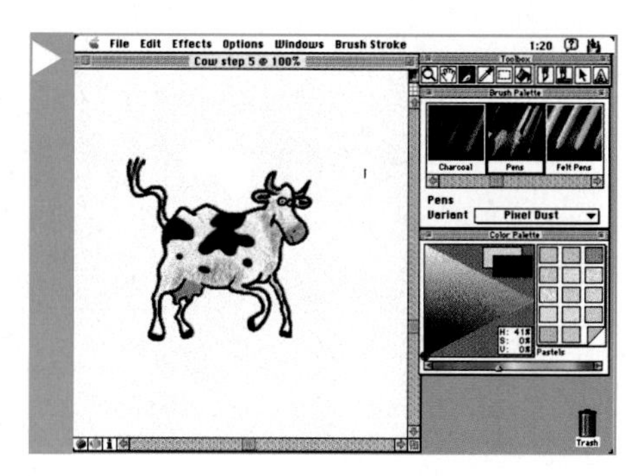

Customizing Your Brushes

CHAPTER 4

If after reading Chapter 3 you thought you had plenty of tools to work with, *wait* until you read this chapter. The tools we covered in Chapter 3 are simply a library of pre-set default brushes the folks at Fractal Design Corporation put together to make your life easier, but you can create an almost endless array of custom brushes to suit your own working style. Your choices for customization include adding variants to existing brushes, or creating whole new brush categories in the Brush palette (including their own name and icon).

CUSTOMIZING A BRUSH

In Painter, several factors combine to create a brush:

- **Brush size.** Determines the width, tip, and angle of a brush stroke.
- **Method.** Determines the nature of the brush stroke
- **Brush behavior.** Refines brush strokes and determines how colors interact when they build up on each other.
- **Expression.** Controls color density, stroke width, and how brushes interact with paper texture.

Let's see how they all work.

BRUSH SIZE

The width, tip, and angle of your brush strokes are controlled from the Brush Size palette. To open the palette, shown in its expanded form in Figure 4.1, select Brush Size (Command+4) from the Windows menu.

- **Stroke contour.** The strip of six icons in the upper left of the window allow you to select the contour of a brush nib.

Strokes using this nib provide more color at the center than at the edges of a brush, as with the **Sharp Chalk** variant.

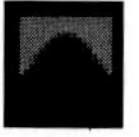

This nib produces concentrated color in the center of a stroke, as with the **Artist Chalk** variant.

This nib gives strokes with a small area of color in the center of a stroke, as with the **Crayons**.

This nib strokes with a moderate amount of color in the center, as with most of the **Pencil** variants.

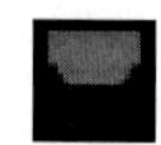

Strokes with this nib pool color at the edges, as with many of the Watercolor brushes.

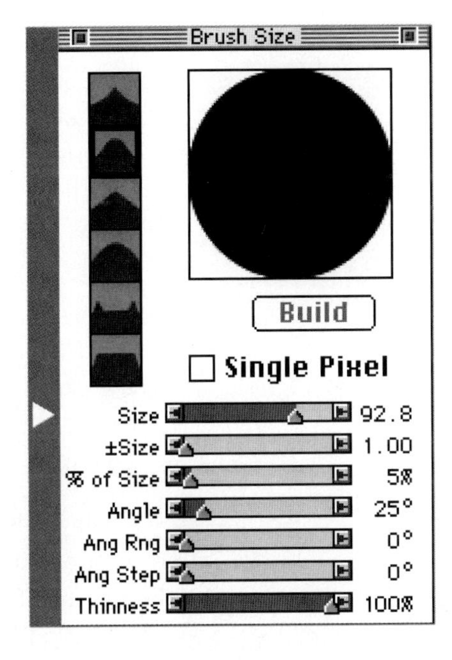

FIGURE 4.1 *The expanded Brush Size palette.*

Strokes from this nib provide flat color throughout, as with the **Calligraphy Pen** variant.

- **Preview window.** The preview window in the upper right of the palette displays stroke angle, width (black), and the spread of color through a stroke (gray).

- **Build.** Click on this button to have Painter build a brush with the options you have selected. You cannot paint with the parameters you chose without first clicking on **Build**.

- **Single Pixel.** Check this box to create very, very fine brushes that are 1 pixel wide.

- **Size** increases (right) or decreases (left) the width of your brush stroke.

- **±Size** controls the spread of color through a stroke. Move the slider left to decrease the range of a stroke width, right to increase it. When you move this slider, the black circle in the preview window shows the minimum stroke width, the gray circle shows the maximum stroke width.

- **% of Size** controls the transition of a stroke from thick to thin, and thin to thick. A lower percentage indicates a smoother transition, while a higher percentage provides a much more blunt transition.

- **Angle** controls the brush direction of a chosen nib. Use it in with the **Thinness** option, which controls the width of the angle.

- **Ang Rng** selects the maximum range of angles available in a stroke. Moving this slider to 45 degrees lets a stroke range from 0 to 45 degrees.

- **Ang Step** controls the number of angles in a brush. A lower setting provides more brush angles, a higher setting provides fewer brush angles.
- **Thinness** adjusts the width of stroke's angle (determined by the **Angle** slider).

METHOD

Method determines the nature of your brush stroke. Each of the default selections in the Brush palette already have a method assigned to them that gives them the characteristics of their traditional parallel.

A tool's method is chosen from the **Method** pop-up menu on the extended Brush palette, shown in Figure 4.2.

The selection of 27 methods gives you powerful customizing ability, but when you first look at the menu you may gasp and say, "That whole menu?" It may seem easier to go to Acme hardware and buy some brushes, but the organization is very logical. Once you understand the five categories, it's a breeze.

Strokes are created using two sets of properties: a stroke method category plus stroke characteristics. Within each method (Column A in Table 4.1) you'll find repeating stroke characteristics (Column B in Table 4.1), including soft, flat, hard, grainy, edge, and variable.

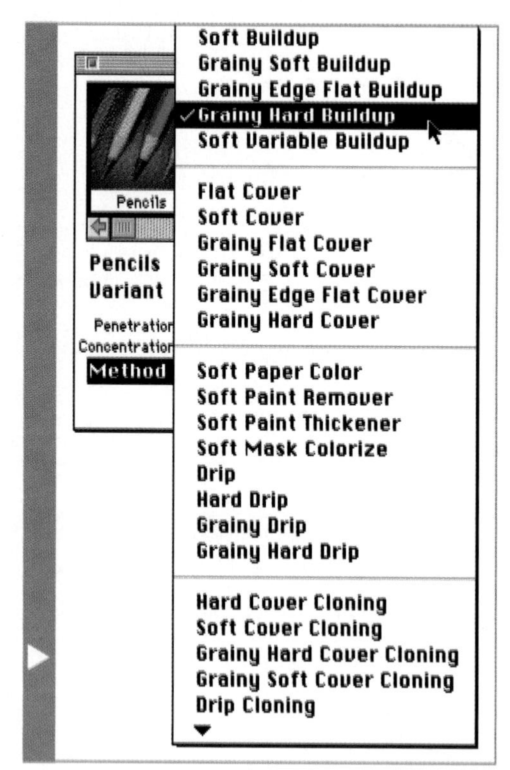

FIGURE 4.2 *The Method pop-up menu on the extended Brush palette.*

TABLE 4.1 *Stroke categories and characteristics.*

Column A Method Categories		Column B Stroke Characteristics	
	*Buildup methods* give you brushes whose strokes "build up" on the ones under them to produce a more opaque stroke. Buildup methods tend to generate darker, muddier results. The **Felt Pens** variants use Buildup methods.		*Soft* produces smooth strokes.
			*Flat* gives you hard-edged strokes.
	*Cover methods* paint over—or cover—earlier layers of paint, instead of building on underlying layers like the Buildup methods. Rather than build up to a blacker, muddier tone, Cover methods simply become more opaque as more paint is applied.		*Hard* creates rough-edged strokes.
			*Grainy* produces strokes that react to your paper surface.
	*Editing methods* affect underlying strokes by erasing them, smearing them, or darkening them. Please note the names of these methods use terms like "Paint Thickener" and "Drip" rather than "Editing."		*Edge* gives you strokes with a dense edge.
		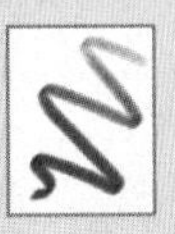	*Variable* creates strokes that start with more transparency.
	*Cloning methods* let you clone (or copy into a new file) an existing image and re-generate it.		
	*Wet methods* create the effects of using water color paints. Wet methods only work in the Wet Paint layer.		

Now you simply decide what you want in a stroke, and choose the category and characteristics that best achieve that goal. It's like ordering from a menu in a family-style restaurant: Choose one option from Column A (in this case one of the five Method Categories), and one or more from Column B (in this case the Characteristics).

For example, in Figure 4.3, Grainy Hard Buildup gives you strokes that react to the paper texture (Grainy—Column B), have rough edges (Hard—Column B), that eventually build up over each other to muddier, blacker tones (Buildup—Column A). Grainy Soft Cover gives you a paper-grain sensitive (Grainy—Column B), smooth (Soft—Column B) strokes that hide underlying strokes (Cover—Column A). Getting the hang of it?

Let's try one more. Grainy Hard Drip creates paper-grain sensitive (Grainy—Column B), rough-edged (Hard—Column B) strokes that are smeared (Drip—Column A). "Huh?" you may say. "Drip isn't a category." Well, you're right.

There are a few items on the **Methods** pop-up menu that, due to their names, defy our little Column A/Column B system. Let's quickly mention them.

Paper Color (Editing method) removes paint strokes down to the original paper color.

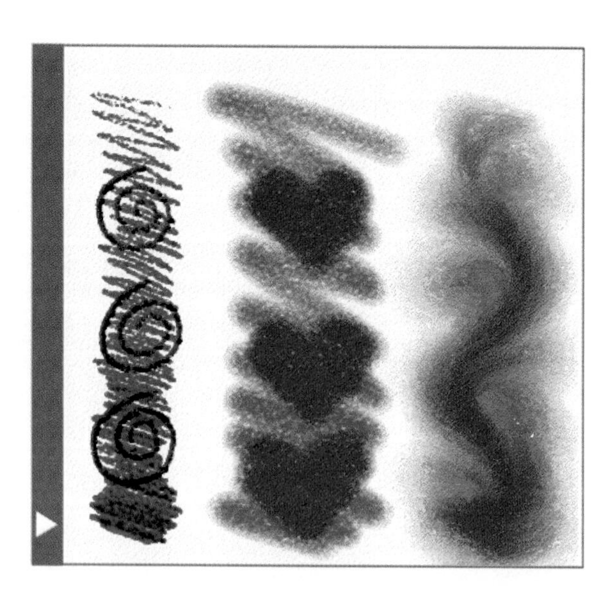

FIGURE 4.3

Examples of some methods.

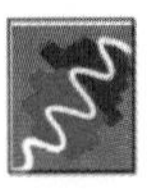

Paint Remover (Editing method) removes paint and replaces it with white.

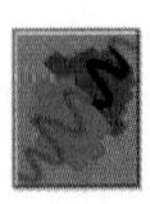

Paint Thickener (Editing method) increases the concentration of a color.

Mask Colorize (Editing method) paints within the frisket (mask) layer from Photoshop and ColorStudio files opened in Painter.

Drip (Editing method) smears strokes.

Wet Buildup (Wet method) produces watery strokes on the Wet Paint layer.

Wet Abrasive (Wet method) places color over existing paint on the Wet Paint layer.

Wet Remove Density (Wet method) is the eraser for the Wet Paint Layer.

Got it? Great! Now let's learn how to refine brush strokes even *more* using the Brush Behavior palette.

BRUSH BEHAVIOR

No, brushes can't misbehave, but their strokes can be refined. That's what the Brush Behavior palette does, along with determining how colors interact when you are using a Buildup method brush.

Open the Brush Behavior palette, shown in Figure 4.4, by selecting **Brush Behavior** from the **Windows** menu, then expand it using the zoom box in the upper right corner.

Looks awfully technical, doesn't it? Well, we thought so too, so we've included a few little graphics to perk up our discussion a little more. Let's take a look at these sliders and check boxes.

Dab Location Variability refers to the pattern of brush "dabs" that form a brush stroke, for example the bristle pattern of a bristle brush. Increasing the **Amount** value increases the randomness of the dabs, and ultimately gives you Seurat-like results.

Dab-to-Dab Spacing controls the space between dabs in a brush stroke. Increase the **Spacing/Size** value to make strokes denser and more continuous. **Min Spacing** further refines your "dab factor" by specifying the smallest number of pixels between dabs.

Brush Paint Reservoir adjusts the amount of paint held on a brush and the way the paint interacts when it builds up. Increase your **Resaturation** value to make the color last longer through a stroke. Increase your **Bleed** value to make colors blend more as they build up.

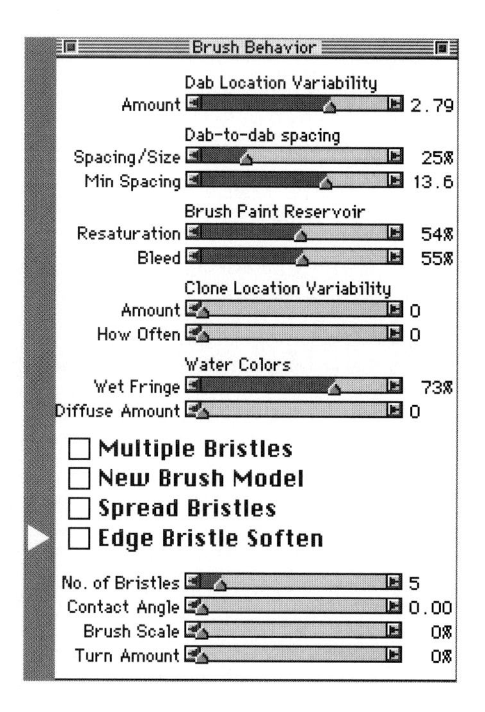

FIGURE 4.4
The expanded Brush Behavior palette.

Clone Location Variability controls factors associated with Cloning methods. Increasing the **Amount** value softens brush strokes and makes them less precise. Decreasing **How Often** generates rougher strokes.

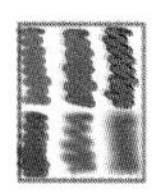

Water Color values affect Water Color (Wet method) brushes. Increasing **Wet Fringe** increases the amount of pooling on the Wet Paint Layer. Increasing **Diffuse Amount** increases the feathering of strokes on the Wet Paint layer.

Multiple Bristle Brushes

Real-time, multiple bristle brushes are brushes that give you incredibly realistic oil paint and acrylic paint effects. They are most effective when used with Surface Texture (see Chapter 5). The default real-time brushes are included among the **Brush** variants. The options on the lower half of the Brush Behavior palette let you edit existing bristle brushes or build your own. All of the default bristle brushes use the Cover method, so their strokes will cover existing paint.

- **Multiple Bristles.** Check this box to generate brushes that paint with visible bristle marks.
- **New Brush Model.** Select this option for real-time multiple bristle brushes.
- **Spread Bristles.** Use this option with **New Brush Model** to join at the beginning or end of a stroke bristles that have been spread. Deselect it to have bristles run parallel to each other.
- **Edge Bristle Soften.** Check this box to soften the bristles on the edge of a brush.
- **No. of Bristles** adds bristle hairs to a brush.
- **Contact Angle** widens the stroke of real-time brushes and increases the number of bristles.
- **Brush Scale** increases or decreases the stroke size of real-time brushes.
- **Turn Amount** smoothes (higher value) or roughens (lower value) curves painted with a bristle brush.

Still not enough control for you? Well, we still have one more trick left up our sleeve—the options on the Expression palette.

THE EXPRESSION PALETTE

The Expression palette, shown in Figure 4.5, controls how your brushes interact with paper texture, color density, and stroke width. Many of the settings enable mouse users to achieve the effect of using a pressure-sensitive stylus, but others are also useful for special effects.

- **Size** controls how Painter determines brush size.
- **Jitter** increases or decreases the randomness of your brush strokes.
- **Penetration** controls how paper texture is shown through a brush stroke.
- **Concentration** determines how Buildup method brushes operate.
- **Color** allows you to have two-color brush strokes. Choose one of these settings to determine when each color is used.
- **Angle** adjusts the direction of dabs in a stroke.

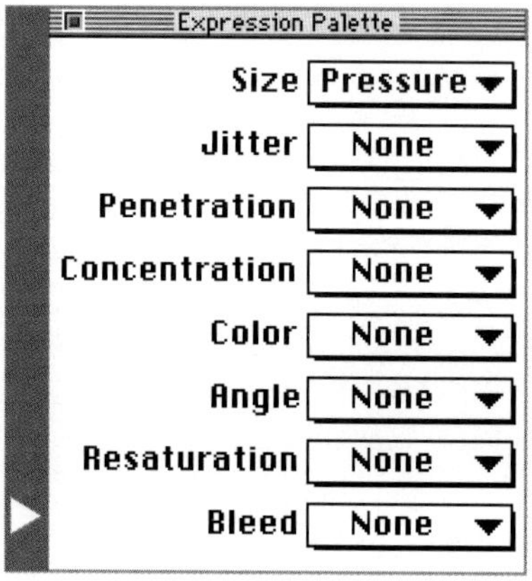

FIGURE 4.5
The Expression palette.

- **Resaturation** controls how much color is retained on a brush through a stroke.

- **Bleed** determines how colors mix together when you are using a Buildup method brush.

Each of these settings let you select how you want Painter to determine the options: none (the stroke is unaffected), stylus velocity (speed), direction, pressure, tilt (CalComp stylus only), bearing (CalComp stylus only), original luminance (for cloning), or randomly.

Well, that's it for the basic techniques for customizing brushes. Even if you never use them, you'll still have an exceptional supply of default tools to work with. If you're a real adventurer, you'll come up with tons of new variants to impress your friends and colleagues with. Before you go off and design a slew of new and exciting tools, let's look at how Painter lets you preview new brush strokes and save the ones you really want to keep.

VIEWING AND SAVING BRUSHES

Painter provides you with the Brush Stroke Designer palette, a wonderful interactive preview tool to view your brush strokes as you create or edit them. Then, you can use the Brush Looks window to keep a visual record of your brush strokes. Finally, you can add your new custom brushes and variants to the Brush palette.

THE BRUSH STROKE DESIGNER

The basic purpose of the Brush Stroke Designer palette is so you can see—right as you're working along—how custom brush and stroke characteristics will look, right down to the colors you want to use them in.

The Brush Stroke Designer is *very* easy to use and is an incredibly useful tool that will make all of the technical customization we just covered very easy to swallow. Basically, it means that you don't have to memorize (or even totally understand) what every customization option is for. Just check it out in the Brush Stroke Designer, and keep fiddling with it until you see the result you want. (Sorry, but if we told you this earlier, you wouldn't have even read any of the other stuff.)

First, open the palette by selecting **Brush Stroke Designer** from the Windows menu. The palette shown in Figure 4.6 is displayed.

You should be looking at a sample brush stroke on a sample background. To change the shape of the sample stroke, simply paint another stroke with your mouse or stylus. To change the stroke color or background, select a color from the primary or secondary color rectangles (respectively) on the Color palette, then click **Set Colors** on the Brush Stroke Designer palette.

A good way to get a feel for how this works is to select existing default variants from the Brush palette and see how they look in the Brush Stroke Designer. Then experiment with them using the customization methods we just discussed. Don't worry—you won't permanently affect your default brushes; unless you save them, your brushes will revert to their original settings.

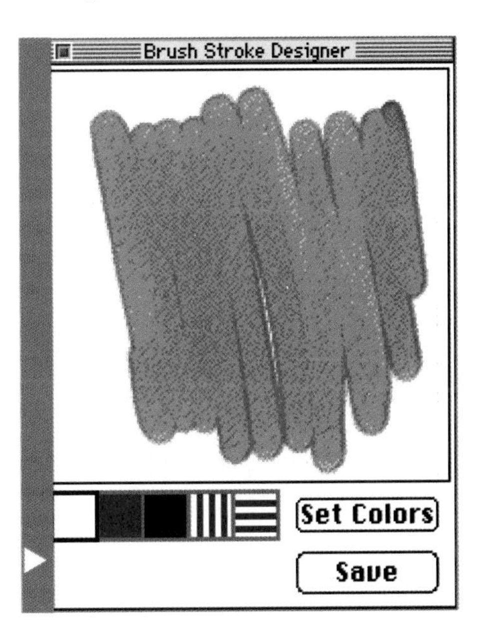

FIGURE 4.6

The Brush Stroke Designer palette.

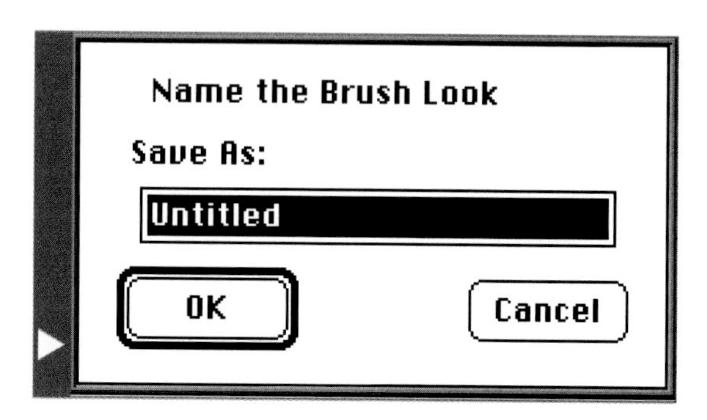

FIGURE 4.7
The Name the Brush Look dialog box.

So what if you come up with a brush you really like? Use it to paint with right away, or save it. You can save it as a variant in the Brush palette, or save it in the Brush Looks window right from the Brush Stroke Designer.

Let's try it: Click on the **Save** button and you'll see the Name the Brush Look dialog box shown in Figure 4.7.

Enter a name in the **Save As** field, and click **OK**. That's it! Your new custom brush is saved in the Brush Looks palette.

BRUSH LOOKS

"Okay," you may be saying. "I've just saved my new brush stroke in the Brush Looks window, but what the heck is that?"

Simple. It's a visual library of changes you made to a brush stroke using any of the customization methods (including the Paper palette, discussed in the next chapter). Open the palette by selecting **Brush Looks** from the Windows menu.

This palette, shown in Figure 4.8, is already chock full of options that are ready to use. Use this palette the same way you use the Brush palette: Scroll through the colorful icons, and click to select one. You can also tear off options, just as you do with variants on the Brush palette.

Click on **Library...** to access a slew of additional brush libraries available from Fractal Design Corporation. If you received the Painter Companion package, you will already have two additional libraries: **Mark's Looks** and **John's Looks**. These are brush libraries made by two of Painter's creators, Mark Zimmer (he created the paint can painting shown on every Painter package) and John Derry (whose art is featured later in this book).

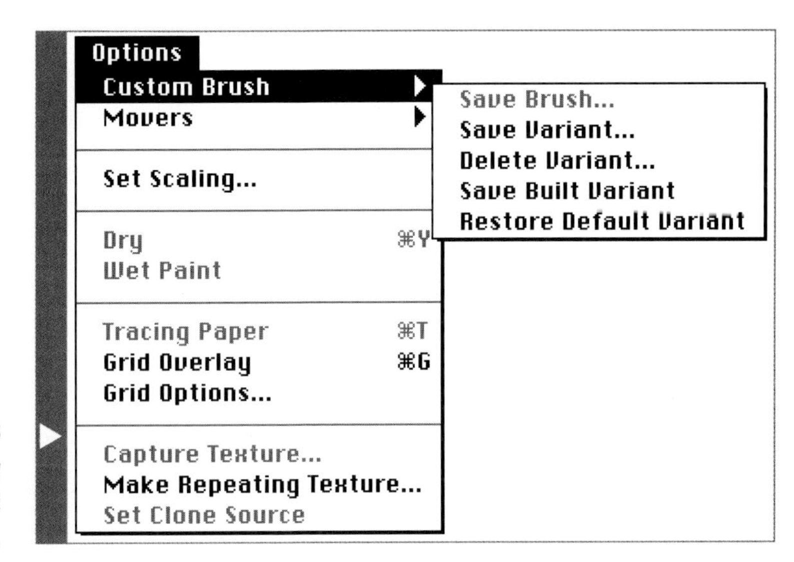

FIGURE 4.8
The cascading Custom Brush menu.

SAVING BRUSHES AND VARIANTS

You also have the option of saving a custom brush directly to the Brush palette. To see your choices for saving and deleting brushes and variants, select the cascading **Custom Brush** menu found under the **Options** menu. Figure 4.8 displays your options.

Saving New Brushes

It's also easy to create a whole new brush category. Of course, you'll want to create a picture to appear alongside the existing pictures on the Brush palette, so do that first (or, you can use any picture that can be imported into Painter). Use the **Selection** tool to choose a square portion of the image to be used. Then, select **Save Brush...** from the cascading menu, enter a name for your brush, and click **OK**. Your new brush and its mug shot are now the last option on the Brush palette. Now, create as many new variants for your brush as you like.

Saving and Deleting Variants

To save a brush stroke as a new variant of the currently selected brush, select **Save Variant...** from the cascading menu. Then enter a brush name in the **Save As** field of the Save Variant dialog box. Click **OK**, and it's saved.

To permanently change an existing variant, select the variant, and apply whatever customization you like. Then select **Save Built Variant** from the cascading menu. If you change an existing variant and later decide you liked the original better, simply select **Restore Default Variant** to bring back the original one.

To permanently erase a variant, select the variant you want to delete on the Brush palette. Then choose **Delete Variant...** from the cascading menu. Painter will ask you again if you really want to delete the variant. If you do, click **Yes** to complete the action. If not, click **No** to cancel it.

Remember, if you don't save either to the Brush palette or the Brush Looks palette, your changes will disappear as soon as you select another brush or variant. So be sure to save the effects you 'd like to use again.

Custom Brush and Brush Looks Palettes

It's easy to set up custom Brush palettes or Brush Looks palettes for individual clients or projects. Select either **Brush Mover...** or **Brush Looks Mover...** from the cascading Mover menu (under the Options menu), as shown in Figure 4.9.

Depending on your selection, you'll now see either the Brush Mover or Brush Looks Mover dialog box. Except for the title, they both look and operate alike. Let's use the Brush Looks Mover, shown in Figure 4.10, as our example.

Use this dialog box to move brushes into your new library (**>>Copy>>**), remove brushes from an existing library (**Remove**), close an

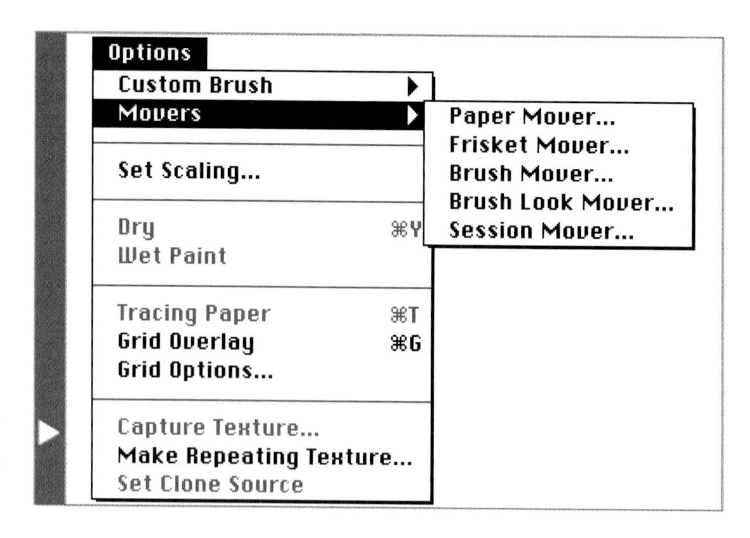

FIGURE 4.9
The cascading Mover menu.

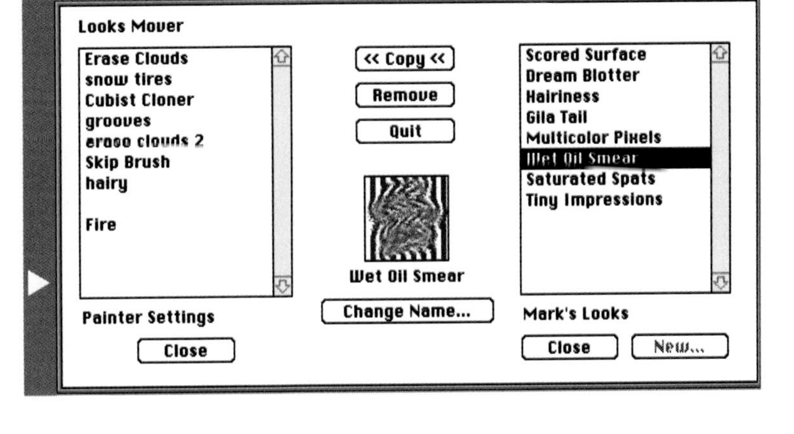

FIGURE 4.10
The Brush Looks Mover dialog box.

open library (**Close**), open an existing library (**Open**), or create a new library (**New...**). Simply select the brush or library you wish to use, close, or change, then click on the button that performs the action. When you're done, click on **Quit** to close the dialog box.

WHEW!

We've finally covered all of the brush customization options available in Painter. If you can think of anything that Fractal Design left out, call them up—I'm sure they'd love to hear about it. But if you're like us, your head is probably spinning from all of the choices already available, so take a few minutes to go for a walk or splash cold water on your face before moving on to the next chapter.

PRACTICE SESSION

1. Open a new file, and select black for the background. Select the **Impressionist Artists** brush from the Brush palette. Change the **Method** to **Hard Drip**. Choose a brown square from the Impressionist color page on the Color palette. Now draw the wood for a campfire.

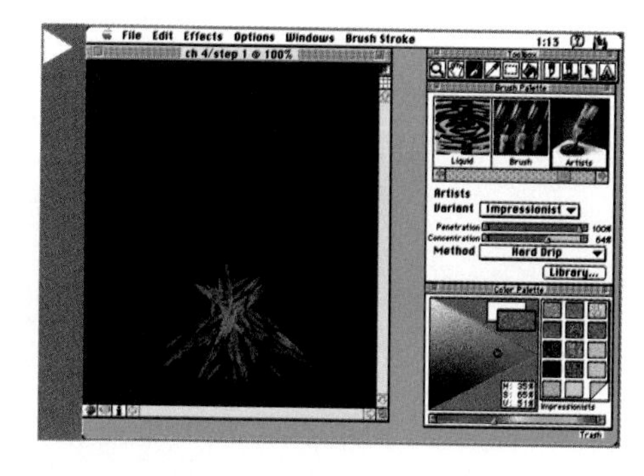

2. On the Brush palette, select the **Coarse Smeary Bristles** variant of the **Liquid** brush. Reduce the Penetration to 50%, and the increase the Concentration to 85%. Change the **Method** to **Grainy Drip**. Next, paint on some red, orange, and yellow, applying darker colors toward the source of the fire. We've selected our colors from the Fire Colors page of color squares.

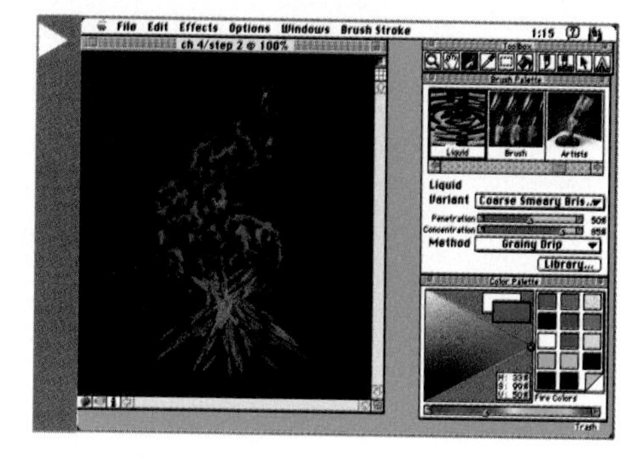

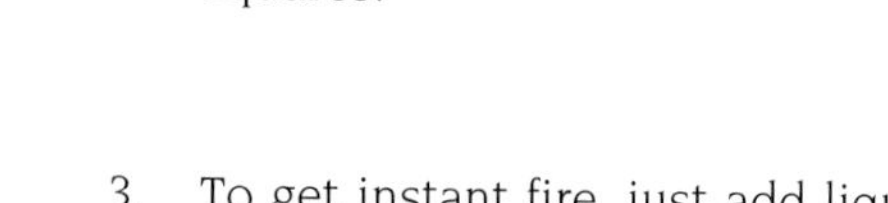

3. To get instant fire, just add liquid: Select the **Distorto Liquid** tool, open the Brush Size palette, and decrease the **Size** slider to about 20. Click **Build**, then smear your fire upward.

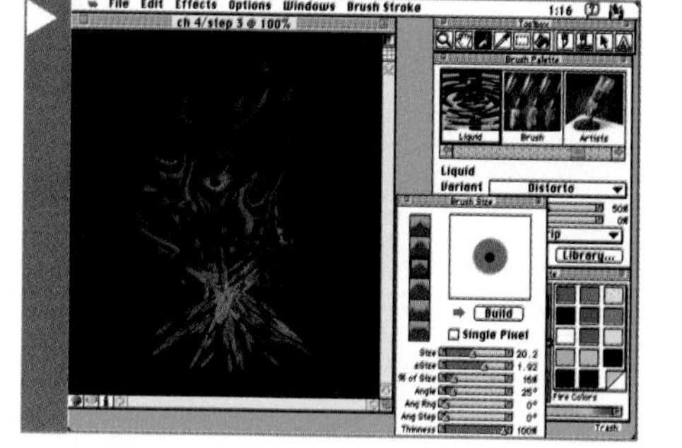

Color

CHAPTER 5

Colors are our perception of different wavelengths of light. Almost all colors can be created by using one of three color-mixing systems, each of which is best suited for a different purpose.

- **RGB** is typically used to create transmitted colors, and is the method used by color monitors and color televisions. RGB shows colors by using clusters of red, green, and blue phosphors, often referred to as *pixels*.

- **HSV** relates to the way the human eye perceives color. HSV stands for hue, saturation, and value (often called *brightness*). *Hue* refers to the property of a particular color relating to its frequency, or wavelength, of light. *Saturation* is the extent to which a color is comprised of a selected hue, rather than a combination of hue and white, as in the difference between red (a heavily saturated color) and pink (a less saturated color). *Value* is the degree of lightness or darkness in a color. Painter uses HSV on its Color palette because this color-wheel based system is most familiar to artists.

- **CMYK** is best suited for representing reflected colors—for printing colors. Generally used for producing printing plates for four-color process printing, CMYK is a color model using cyan, magenta, yellow, and black inks for different colors.

Remember, Painter mixes paint on the Color palette using HSV and saves files in RGB format. It *does not* use CMYK. If you are planning to import your files into a page layout program or output RC paper or film for four-color process printing, you must save your Painter files as DCS files, which are CMYK.

MORE USES FOR THE COLOR PALETTE

The basic operation of the Color palette is covered in Chapter 3. This section discusses some more advanced uses for that palette, most of which are found when you click on the Color palette's zoom button to reveal the expanded Color palette, shown in Figure 5.1.

PRIMARY AND SECONDARY COLORS

Depending on the brush you choose, your strokes can be comprised of a primary color, a secondary color, and the range of colors between them.

Click on the front rectangle on the Color palette to select your primary painting color, and on the back rectangle to select your secondary painting color. Figure 5.2 shows blue chosen as the primary color (front rectangle) and red (back rectangle) as the secondary color.

The use of primary and secondary colors is controlled by the Expression palette. When **None** is selected in the **Color** field of the Expression palette, you can only paint using one color at a time. Any of the other selections allow you to paint in two colors and

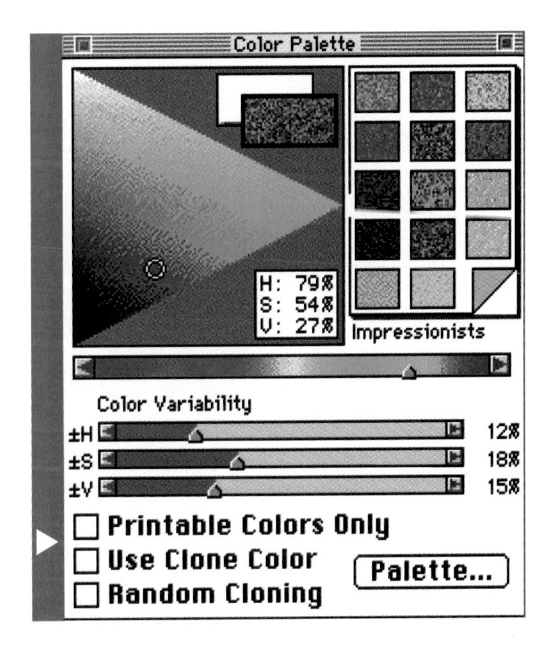

FIGURE 5.1
The expanded Color palette.

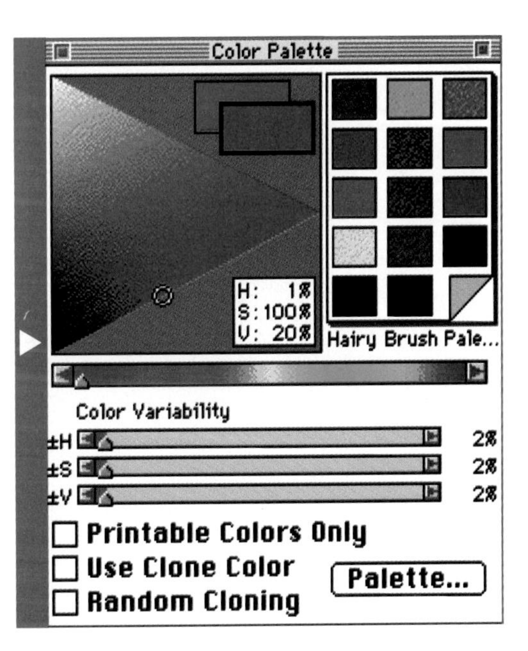

FIGURE 5.2
The Color palette with blue selected as a primary color and red selected as a secondary color.

determine when the primary color is used and when the secondary color is added.

PAINTING WITH MULTIPLE COLORS

You can also set up your Color palette to paint using more than two colors by using the **±HSV Color Variability** sliders on the Color palette.

- Increase the **±H** (hue) percentage to increase the number of hues in a brush stroke.
- Increase the **±S** (saturation) percentage to increase the number of saturations in a brush stroke.
- Increase the **±V** (value) percentage to increase the limit of luminances in a brush stroke.

Your kaleidoscopic selection is previewed in the front rectangle, as in Figure 5.3. The Impressionists color page was created with this technique. Hold down the **Option** key while clicking on a color square to add your multi-colored selection to a color page (remember to save it if you want to keep it).

PRINTABLE COLORS

Although you have a palette of 16 million colors to paint with, an offset printing press can't always print every color you come up with. To remedy this, click in the **Printable Colors Only** check box to select it. If you have selected a printable color, your whole color-selection rectangle will be one color. If you have not selected a printable color, the on-screen color is displayed in the left of the rectangle, and the printable

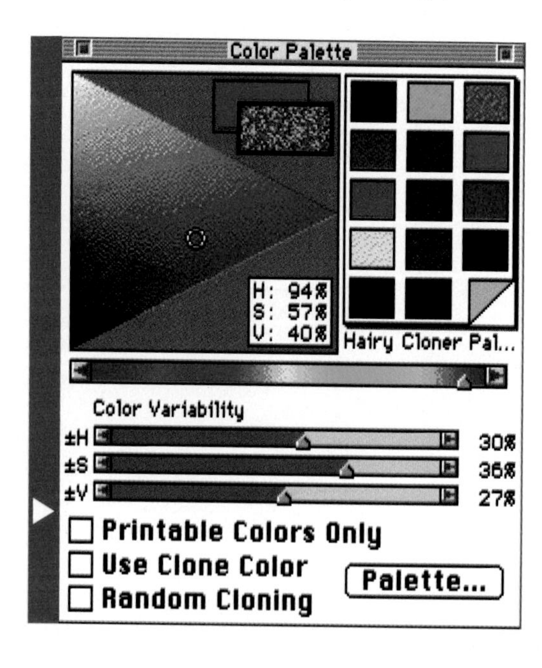

FIGURE 5.3
Selecting a multicolored brush stroke.

color in the right, as in Figure 5.4. The colors you paint with will now be the printable colors displayed on the right of the rectangles, not the on-screen colors on the left.

If the color you've selected is, in fact, printable, then your rectangle will be displayed as a solid color.

Oops! I Forgot to Check the Box

You've just spent three weeks creating the masterpiece of your lifetime and are ready to send it to your printer. Oh, no! You forgot to check **Printable Colors**, and you have no idea how your piece will print. Not to worry—you can change your 16 million colors to printable colors at any time in a project (although it's always best to do it before you start working).

Open the **Effects** menu and select **Enforce Printable Colors...** from the **Tonal Effects** cascading menu. Click **OK** in the dialog box shown in Figure 5.5, and it's done.

You may also apply printable colors to a selected area of an image by selecting the area *before* selecting **Enforce Printable Colors**.

CLONING COLORS

You may also clone, or copy, a color or portion of colors from one painting to another, or even within the same painting.

Click on the **Use Clone Color** check box on the Color palette. Then select one of the variants of the **Cloner** brush on the Brush palette (see Chapter 9 for more details on cloning brushes). Click once in the source area. Then, while holding down the **Control** key, click and drag over the area you

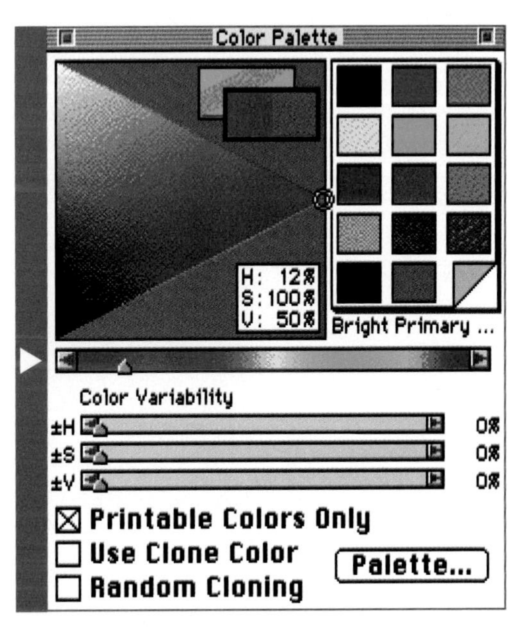

FIGURE 5.4 *Printable colors are displayed to the right of the rectangle, on-screen colors to the left.*

FIGURE 5.5
The Enforce Printable Colors dialog box with a preview.

want to paint. Your source image will re-create itself using the variant you selected, as in Figure 5.6.

COLOR FOR VIDEO

As with offset printing presses, not all colors that are displayed on your monitor can be used in video. However, most colors on your monitor will be video legal (except bright yellows and cyan blues).

Open the **Effects** menu and select **Video Legal Colors...** from the **Tonal Effects** cascading menu. You'll see a preview of the video-legal image in the dialog box shown in Figure 5.7. Select either the **NTSC** (United States) or **PAL** (European) video system from the pop-up menu, click **OK**, and it's done.

You may also apply video legal colors to a selected area of an image by selecting the area before selecting **Video Legal Colors**.

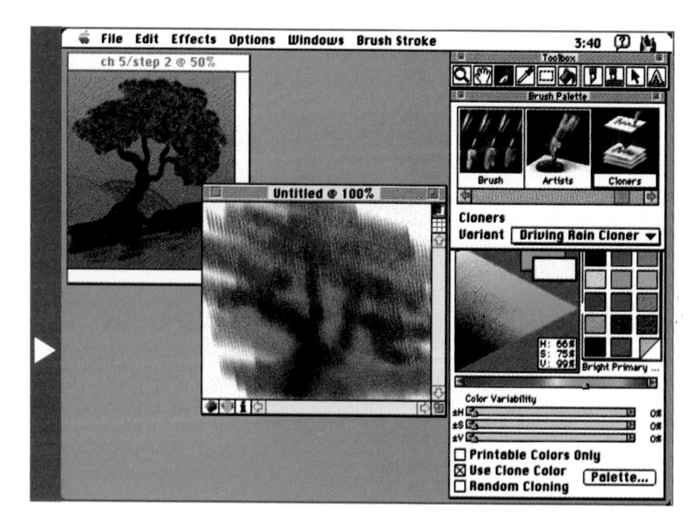

FIGURE 5.6
A source image (left), and its cloned colors using the Driving Rain Cloner variant.

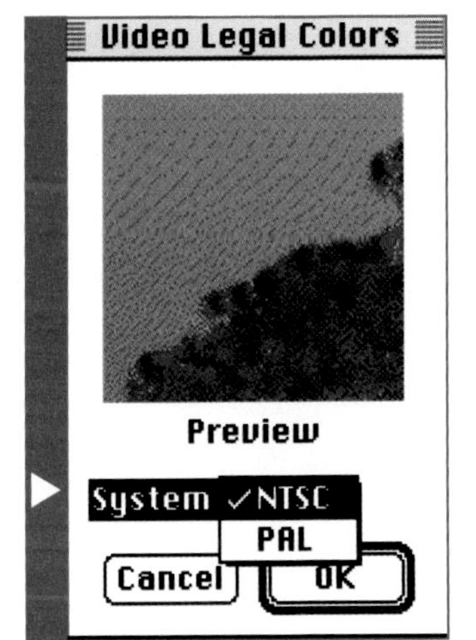

FIGURE 5.7
The Video Legal dialog box with a preview of the image.

THE FILL PALETTE

The Fill palette is great for dumping color into an enclosed area, a selected area, a frisketed area, or an entire image. To open it, select **Fill Palette** from the **Windows** menu or double-click on the **Bucket** tool in the Toolbox.

Select the type of area you want to fill from the top of the palette by clicking once on the icon. You also have some options as to the type of fill to use:

- **Flat Shade** fills an area with the flat tone selected as your primary color on the Color palette.
- **Color Ramp** fills an area with a gradient fill, from primary color to secondary color. Select a Ramp Direction radio button to indicate the angle of your fill.
- **Clone Source** fills an area with a selected part of another image—a "clone source" (see Chapter 9 for more details on cloning images).

Figure 5.9 shows a selected area being filled with a Color Ramp.

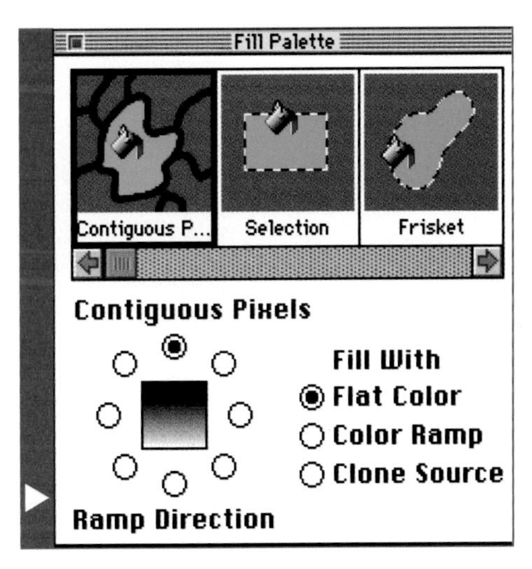

FIGURE 5.8
The Fill palette.

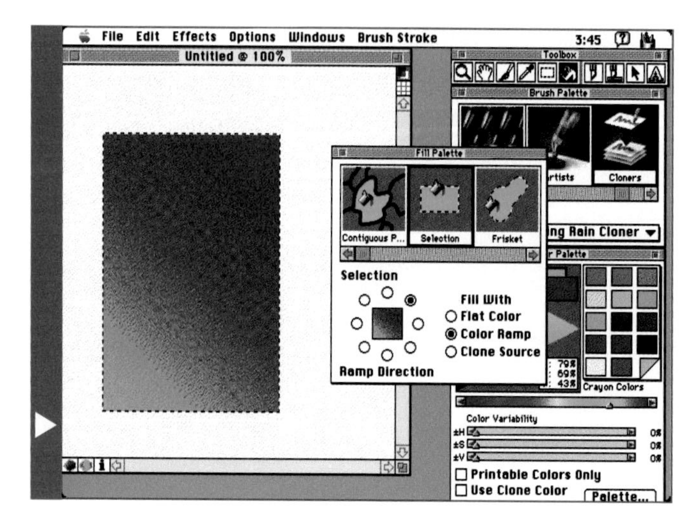

FIGURE 5.9
Filling an area with a **Color Ramp**.

SOFT MASK COLORIZE

Soft Mask Colorize is a great tool for creating cartoon-like effects. To use it, you must work with files created in ColorStudio or Photoshop that use a mask layer.

Access this tool from the **Methods** pop-up menu on the extended Brush palette, as shown in Figure 5.10.

Soft Mask Colorize uses the mask layer as sort of a stencil, coloring the image using your primary colors (white

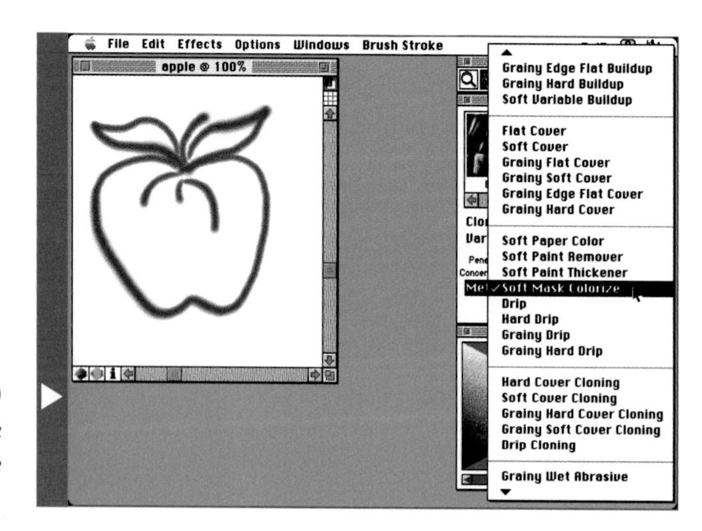

FIGURE 5.10
Selecting **Soft Mask Colorize** *from the* **Methods** *pop-up menu.*

FIGURE 5.11 *Photoshop mask (left), and* ***Soft Mask Colorize*** *with yellow as a primary color and blue as a secondary color (right).*

areas of the image) and secondary colors (black areas of the image), blending primary and secondary colors on gray areas, as in Figure 5.11.

If you find yourself using **Soft Mask Colorize** often, add it to the Brush palette using the technique described in Chapter 4.

PRACTICE SESSION

1. Open a new file (Painter's default size is just fine). On the Color palette, select a light blue as the primary color (front rectangle) and a brown as the secondary color (back rectangle). You may use either the color triangle or an existing color page to select these colors.

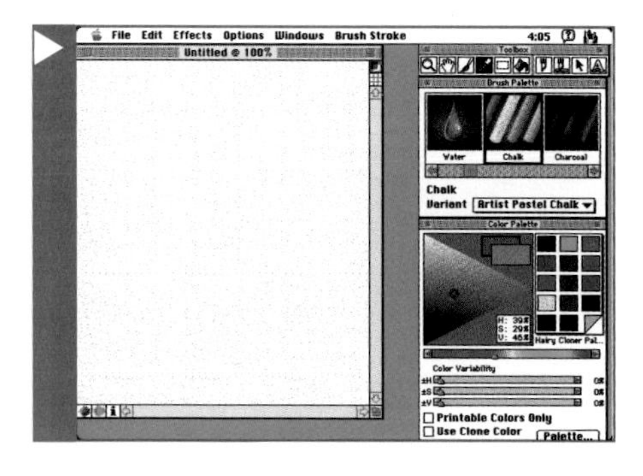

2. Open the Fill palette by double-clicking on the **Fill** tool in the Toolbox. Under **Fill With**, click on the **Color Ramp** radio button, and select the **Ramp Direction** radio button located at 12 o'clock. Scroll to the **Entire Image** icon, select it, and click on your page to fill it with the selected color ramp.

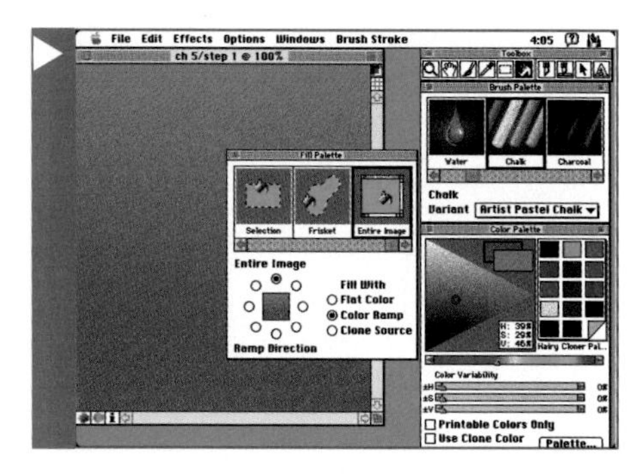

3. Use the color triangle and the **±HSV** sliders to create some multicolored strokes. Use those color strokes with the **Artists Pastel Chalk** variant to sketch out a little landscape using multicolored strokes. Notice that with a combination of the texture-sensitive pastels and the multicolored strokes, you'll only need to make about four selections from the Color palette to sketch out this little landscape.

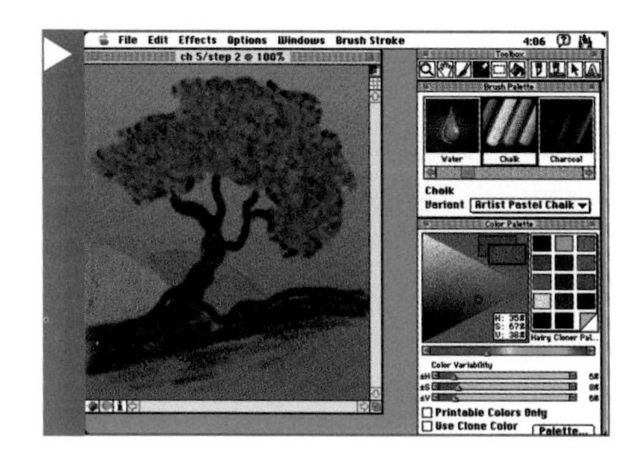

Scratching the Surface

PAPER TEXTURE AND SURFACE CONTROL

CHAPTER 6

One of the best features in Painter—there are so many of them—is the ability to have your tools interact with a plethora of surface textures. It's one thing to be able to paint electronically with realistic brushes. It's amazing to be able to do this on a vast assortment of canvases and other surfaces and to see your tools interacting with these surfaces. After reading this chapter, you'll also be able to apply special effects to your painting surfaces, from marbling and distorting images to adjusting tones and adding light sources.

TEXTURES: THE PAPER PALETTE

Opening the Paper palette (under the **Windows** menu) is a sensual experience. Really. You can almost feel your brushes interacting with whatever paper grain you have selected.

When you select a paper grain by clicking on its icon, you won't see the background of your image change to that texture. Instead, you'll see the texture reflected in your brush strokes, if you are using a paper-texture sensitive tool. (Any brush that uses a **Grainy Method** reacts to paper texture.) Figure 6.1 shows the **Chalk** brush being used with a variety of textures available in the default Paper palette.

Use the zoom box to expand the palette and you can increase the size of the paper grain by increasing the value on the **Scale** slider. Check the **Invert Grain** check box (three guesses as to what this one does) to invert the

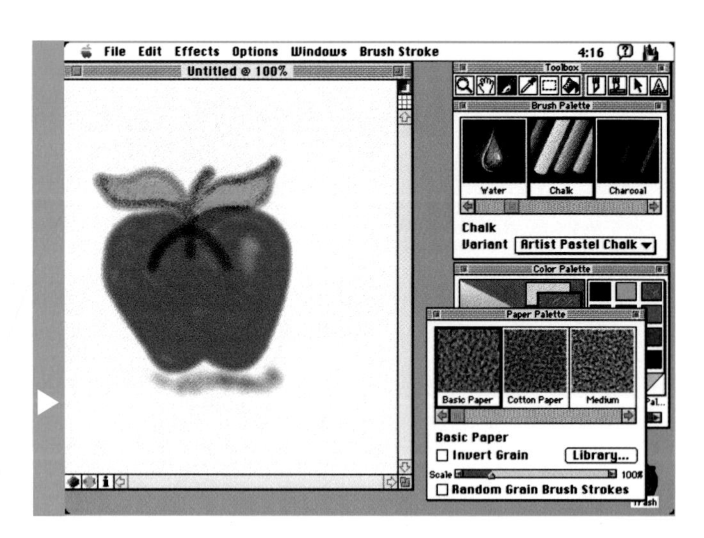

FIGURE 6.1
*Using the **Chalk** brush with the default Paper palette.*

grain of your paper. **Random Grain** randomizes the texture and gives you an unrepeating version of a texture. After you change the scale, invert, or randomize a paper grain, you can even tear off the new variant you created, just as you tear off a variant from the Brush palette.

To access an even cooler assortment of textures, click on the **Library** button, and select from additional texture files: **More Paper Textures**, **Simple Patterns**, **Texture Sample**, **Wild Textures**, and **More Wild Textures** (your default file is **Paper Textures**). You can have tear-off windows from different libraries open at the same time. Figure 6.2 shows tear-offs from several libraries and in differing percentages.

APPLYING PAPER GRAIN TO AN ENTIRE IMAGE

In addition to applying grain to individual strokes, you can apply a three-dimensional paper grain to an entire image. This works either before, during, or after adding brush strokes to an image.

Using the Paper palette, select the grain and other options you want to apply. Then open the **Effects** menu and select **Apply Surface Texture...** from the **Surface Control** cascading menu. The Apply Surface Texture dialog box, shown in Figure 6.3, gives you a preview of how your image will look with the selected texture. (If you have a slower computer, please be patient while this dialog box makes its appearance.)

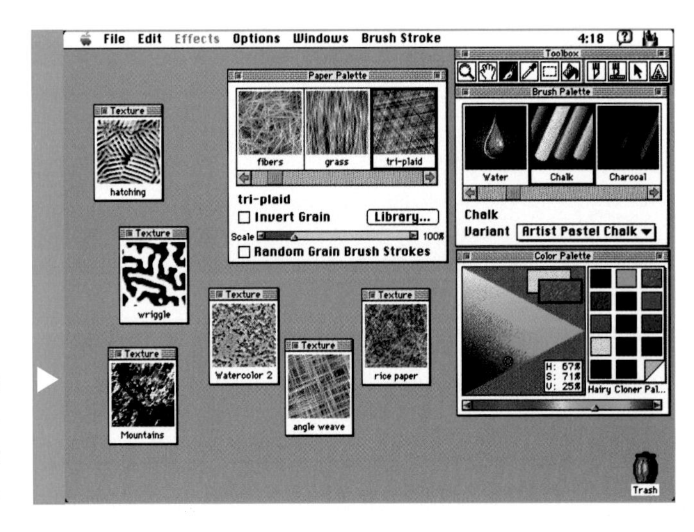

FIGURE 6.2
Tear-off windows from different paper texture libraries.

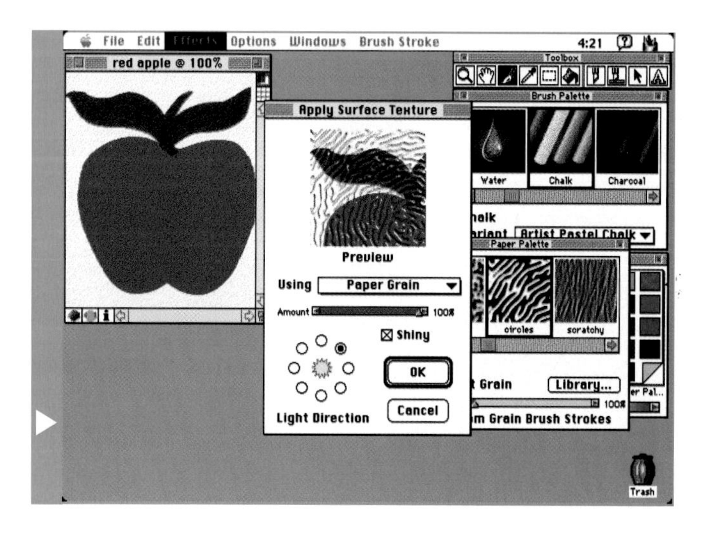

FIGURE 6.3
The Apply Surface Texture dialog box.

Make sure **Paper Grain** is chosen on the **Using** pop-up menu, adjust the **Amount** slider to the percentage of grain you want to apply, and click **OK**. Voila! Instant texture.

If you choose **Image Luminance** in the **Using** pop-up menu, Painter uses the brightness of an image to decide where to place texture.

Reserve some time for either of these options to process.

APPLYING COLOR AND PAPER GRAIN

Use the **Color Overlay** feature, also found under the **Surface Control** cascading menu, to add both color and texture at the same time to either an entire image or a selected portion.

In the Color Overlay dialog box, (Figure 6.4), select a model: **Dye Concentration** allows color to be absorbed by the paper, **Hiding Power** allows the color to cover an underlying image.

Adjust the **Opacity** slider until you see the results you want in the Preview window. Next, select a mode from the **Using** pop-up menu:

- **Uniform Color** overlays a flat, untextured tint.
- **Paper Grain** overlays a texture selected in the Paper palette. (You may switch to the open Paper palette from this dialog box.)
- **Frisket** adds texture around a frisket (see Chapter 7 for more information on friskets).

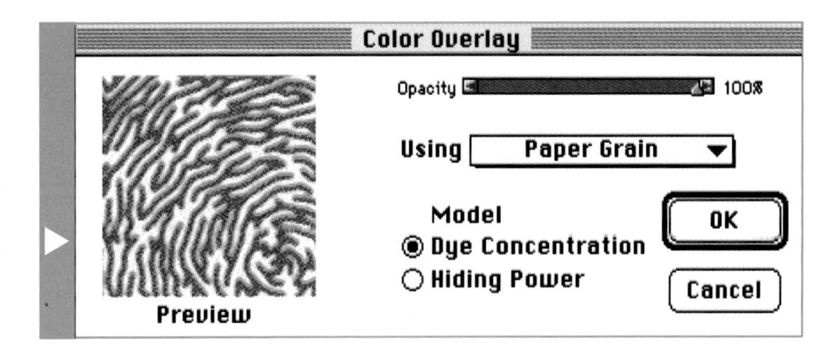

FIGURE 6.4
The Color Overlay dialog box.

- **Image Luminance** generates a texture based on the brightness of an image.

- **Original Luminance** texturizes a cloned image based on the brightness of a source image (see Chapter 9 for more information on cloning).

When the Preview box shows the results you want to achieve, click **OK**.

CREATING AND EDITING PAPER TEXTURES

If that's not enough for you (boy, are you demanding), you can create your own paper textures and libraries, or edit existing ones.

Repeating Textures

Use the **Make Repeating Texture** choice under the **Options** menu to make custom surfaces from a selection of preset patterns. From the Make Repeating Texture dialog box, shown in Figure 6.5, make any of the following adjustments:

- Select a pattern type from the **Pattern** pop-up menu (**Halftone**,

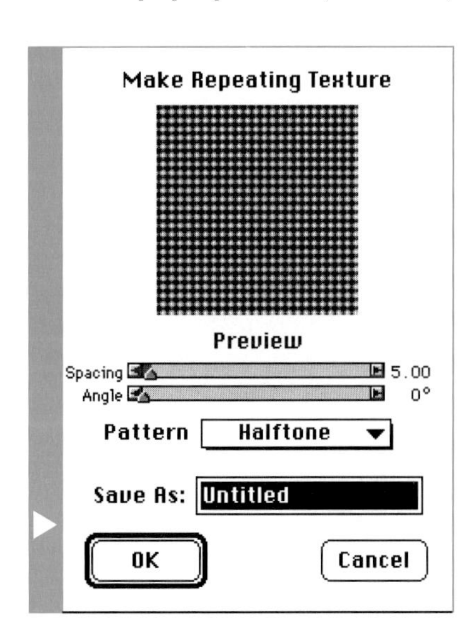

FIGURE 6.5
The Make Repeating Texture dialog box.

New Halftone, **Line**, **Diamond**, **Square**, **Circle**, **Ellipse**, or **Triangle**).

- Increase the value on the **Spacing** slider to increase the space between each pattern element.

- Change the value on the **Angle** slider to change the angle of the pattern.

Your changes are displayed in the Preview window. When you achieve the results you want, name the pattern, click **OK**, and it is added to the end of the open paper texture library.

Capturing a Texture

Let's say you've created a brush stroke or a series of strokes that you want to use as an underlying texture for a series of digital paintings the Metropolitan Museum of Art has commissioned you to paint. Well, Painter makes it even easier than you would have thought to use that texture again and again.

Simply select the area you want to add to a library and choose **Capture Texture...** from the **Options** menu. Use the **Crossfade** slider to indicate how much the selected area repeats in the texture, enter a texture name, and click **OK**. Your texture is now added the end of the open paper texture library.

SURFACE CONTROL

The section on texture talked about applying grains and textures to the surface of an image. *Surface control* refers to other types of effects that can be applied to the surface of an image, such as adjusting tone, distorting an image, applying a light source, and adding other special effects.

TONAL CONTROL

Did your mother ever tell you to change your tone? Well, here's your chance to make Mom real happy.

Under the Effects menu you will find the Tonal Control cascading menu. You have several options here that we haven't covered yet. All of these options can be applied to an entire image or a selected or frisketed part.

- **Brightness/Contrast** adjusts the brightness and contrast from the dialog box shown in Figure 6.6.

- **Equalize** balances the brightness and contrast settings to optimize them. It finds the lightest and darkest values in an image, averages them, and redistributes the values in between. Use the black and white triangle sliders under the histogram (the black mountain-like image) to adjust your image. Adjust the **Brightness** slider to increase or decrease gamma (midtone values—everything but black and white). You'll see the changes on-screen as you move the sliders. Click on **Apply** if you want to keep your changes. (Huh?) Forget all of that, just look at Figure 6.7 to see what it does.

FIGURE 6.6 *The Brightness/ Contrast dialog box.*

- **Posterize** reduces the amount of colors (or grayscales) in an image. Simply enter the number of colors you want your image reduced to in the Posterize dialog box and click **OK**. Figure 6.8 shows an image before and after posterization.

- **Negative** turns your image into a negative, as in Figure 6.9.

ORIENTATION AND DISTORTION

These options are great for getting Picasso-like results. Under the **Effects** menu is the **Orientation** cascading menu, allowing you access to the following manipulations:

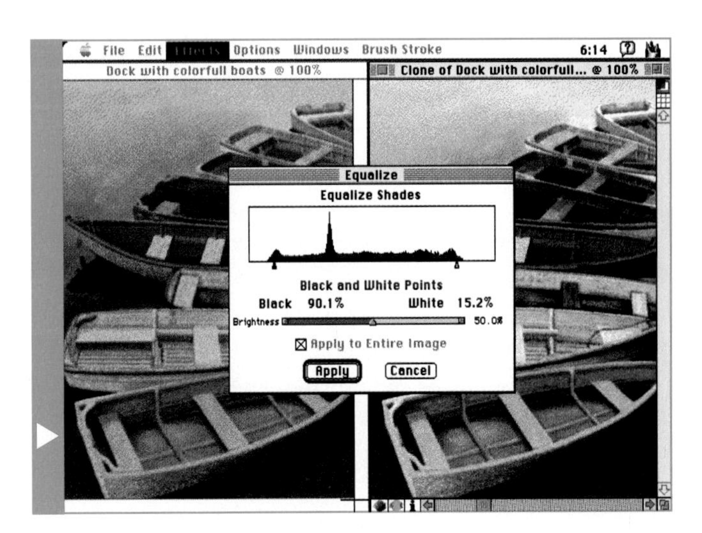

FIGURE 6.7 *An image before (left) and after (right) equalization.*

FIGURE 6.8
An image before (left) and after (right) posterization.

- **Rotate** turns your image (or selected area) in increments of 1 degree. Enter the value in the dialog box, and click **OK**.

- **Scale** changes the dimensions of the image or selected area. Either click and drag on the handles that appear around the image, or enter horizontal and vertical scale values in the dialog box. Click **Constrain Aspect Ratio** to proportionally scale an image. Click **OK** to keep your changes.

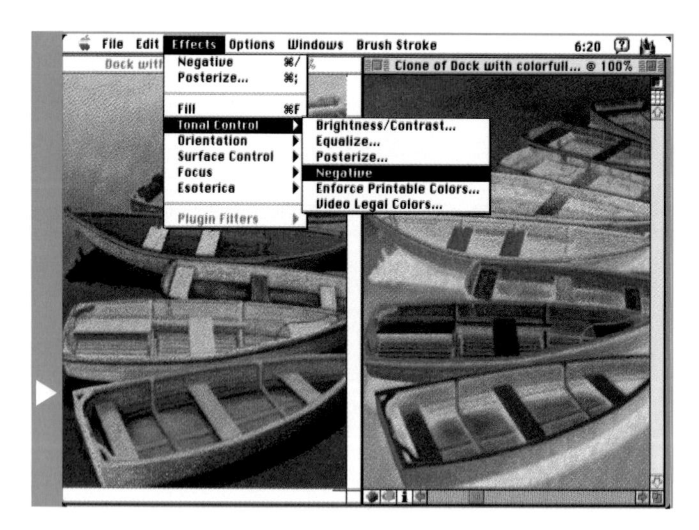

FIGURE 6.9
An image before (left) and after (right) using the ***Negative*** *option.*

- **Distort** warps the image in a selected area. Click and drag on the handles that appear around the selection. If you click on the **Better** check box, you get a more accurate distortion, but it takes much longer to render. Click **OK** to keep your changes.

- **Flip Horizontal** works on an entire image or a selected area.

- **Flip Vertical** works on an entire image or a selected area.

DYE CONCENTRATION

Dye concentration adjusts the intensity of color in all or a selected part of an image. The Adjust Dye Concentration dialog box, shown in Figure 6.10, is also another place you can add texture to an image. Access this dialog box from the **Surface Control** cascading menu under the **Effects** menu.

Select from the following options in the **Using** pop-up menu:

- **Uniform Adjustment** adjusts color. It does not add texture.

- **Paper Grain** adjusts color while adding a texture selected from the open Paper palette.

- **Frisket** adds texture around a frisket (see Chapter 7 for more information on friskets).

- **Image Luminance** generates a texture based on the brightness of an image.

- **Original Luminance** texturizes a cloned image based on the brightness of a source image (see Chapter 9 for more information on cloning).

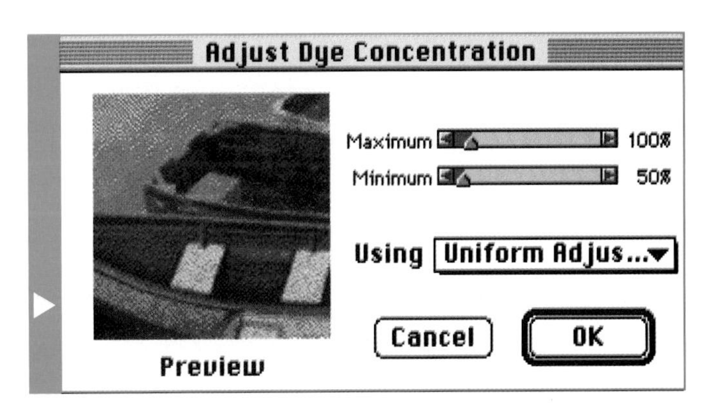

FIGURE 6.10
The Adjust Dye Concentration dialog box.

Use the **Maximum** and **Minimum** sliders to adjust the intensity of color in an image. When the Preview box reflects the results you want, click **OK** to accept the changes.

LIGHTING

Use this feature, also found under the **Surface Control** cascading menu, to add one or more light sources to all or a selected part of an image. You can even select the color of the light source.

This option is only available to users working on a computer with a floating point unit (math coprocessor). If you do not have a floating point unit built into your computer,this option will be grayed out.

Use the scrolling palette in the bottom left of the Apply lighting dialog box to select the type of lighting you want to apply.

To edit the light source, adjust the sliders until the results you want are displayed in the Preview box.

To add color to the light source, click in the **Light Color** square. Select a color from the color picker, and click **OK**. Use the same process to select an **Ambient Light Color** (the surrounding light).

If you've edited an existing light source and would like to save it, click on the **Save** button, enter a name for your new lighting, and click on **OK**. Your new lighting is now added to the scrolling palette.

When your lighting is absolutely perfect, click **OK** to accept the changes. Please be aware that, although it's a really neat feature, this is one of the slowest options in Painter (unless you are using a DSP-equipped AV or a Power Mac). You may want to use it just before a lunch break. If you are lucky, it may be ready in time for dinner.

FOCUS

The options on the Focus cascading menu allow you to sharpen and blur your image or a selected portion of it.

- **Sharpen** increases contrast of adjacent pixels to increase the clarity of an image. Be careful with this one, you can get some really wild results if you oversharpen. Figure 6.11 shows the sharpening of an image.
- **Soften** is the opposite of **Sharpen**, and has the same effect as putting a filter on a photographic lens, as in Figure 6.12.
- **Motion Blur** creates the illusion of movement by making an image appear as if you had pho-

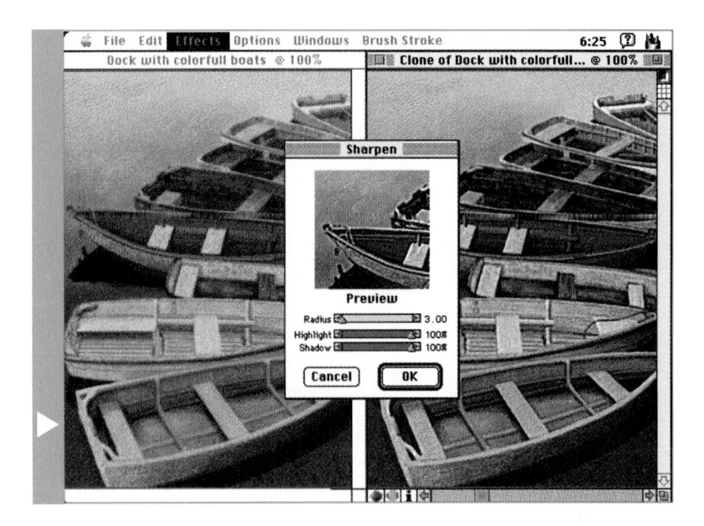

FIGURE 6.11
An image before and after sharpening.

tographed it while it was moving, as in Figure 6.13.

- **Glass Distortion** makes your image appear as though you were viewing it through glass, as in Figure 6.14.

OTHER SURFACE EFFECTS

Now we're getting into an even wilder set of tools found on the **Esoterica** cascading menu (under the **Effects** menu).

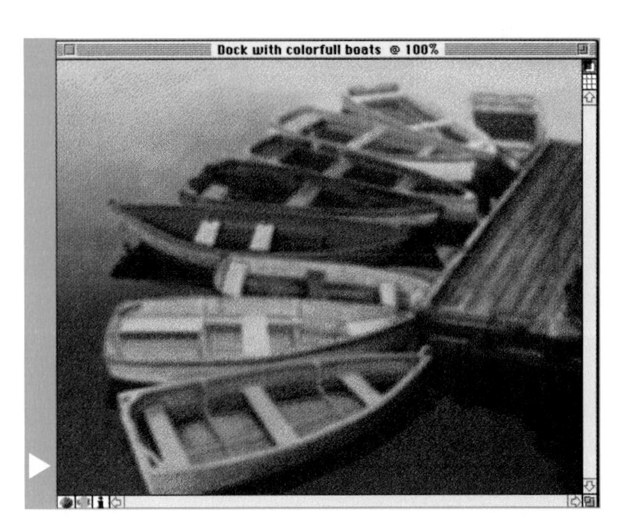

FIGURE 6.12
Softening an image.

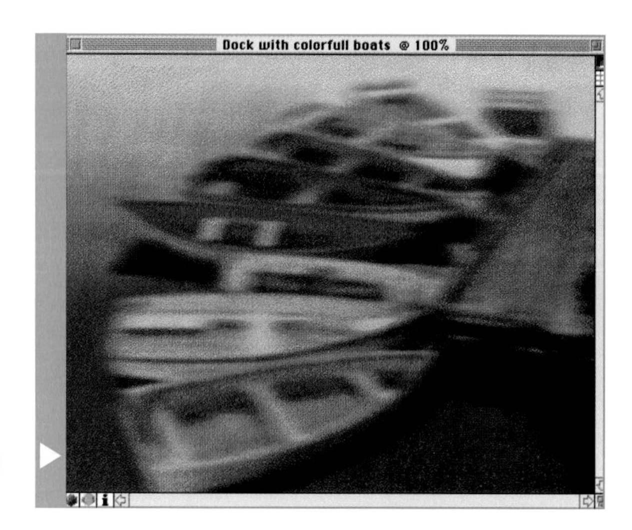

FIGURE 6.13
Using **Motion Blur**.

Marbling

Marbling turns any image (all or a selection) into a marbled masterpiece. Specify the **Rake Path** (direction of marbling) to get the effects you want. Figure 6.15 shows an example.

Blobs

True to its name, **Blobs** uses either a color or an item on the current clipboard to place floating blobs on an image. Blobbed images are great candidates for marbling. Figure 6.16 is blobbed.

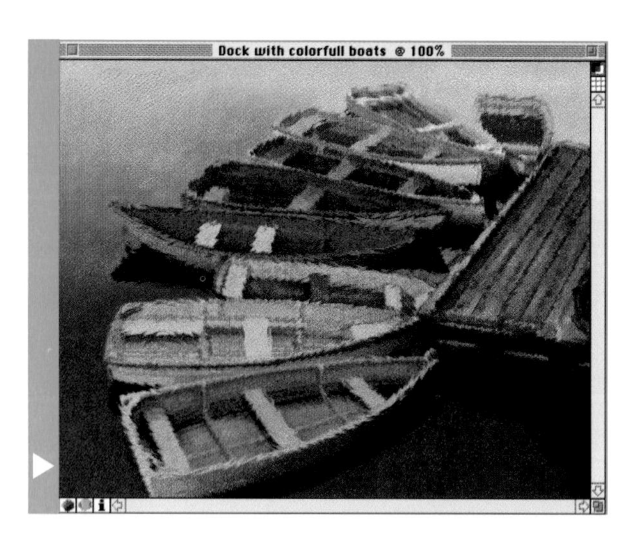

FIGURE 6.14
Using **Glass Distortion**.

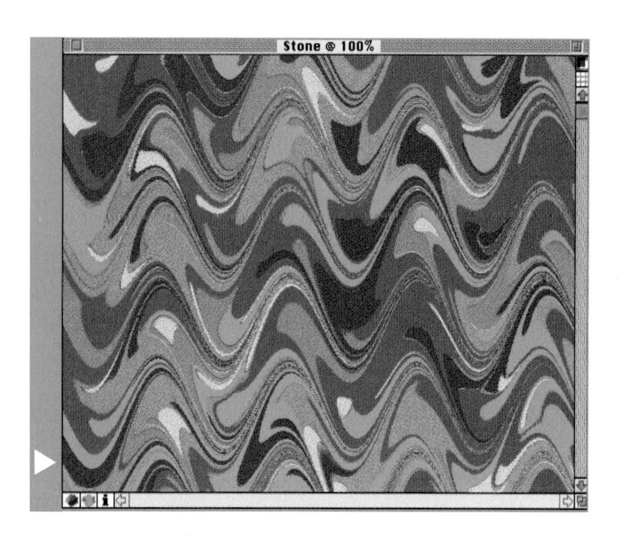

FIGURE 6.15
*Applying **Marbling**.*

This option is only available to users working on a computer with a floating point unit (math coprocessor). If you do not have a floating point unit built into your computer,this option will be grayed out.

Highpass

Highpass lets higher-frequency areas show through while suppressing lower-frequency areas. It has the effect of highlighting areas of brightness and

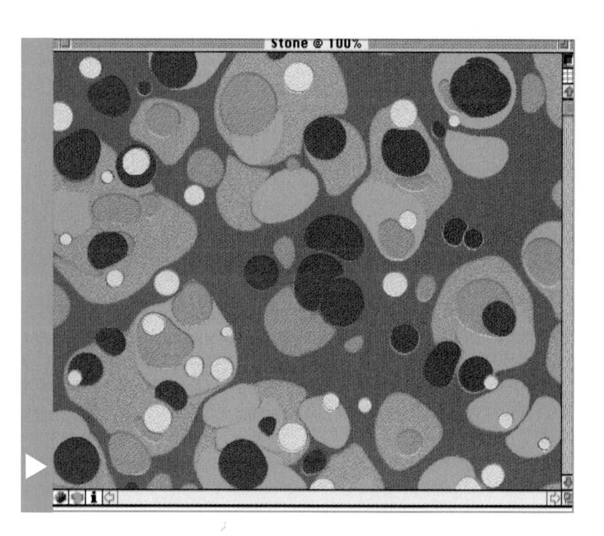

FIGURE 6.16
A blobbed image.

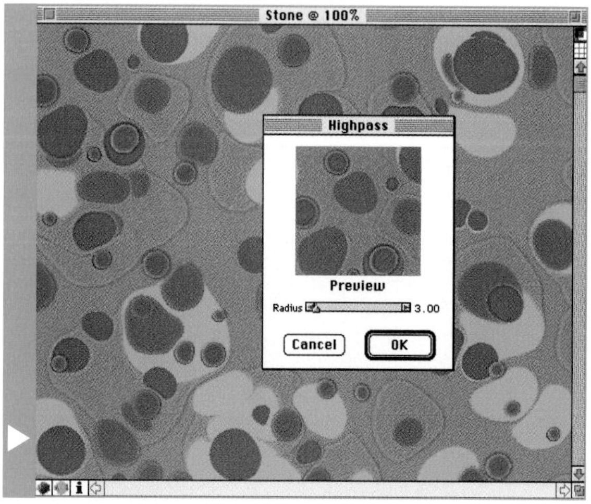

FIGURE 6.17
Applying ***Highpass***.

increases contrast in areas that are lacking contrast, as in Figure 6.17.

Grid Paper

Grid Paper adds grid lines to all or part of an image. These lines are editable as if they were applied by painting them on.

PLUG-INS

If you chose to access third-party plug-ins while installing Painter, you can access them through the **Plug-in** cascading menu under the **Effects** menu. If you did not locate any plug-ins during installation, this option is grayed out.

Enough of this chatter. Let's try some of this stuff.

PRACTICE SESSION

1. Let's quickly resketch the tree in the previous chapter, adding a few new effects. Open a new file (Painter's default size is just fine). Select the upper two-thirds of the screen and fill it with a **Ramp** ranging from dark blue on top to light blue on the bottom. Next, select the lower third of the image and apply a **Ramp** fill using two medium browns or rusts.

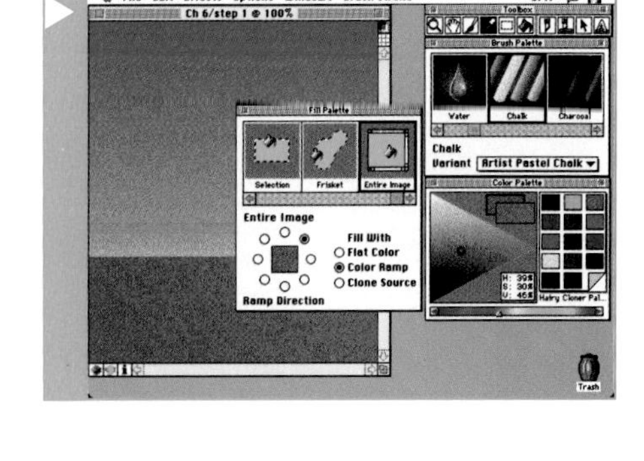

2. Now for some clouds. Select **Surface 2** from the More Paper Textures library on the Paper palette and create a multicolored off-white stroke on the Color palette. Use the **Spatter Airbrush** to add some clouds to the sky. You can actually use any brush you want, but remember it must use a **Grainy** Method to paint with the selected paper texture.

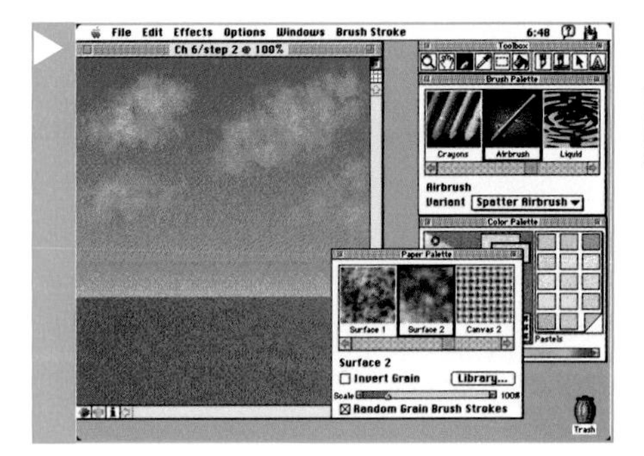

3. Select the sky area, and select **Distort** from the **Orientation** cascading menu. Grab one of the side handles, and stretch the image horizontally. This is a tip from John Derry at Fractal Design Corp., who says this is the best way to remove evidence of an artist's hand from a skyline.

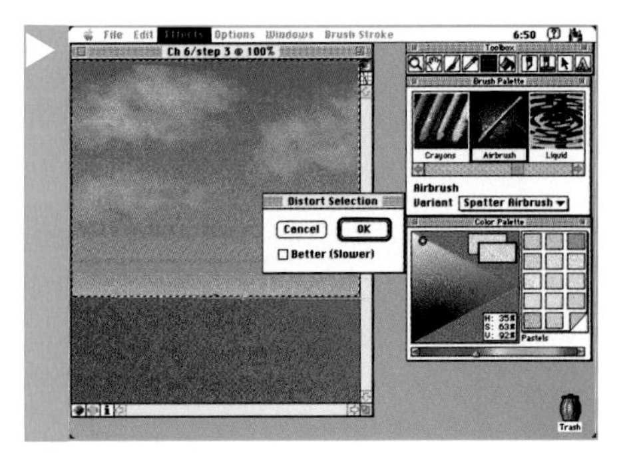

PRACTICE SESSION CONTINUED

4. Use any cover brush, such as the **Camel Hair Brush** variant, to block out the mountains. Then use the **Artist Chalk** tool, a multicolored stroke, and the **Scratchy** texture from the More Wild Textures library to cover the blocked area with a darker textured stroke.

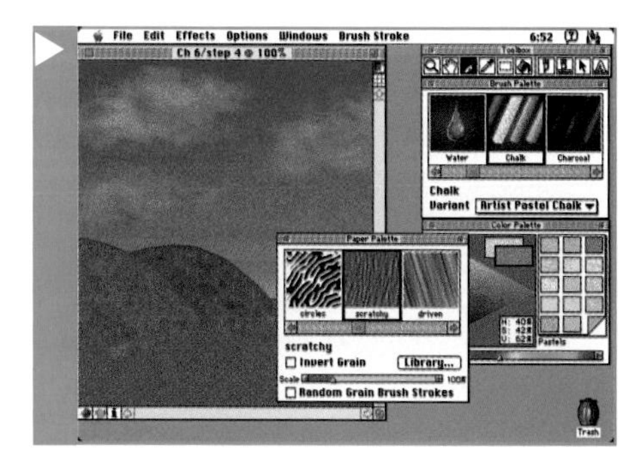

5. Next, block out your tree and foliage. Use the **Mountain** texture (Texture Sampler library) and the **Colored Pencil** brush for the bark of the tree, blend the foreground a little with the **Grainy Water** brush, and use the **Artists Pastel Chalk** with the **Scatter** texture for the foliage.

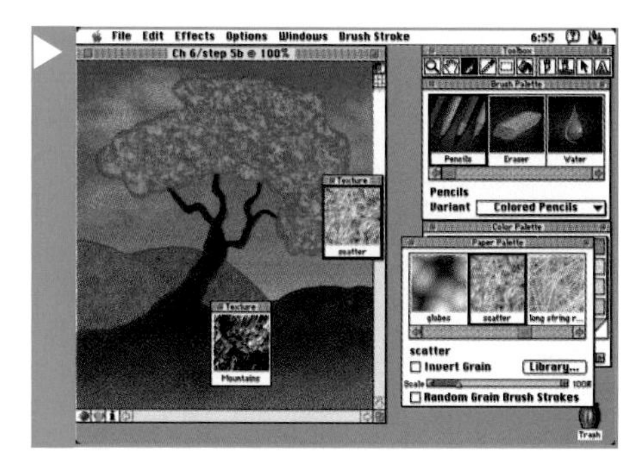

6. Use **Apply Surface Texture** on the **Surface Control** cascading menu to apply **Rice Paper** texture from the Wild Textures library to the entire image. Deselect the **Shiny** option.

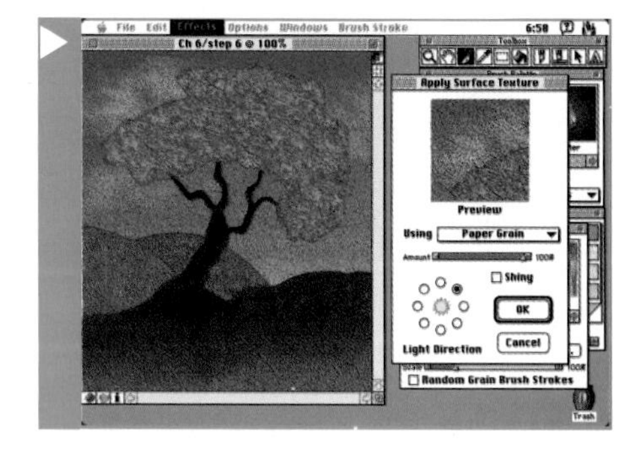

Friskets

CHAPTER 7

A *frisket* is a mask applied to certain areas of an image to protect them while you work on other areas of the image. If you've also been concerned about why you can only select rectangular areas with the **Selection** tool, you'll be happy to know that you can use a frisket to select irregularly shaped areas of an image. Friskets are not only handy for protecting areas of a painting, but also for applying special effects, textures, text, and fills to specific areas of an image.

FRISKET TOOLS

All of the tools found in the extended Toolbox are frisket tools. We'll briefly introduce them here, and cover them throughout this chapter.

The **Frisket Knife** tool draws freehand friskets. Click and drag with this tool to use it.

The **Frisket Line** tool draws polygonal friskets. Click on the origin point of a frisket, and continue clicking until you close your polygon. If you click and hold, Painter displays a guide showing you where your line segment lays. Holding the **Shift** key while clicking constrains your line segments to 45-degree angles. When you have completed your polygon, press **Enter**.

The **Frisket Pointer** tool selects existing friskets. To select a frisket, click on it, and is will be displayed with handles around it. Hold down the **Shift** key while clicking on friskets to select multiple friskets. Deselect a frisket by clicking anywhere outside an existing frisket, or by choosing **Deselect** from the Edit menu.

The **Frisket Text** tool creates friskets made of type for some incredible effects.

Figure 7.1 shows these tools in action.

MULTIPLE FRISKETS

You may add more than one frisket to an image. You can also create multiple friskets and work with them simultaneously.

To create "connected" multiple friskets, select the **Frisket Knife** or **Frisket Line** tool while holding down the **Command** key. Your frisket cursor is displayed with a plus sign next to it, indicating that you're adding multiple friskets. Draw as many friskets as you

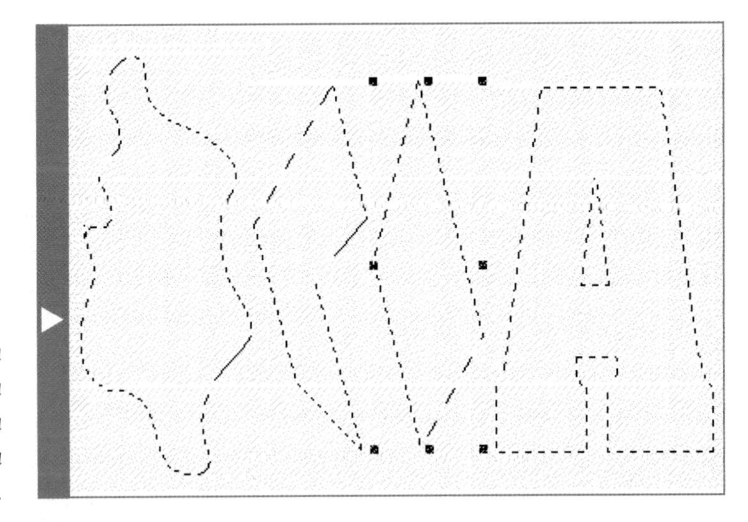

FIGURE 7.1
From left to right, a freehand frisket, a polygonal frisket, a selected frisket, and a text frisket.

like, and remember that when you add multiple friskets, effects and fills are applied to *all* of these friskets.

THE FRISKET PALETTE

Friskets are controlled from the Frisket palette, shown in its extended form in Figure 7.2. Open the palette by selecting **Frisket Palette** from the Windows menu, or by double-clicking on the **Frisket Knife** tool or the **Frisket Line** tool.

The Frisket palette turns friskets on and off, specifies the type of frisket you're using, controls whether or not the edges are feathered, and allows you to import friskets from EPS files.

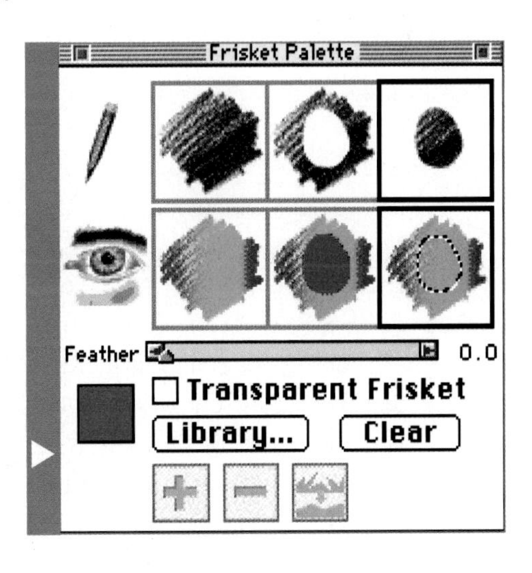

FIGURE 7.2
The extended Frisket palette.

The row of brown icons (next to the pencil) determines how the frisket works on your image.

Turns off the frisket.

Changes the protected area to inside the frisket.

Changes the protected area to outside the frisket (makes "reverse" or "negative" friskets).

The row of multicolored icons (next to the eye) determines how you'll view a frisket on-screen.

Makes the frisket invisible, but still active according to the icon selected in the brown row.

Displays the frisket using a flat color. The area covered with the color is the protected area. Click on the **Transparent** button to make your image visible through the selected color. To change the color of a frisket, click on the color square (lower right of the palette), and select a new color from the color picker that is displayed. Click **OK** to accept your choice.

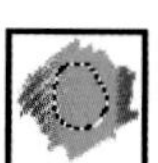

Displays the frisket using a selection marquee (dotted line), indicating that you want to use this frisket as an irregularly shaped selection. Copy a frisket selection by holding the **Option** key and dragging the image to a new location. You may apply fills, textures, and special effects to frisket selections.

IMAGE WINDOW ICONS

Frisket palette options can also be accessed from the frisket icons on the lower left of every image window, as shown in Figure 7.3.

Click and hold on the brown icon to bring up the top row of frisket use options, on the multicolored icon to bring up the row of frisket display options. The currently selected option for each row is displayed in the image window.

EDITING FRISKETS

Friskets add a new dimension to your work by allowing you to isolate different areas of a painting. They are also very flexible tools that can easily be edited and manipulated.

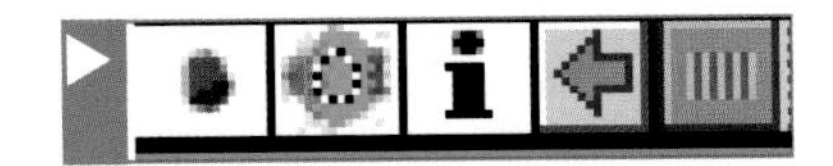

FIGURE 7.3
The two left icons are the frisket icons in the image window.

Some of the basic manipulations are:

- **Select.** To select a frisket, click on it with the **Frisket Selection** tool. If the first icon on the second row (on the Frisket palette) is chosen, your frisket is displayed only by its control handles. If the second icon is selected, it is masked with the frisket color. If the third icon is chosen, your frisket has a selection marquee displayed around it.

- **Multiple selections.** To select more than one frisket at a time, hold down the **Shift** key while clicking on each one or do a marquee select by clicking and dragging over several friskets.

- **Deselect.** Click anywhere on the image where there is *not* a frisket. To deselect just one of several selected friskets, hold down the **Shift** key while clicking on the one you want to deselect.

- **Delete.** To delete a frisket, select it with the **Frisket Selection** tool and press **Delete**. If you select it with the rectangular **Selection** tool instead of the **Frisket Selection** tool, the contents of the frisket are deleted and the frisket remains on your image.

- **Resize.** Select the frisket, then drag one of the selection handles. Holding the **Shift** key while dragging a *corner* handle, proportionally resizes an image.

- **Move.** Select a frisket, then drag it to a new location.

- **Skew.** Hold down the **Command** key while dragging a *side* handle.

- **Rotate.** Hold down the **Command** key while dragging a *corner* handle.

Figure 7.4 gives you an idea of what these manipulations look like.

EDITING FREEHAND FRISKETS

You've just spent a lot of time drawing a complicated freehand frisket, but you're off by a hair on one area or another. Do you curse, throw things, and keep trying? Well, that's one option. Another option is to simply edit.

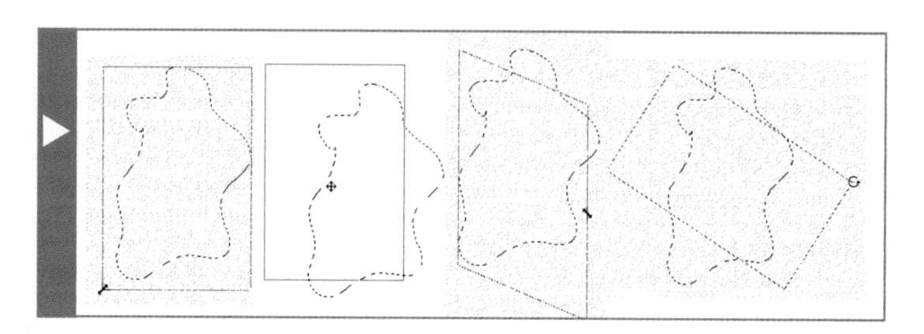

FIGURE 7.4
From left to right, resizing, moving, skewing, and rotating a frisket.

To edit, make sure the frisket is showing and select the **Frisket Knife** tool (if it's not showing, click on the **Frisket Selection** tool, select the frisket, then choose the **Frisket Knife** tool). Hold down the **Shift** key and redraw the segment you want to change. When you release the stylus and **Shift** key, the frisket is redrawn with your correction.

SMOOTHING FRISKETS

If the corners of your frisket seem too sharp, click the **Frisket Smoother** button on the Frisket palette to smooth them. The more you click on this button, the smoother your corners will be, as in Figure 7.5.

FRISKET A FRISKET

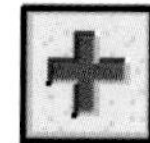

No, that's not a typo. You can actually frisket a frisket. Several times, as a matter of fact. In other words, you can cut holes in existing friskets to open an area or create layered effects.

Add an intersecting frisket to an existing one, then make it a negative frisket by clicking on the **Negative**

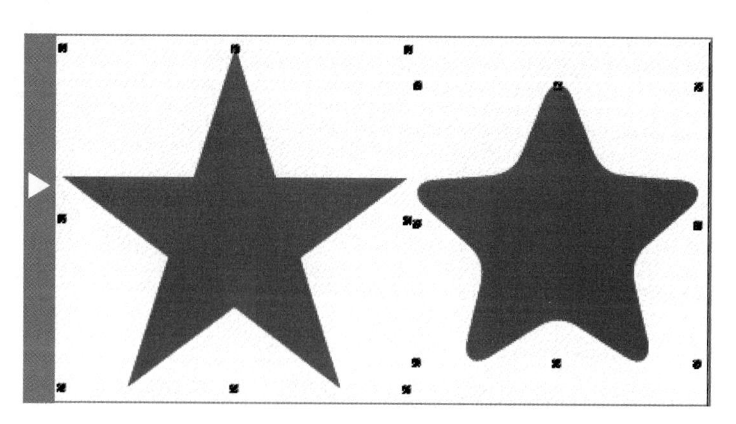

FIGURE 7.5
Smoothing a frisket. The far left image is transformed into a smoother one as the ***Frisket Smoother*** *button is clicked.*

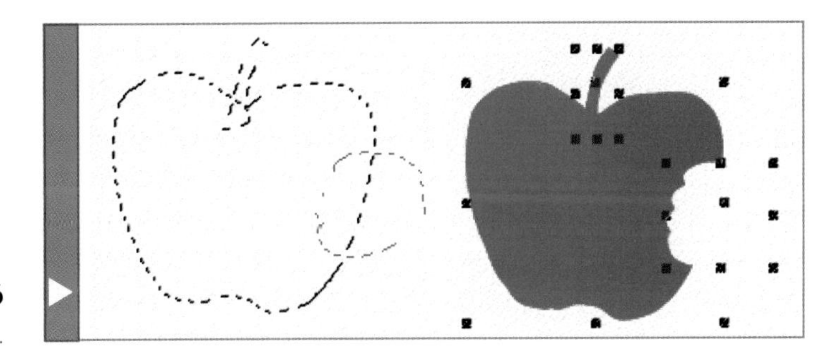

FIGURE 7.6
Friskets with cutouts.

Frisket button on the Frisket palette. Negative friskets only work when a positive frisket is present.

Create layered effects by making multiple cutouts, and adding positive friskets within negative ones (use the **Positive Frisket** button). Negative friskets have a red outline; positive friskets have a black outline. Figure 7.6 shows cut-out friskets.

FEATHERING

The **Feather** slider on the Frisket palette "feathers," or blends, the edges of a frisket, as if with an airbrush. Increase the slider to get the effect shown in Figure 7.7, reduce it to 0 to eliminate the effect.

The effect stays with the frisket, even if it is edited or manipulated, unless you change the setting on the

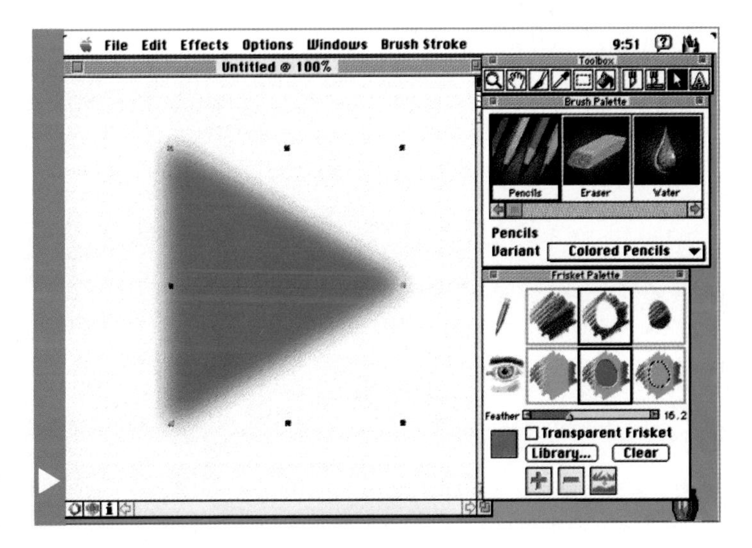

FIGURE 7.7
Feathering a frisket.

palette. If you change the slider setting, it applies to all future friskets until the setting is changed again.

A LITTLE BIT OF MAGIC

You have this great painting with lots of detail, but you want to use friskets on all of the red and yellow areas to apply some finishing touches. Do you (a) spend all day trying to draw tiny little friskets around all of these areas?, (b) just forget about the finishing touches and walk away from the piece?, or (c) select the **Magic Wand** tool from the Edit menu to handle this challenge with a few clicks?

If you answered (a) or (b) to this question, you should give the folks at Fractal Design Corporation more credit. If you answered (c), move over Merlin, you're now armed with your own magic wand.

Select **Magic Wand...** from the Edit menu. You'll see the Magic Wand dialog box, and your cursor becomes a magic wand. This tool selects areas based on the hue, saturation, and value of the pixels. You can use it to select either solid colors, or an entire range of colors.

Click your wand in the area you want to select, and the area is marked with the frisket overlay color. If you're selecting a solid area, click **OK**, and your area is frisketed.

If you're selecting a range of colors, use the HSV sliders to indicate the range you want. Click **OK**, and your color range is frisketed. Figure 7.8 shows the Magic Wand dialog box and a frisketed area.

FIGURE 7.8
Using the Magic Wand to frisket a range of colors.

FRISKET TEXT

This is really the only way to add text to a Painter image. It's a great tool for applying special effects to type, because it's so easy to fill the type with paint, textures, lighting, and other effects.

Double-click on the **Frisket Text** tool and you'll see the Text Specifications dialog box shown in Figure 7.9.

Select the type of font you want to import:

- **Import Type 1.** Imports Type 1 fonts. Using the dialog box, locate on your hard drive the outline font you want to import. If you are running System 7, chances are it is in the Fonts folder located in the System folder. Select the font and click **Open**.
- **Import TrueType.** Imports TrueType fonts. Using the dialog box, select a font from the pop-up menu, then click **OK**.

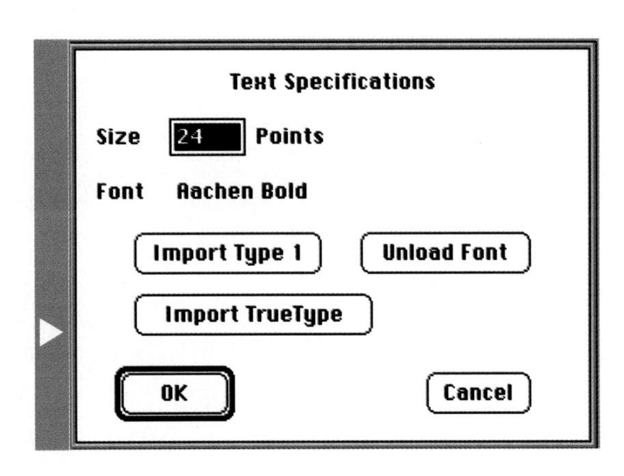

FIGURE 7.9 *The Text Specifications dialog box.*

Select a point size, and click **OK**. Now, click on your image where you want to insert the font, and begin typing. Your type operates like any other frisket—you can size it, skew it, rotate it, or apply any of a number of effects to it.

FRISKET LIBRARIES

Friskets can be saved, imported from EPS files, and arranged into custom libraries. All of these options are accessed from the dialog box displayed by clicking on the **Library...** button on the Frisket palette, shown in Figure 7.10.

SAVING FRISKETS

To save a frisket for later use, select the frisket then open the library dialog box. Click on the **Save** button, enter a name for your frisket, and click **OK**.

Click on the **Save EPS** button to save it as an EPS file, enter a name for your EPS file, and click **OK**.

To open a saved frisket, select a frisket name from the list on the left of the dialog box, then click **OK**.

Use the **Open Library...** button to open existing libraries. The name of the current library is displayed over the button.

IMPORTING EPS FILES AS FRISKETS

To import an EPS image for use as a frisket, click on the **Open EPS** button. Locate the file you want to import, and click **OK**. If you'll be using it again, you can save the EPS file in a frisket library.

NEW FRISKET LIBRARIES

To create new libraries, open the Frisket Mover dialog box by selecting **Frisket Mover** from the Movers cascading menu on the Options menu.

Click **New...** on the dialog box shown in Figure 7.11. Enter the name of your new library, and click **Save**. You may also use this dialog box to delete friskets from libraries and to move them to and from existing libraries.

To delete an entire library, you must locate it on your desktop and drag it into the trash.

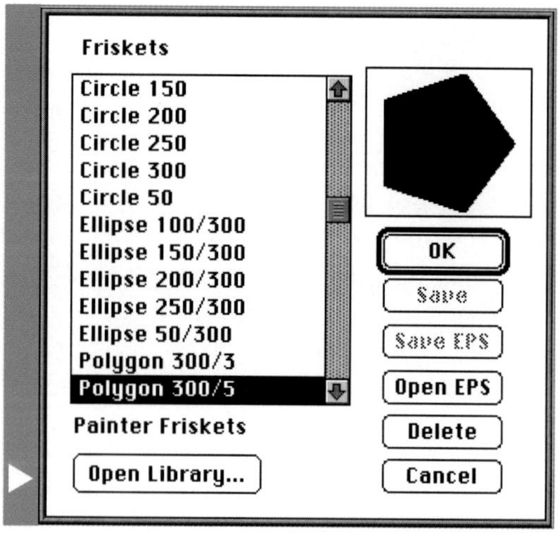

FIGURE 7.10

The Frisket library dialog box.

PRACTICE SESSION

1. Sketch out the beginnings of a self-portrait, or any face, for that matter. Use your **Knife Frisket** tool to draw the outlines for cheek color and eyebrows. Select the cheek friskets and feather them (about 6 or 7).

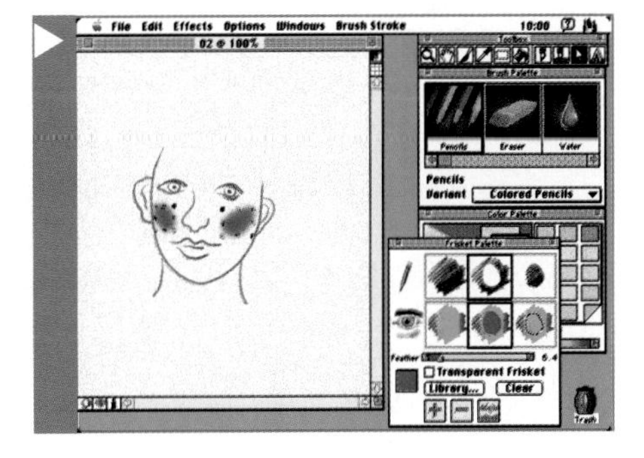

2. Select the a reverse frisket (the right icon on the top row and the middle icon on the second row), and paint on some pink for the cheeks. After you shut off the frisket, you'll notice the feather gave you blended edges without your having to smudge them or airbrush them on.

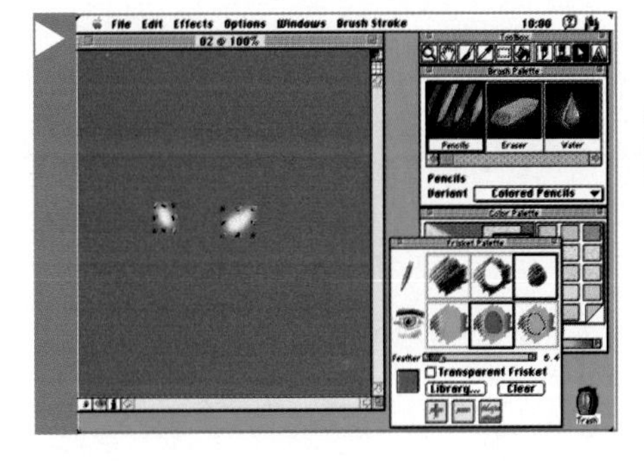

3. Now reverse frisket the eyebrows (if you choose to feather them, don't select a value greater than 1 or 2) and fill them in with color.

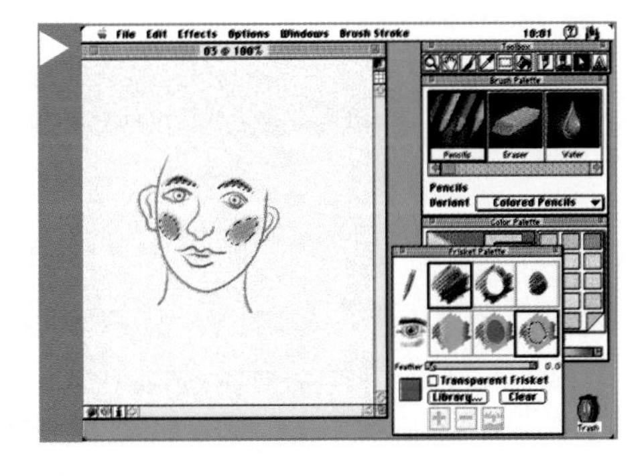

PRACTICE SESSION CONTINUED

4. Turn off all friskets (deselect them and make sure you are in unfrisketed painting mode by selecting the top left frisket icon) and give yourself the hairdo you always wanted to try, but were afraid to.

5. Select the **Frisket Knife** tool and cut a frisket around the face and hair.

6. Activate the frisket by selecting the middle icons on both the top and bottom rows on the Frisket palette, and feather it about 7 or 9.

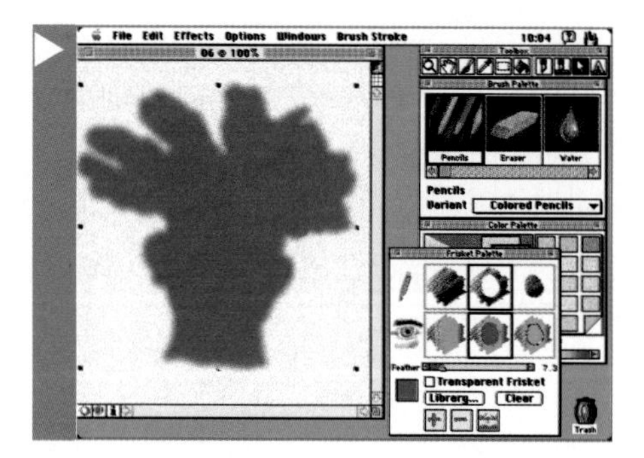

PRACTICE SESSION CONTINUED

7. Open the Paper palette and select the **New 1** texture from the default library. Click on **Random Grain Brush Strokes**, select a multicolored stroke from the Color palette, and use the **Spatter Airbrush** tool to cover the image. (If you remember Chapter 4, you'll notice the Spatter Airbrush uses a Grainy method, which means it reacts to paper grain.)

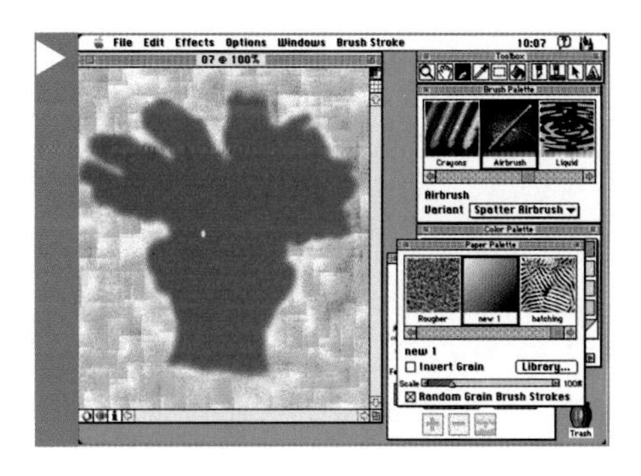

8. Select the **Frisket Knife** tool and cut a frisket over the right side of your painting. To make it more interesting, you may want to make the center line a little wavy. Remember, you can edit a freehand frisket line by holding down the **Shift** key while redrawing a segment.

9. Select the new frisket and choose the two middle options on the Frisket palette. Since the last frisket you drew was feathered, you'll have to adjust the **Feather** slider to 0 to turn off feathering.

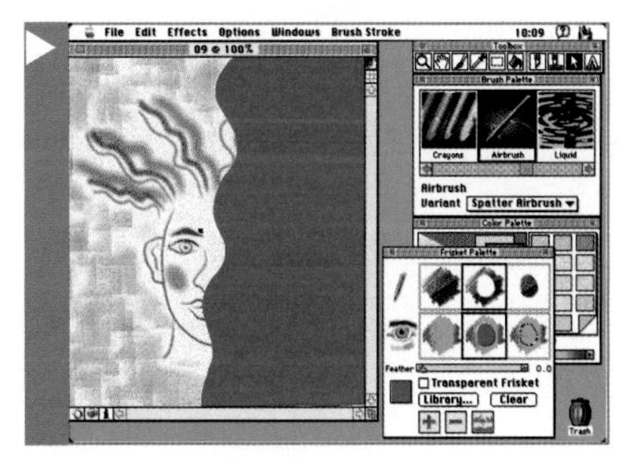

PRACTICE SESSION CONTINUED

10. With the frisket still selected and activated, choose **Negative** from the Tonal Control cascading menu under the Effects menu. Deactivate your frisket (click on the two left icons on the Frisket palette) and deselect the active area (double-click on the rectangular **Selection** tool). There you are—a self portrait showing your light side and your dark side.

Clones and Scanned Images

CHAPTER 8

CLONING AROUND

A *clone* is an exact copy of an image used to metamorphose images to any medium, apply special effects, combine elements, and trace photographs. Although it seems complicated, cloning is a simple process: Create a clone (exact copy) of an image, then use Painter's bells and whistles to transform the copied image into one using a different medium.

Painter accepts scanned and manipulated images from many popular photo retouching, color, and paint programs, including ColorStudio, Sketcher, and Photoshop.

CLONING AN IMAGE

Any time you want to use a cloning feature, whether a brush variant or a menu option, you must first create a clone of your image.

Open an existing image to be used as your source image. Select **Clone** from the File menu, and your image is duplicated. Figure 8.1 shows an image and its clone.

If you look carefully, you'll see the source image is named "Piece of Can." The clone is named "Clone of Piece of Can."

When you are working with cloned images, you must leave *both* the source and clone documents open, since the clone is "mapped" (linked) to the source.

If you close your source and clone images, then later reopen them, you'll have to reestablish the link. To do this, open the source document using the **Open** command from the File menu. To select, clone, and link it to the source document, hold down the **Option** key while selecting **Clone** from

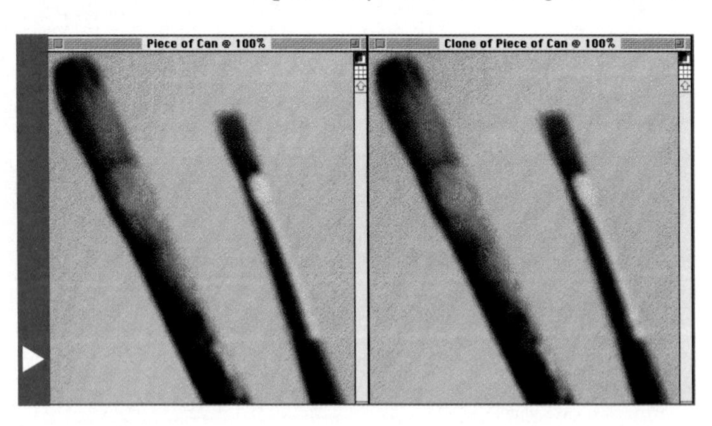

FIGURE 8.1
Cloning an image.

the File menu. Choose the clone document from the open dialog box. The first image you opened is the source, and the second one is the clone.

If you already have your two images opened, make the source document active (click on it or its title bar). Choose **Set Clone Source** from the Options menu, and your second image becomes the clone.

USING CLONER BRUSHES

When using a Cloner variant from the Brush palette, you may either clone entire images, or select parts of an image to be cloned.

To select a part of an image, open both your source and destination documents, making your source image active. (There are two best ways to make an image active: click on its title bar, or select the name of the document from the bottom of the Windows menu.) Select a **Cloner** variant from the Brush palette. Hold the **Control** key while clicking on the source image. The place you click determines the center of the area cloned.

Make your destination (clone) document active, then begin painting with your **Cloner** brush. Figure 8.2 shows a source image and a destination image with a few strokes of a Cloner brush.

You may select either a part of an image, or an entire image to re-create an image with any **Cloner** brush. When you use these brushes, you control the placement and direction of your brush strokes. Remember, you must keep

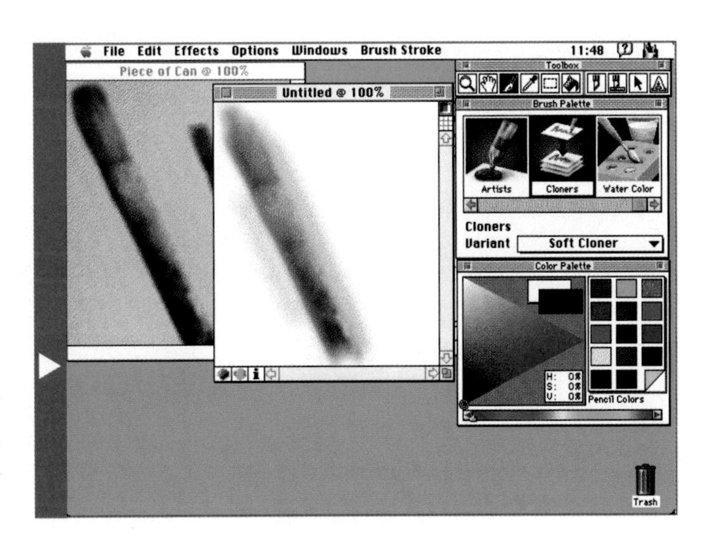

FIGURE 8.2

A source image (left) and a few strokes in a clone using the Soft Cloner brush variant (right).

your source image open while working with a **Cloner** brush. Let's briefly go over your Cloner brush variants.

CLONER BRUSH VARIANTS

Any variant that uses a Grainy Method will react well to the selected paper texture. You may also look at the method to determine what Cover method a variant uses. As with other brushes, you may use any or all of the customization techniques described in Chapter 4 to adjust Cloner brush variants to your specific needs.

Figure 8.3 shows the source image we are using in these examples.

Pencil Sketch Cloner. This variant clones an image using pencil strokes.

Felt Pen Cloner. This variant clones an image using felt pen strokes. Like the **Felt Pen** brushes, strokes from the **Felt Pen Cloner** build up and get darker as you apply them.

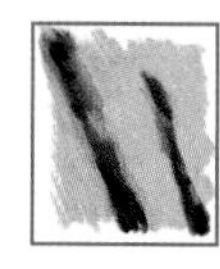

Hairy Cloner. This variant clones an image with strokes like the Hairy Brush variant, showing bristle lines and reacting to paper texture.

Oil Brush Cloner. This variant clones an image using oil paint-like strokes with a soft edge. Each time you lay down a stroke, a dotted line is displayed on your image. Wait until the line renders into a stroke before beginning your next stroke, or you won't get the results you want.

Chalk Cloner. This variant lays down strokes like the Artist Chalk brush and reacts very well to paper texture.

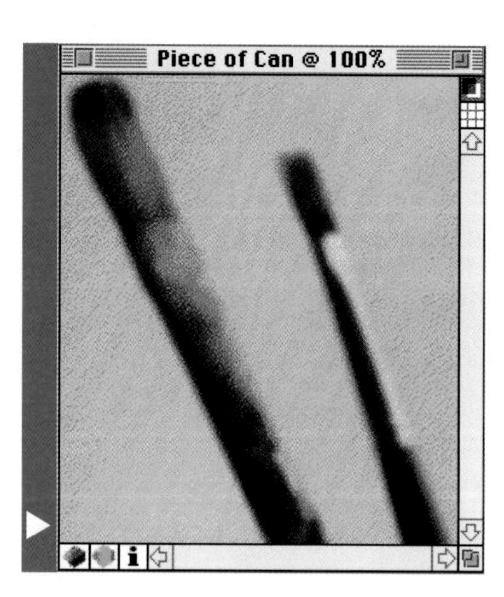

FIGURE 8.3
The original image.

Hard Oil Cloner. This variant clones an image using oil paint strokes with a hard edge. This is a cover brush using a grainy method, so it covers underlying strokes and reacts to paper texture. Each time you lay down a stroke, a dotted line is displayed on your image. Wait until the line renders into a stroke before beginning your next stroke, or you won't get the results you want.

Van Gogh Cloner. This variant clones with multicolored strokes, like the **Van Gogh Artist** brush variant. You will get better results if you use short strokes. Each time you lay down a stroke, a dotted line is displayed on your image. Wait until the line renders into a stroke before beginning your next stroke, or you won't get the results you want.

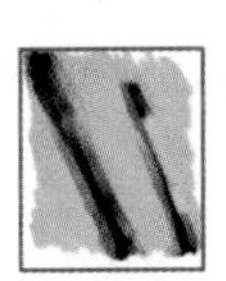

Melt Cloner. This variant clones an image using drippy, smeared strokes.

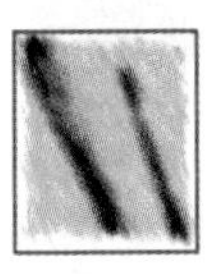

Driving Rain Cloner. This variant clones an image as though it were being viewed through the rain.

Straight Cloner. This variant clones your image without any changes—it *exactly* reproduces the source image.

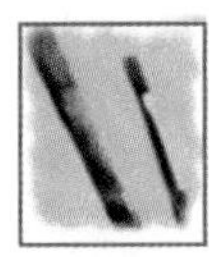

Soft Cloner. This variant clones an image with soft, airbrush-like strokes.

Impressionist Cloner. This variant clones images with short, multicolored strokes like the **Impressionist** variant of the **Artist** brush.

AUTOCLONE

If you have already tried some of the **Cloner** brushes, you may have discovered that it can take a long time to cover a large area. If you want Painter to handle some of the work for you, you can use the AutoClone feature.

Set up your source and destination files and select the brush variant you want to use. You may clone an entire image, or select a portion of it. If you are using the **Seurat** variant, select **Use Clone Color** on the Color palette so your brush will use the colors from your source image.

Select **AutoClone** from the cascading **Esoterica** menu, found under the Effects menu. Your image is automatically cloned using the selected brush variant, as in Figures 8.4 and 8.5.

Painter will continue adding paint to your image until you stop the AutoClone process by clicking anywhere in the image.

AutoClone works best with the **Driving Rain**, **Seurat**, and **Van Gogh** variants.

TRACING PAPER

Painter's cloning feature can also work like tracing paper—you can trace over an image, then get rid of it when you're finished. Use the image to be traced as the source, and create a clone that uses exactly the same dimensions.

Make the clone (destination) document active, select all or part of the image you want to trace, and press **Backspace**. The selected area is deleted, but it is still mapped to the source image, as in Figure 8.6.

Select **Tracing Paper** from the Options menu, and a non-printing "ghost" of the image is displayed, as in Figure 8.7.

Paint over the tracing paper using any tool. When you are through tracing, turn off the **Tracing Paper** option. The ghost is removed, but your traced strokes remain, as in Figure 8.8.

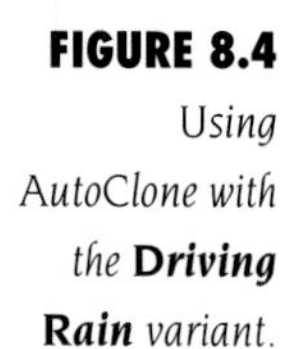

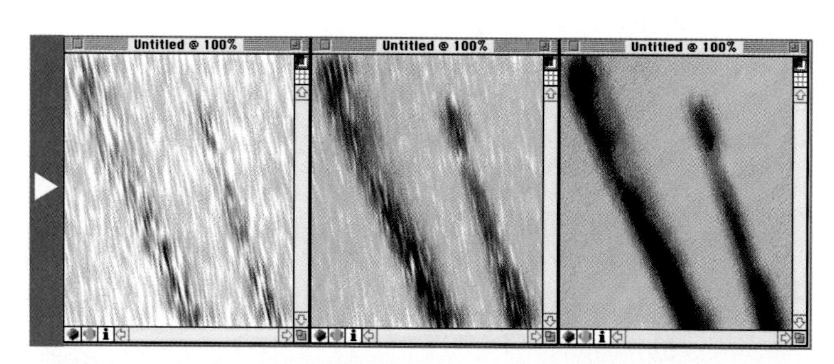

FIGURE 8.4 *Using AutoClone with the* ***Driving Rain*** *variant.*

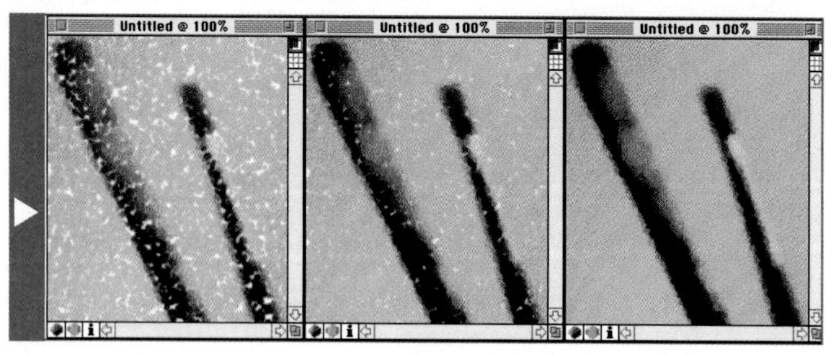

FIGURE 8.5 *Using AutoClone with the* ***Seurat*** *variant.*

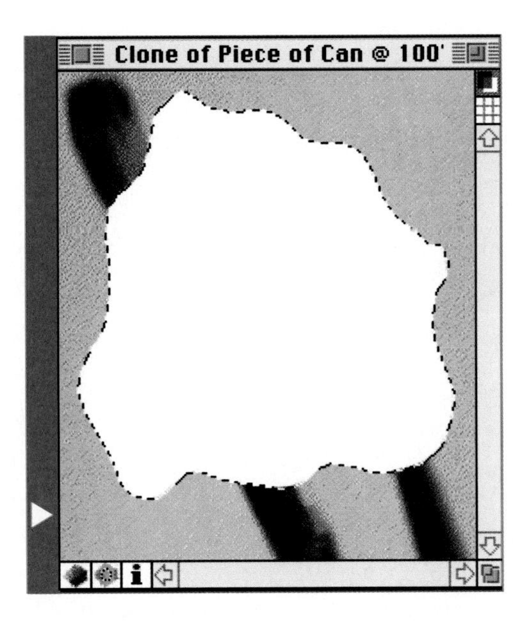

FIGURE 8.6
Selecting a tracing area.

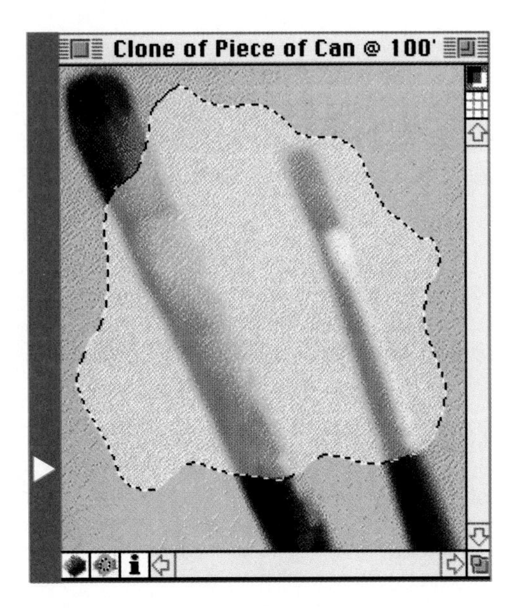

FIGURE 8.7
Turning on ***Tracing Paper****.*

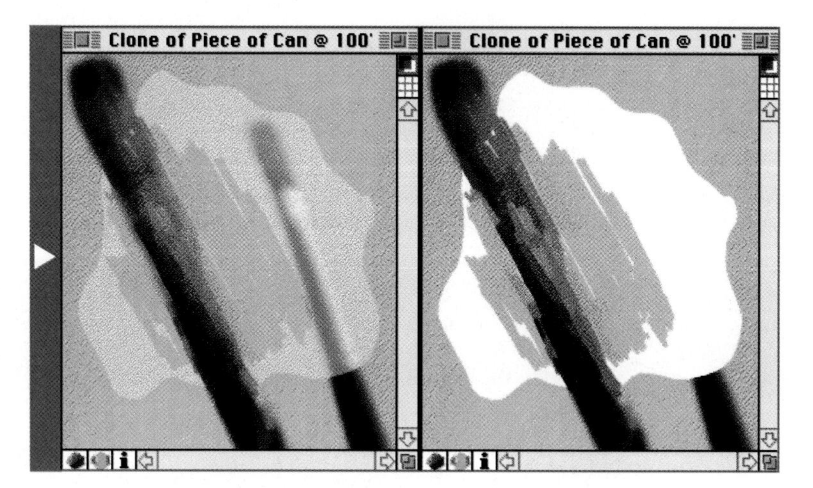

FIGURE 8.8
Place your strokes (left), then turn off the ***Tracing Paper*** *option (right).*

Painter X2

CHAPTER 9

PainterX2 does not ship with Painter—it is an *extension product* that is packaged and sold separately. However, we think it is such an important addition to working with Painter, we included a chapter to cover a few X2 basics.

PainterX2 has many advantages:

- It lets you work with multiple floating selections—items can be worked on, moved, and layered independently, making photo and image composition a breeze. Floating selections stay active, even when deselected, until you determine otherwise.
- Floating selections can be masked, painted into or around, manipulated (scaled, rotated, distorted), and saved in portfolios.
- Color sets are now available, including Pantone Matching System (PMS) colors and unlimited user-definable color sets. Color features also include a new fill tool to **Fill** closed line art.

You must have Painter 2.0 to use PainterX2.

FLOATING SELECTIONS

Floating selections are created from selections, frisket selections, mask layers imported from ColorStudio or Photoshop, or EPS files imported from FreeHand and Illustrator.

While you can import floating selections from other programs, floating selections can only be saved using Painter's native RIFF format. When files are saved to other formats, or opened in other programs, floating selections are composited into the image.

THE BACKGROUND LAYER

The background layer is simply the layer you worked with in Painter 2.0, and the background mask layer refers to any masks on that layer (as described in Chapter 7). Since PainterX2 works in layers, we will frequently be referring to the background layer, as it is the base layer for all images in PainterX2.

USING FLOATING SELECTIONS

Just as friskets are selected and manipulated with the **Frisket Selection** tool, floating selections are selected and manipulated with the **Floating Selection** tool, shown in Figure 9.1.

FIGURE 9.1
The PainterX2 tool palette, with the **Floating Selection** *tool selected.*

CREATING FLOATING SELECTIONS

Floating selections can be created from an image selected with the **Selection** tool, **Frisket Knife** tool, or imported EPS files or masks. Select the **Floating Selection** tool from the Tool palette, click on the selected image, and the image is now a floating selection, as in Figure 9.2.

You may also create a floating selection from a mask on the background layer. Make the mask active, then use the **Selection** tool to select it, or a part of it, as in Figure 9.3.

Click on it with the **Floating Selection** tool, and the mask is now a floating selection, as in Figure 9.4.

PORTFOLIO

The Portfolio palette is basically a library for your floating selections. To open the palette, shown in Figure 9.5, select **Portfolio** from the Windows menu.

To place a floating selection on the palette, select the floating selection with the **Floating Selection** tool. Hold down the **Option** key, and drag the image onto the palette, as in Figure 9.6.

Enter a name in the Save Item dialog box, click

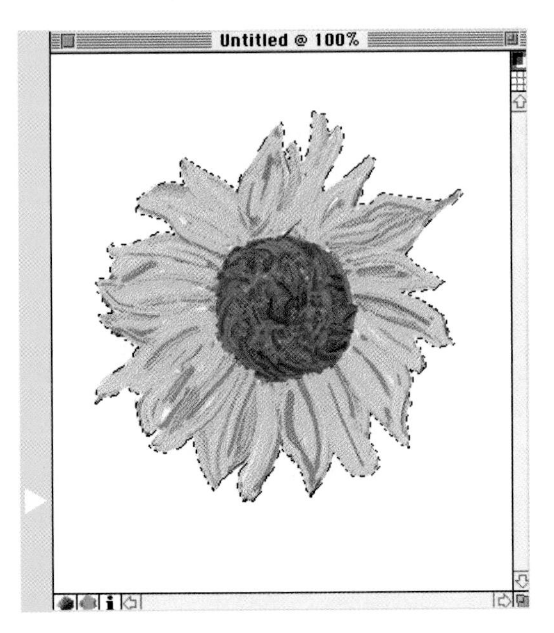

FIGURE 9.2
Creating a floating selection.

FIGURE 9.3 *Selecting a mask on the background layer.*

This dialog box is accessed through the cascading **Movers** menu under the Options menu. It works just like all other Mover dialog boxes, so we won't waste your time going over it again.

OK, and your selection is now included in the Portfolio.

To delete an item from the Portfolio palette, simply click on it, and press **Delete**.

You may also delete items—as well as move, copy, and create new portfolios—using the **Portfolio Item Mover**, shown in Figure 9.7.

MANIPULATING FLOATING SELECTIONS

Floating selections are very easy to work with, and very easy to manipulate. Select them with the

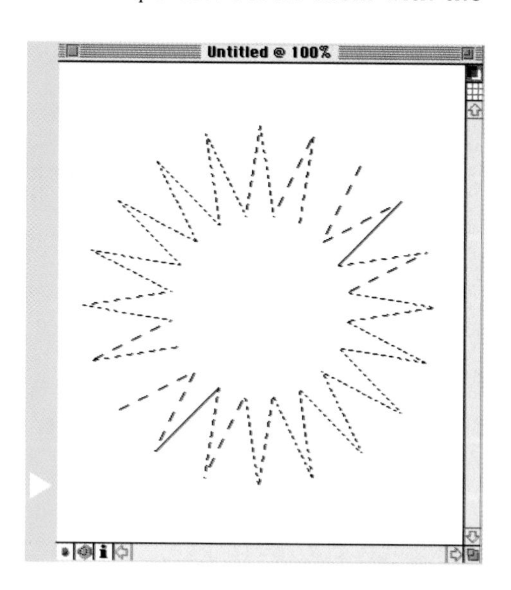

FIGURE 9.4 *A mask as a floating selection.*

FIGURE 9.5
The Portfolio palette.

Floating Selection tool, and deselect them by clicking anywhere else in your image. Use the same click-and-drag technique to move a floating selection as you would any other selected item.

Delete a floating selection from your image by selecting it and pressing the **Delete** key.

To duplicate a floating selection, select it, hold down the **Option** key, and drag the duplicate to its new location.

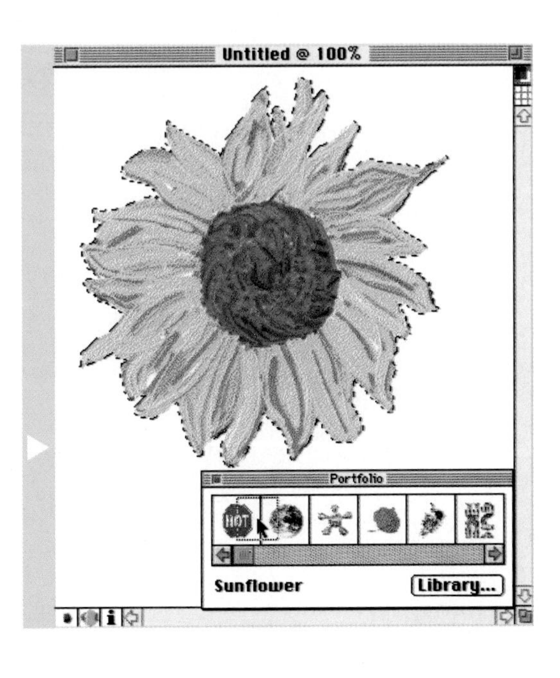

FIGURE 9.6
Placing a floating selection on the Portfolio palette.

Floating selections can also be layered and grouped. The Floating Selections palette, shown in its extended form in Figure 9.8, handles those functions and several others. To open this palette, select **Floating Selections** from the Windows menu, or double-click on the **Floating Selection** tool.

- **Layering.** The top row of buttons controls the layering of floating selections. Clicking on **Back** moves a floating selection to the back, or bottom, layer; **Front** moves it to the front, or top, layer. The **<<** and **>>** buttons incrementally move selections to the back or front, respectively.

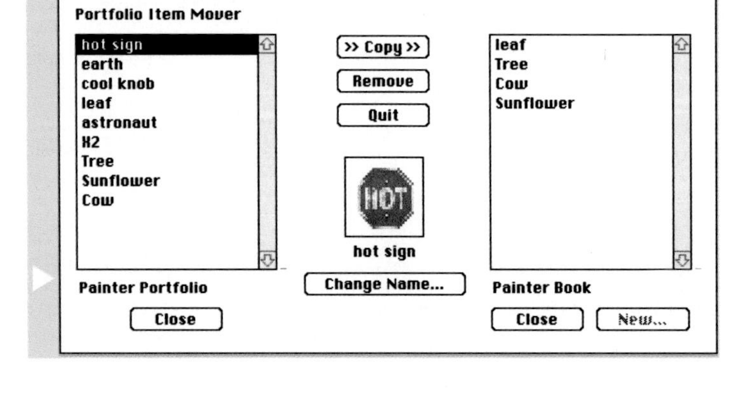

FIGURE 9.7 *The Portfolio Item Mover.*

- **Opacity.** The **Opacity** slider makes a selection more or less transparent.

- **Feathering.** Use the **Feather** slider to adjust the feathering on the edges of a mask.

- **Item Masking.** This pop-up menu determines how an item is displayed in relation to its mask. Figure 9.9 shows all three options.

  - *Unmasked* turns off the masking data.

  - *Masked Inside* masks the image inside the mask.

  - *Masked Outside* masks the image outside the mask.

- **Into Image.** This pop-up menu determines how a floating selection is integrated into the background image. Figure 9.10 shows all three options.

  - *Unmasked* leaves the selection unaffected by the background mask.

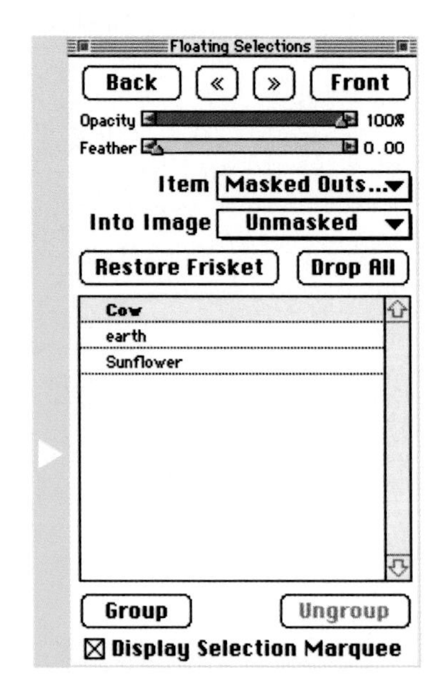

FIGURE 9.8 *The extended Floating Selections palette.*

FIGURE 9.9
The ***Item Masking*** *options from left to right: an item unmasked, masked inside, and masked outside.*

- *Masked Inside* lets the selection show outside of the background mask.
- *Masked Outside* lets the selection show inside the background mask.

- **Restore Frisket.** Click on this button to reverse changes made with a masking brush.
- **Drop All.** Click on this button to drop all floating selections and integrate them into the background image. (To drop only one floating selection, select the item, and choose **Drop** from the Edit menu.)
- **Item List.** This list contains all floating selections in a document. The currently selected item is listed in boldface. You may perform a number of actions from this list:
  - *Selecting a floating selection.* Another way to select an item is to click on its name in the Item List.
  - *Deleting a floating selection.* You may delete a floating selection by selecting its name on the list, and pressing **Delete**.
  - *Renaming a floating selection.* To rename a floating selection,

FIGURE 9.10
The ***Into Image*** *options from left to right: an item unmasked, masked inside, and masked outside.*

double-click on its name. Enter a new name in the Item Attribute dialog box, and click **OK**.

- **Group.** Use this button to group floating selections. Make sure the floating selections you want to group are listed consecutively in the Item List (use the Layering buttons to make adjustments, if necessary). Click on the name of the first floating selection in the list to be grouped, then hold down the **Shift** key while clicking on the last floating selection to be grouped. Click on the **Group** button, and the grouped selections are now listed under a group label in the Item List. You may change a group's name (the same way you change an item's name) and you may have multiple groups.

- **Ungroup.** Click on this button to ungroup a group of floating selections.

- **Display Selection Marquee.** Check this option to display a selection marquee around a selected floating selection.

IMAGE COMPOSITING OPTIONS

You may select from a number of compositing options to determine how floating selections interact. Compositing methods are selected from the Item Attributes dialog box, opened by double-clicking on the name of the floating selection (the one

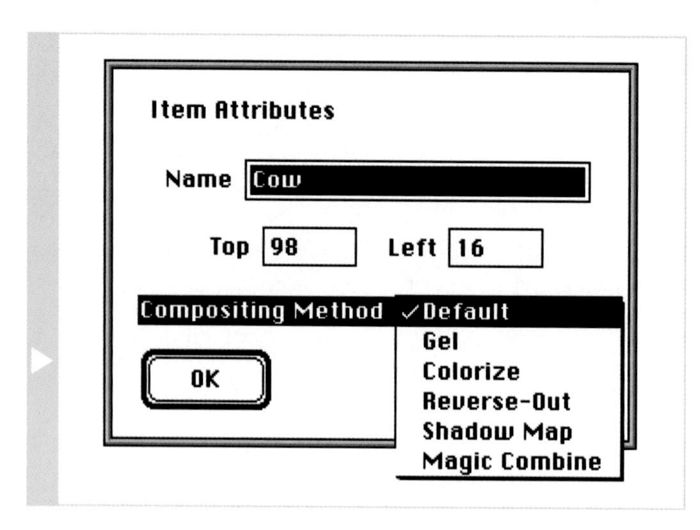

FIGURE 9.11
*The Item Attributes dialog box with the **Compositing Method** pop-up menu.*

you are applying it to) in the Item List on the Floating Selection palette. Figure 9.11 shows the Item Attributes dialog box with the **Compositing Method** pop-up menu.

To composite images, select the floating selection you want to composite. If you are compositing it with another floating selection, make sure it is under the *selected* item. Otherwise, the selected floating item is composited with the background layer. Bring up the **Item Attributes** menu and choose from the following compositing methods:

- **Default.** The floating selection covers the image below it.
- **Gel.** This option tints the image below it using the color of the top image.
- **Colorize.** Colorizes the underlying image using the HSV values of the top image.
- **Reverse-Out.** Provides a drop-out effect, using negative color values (for example, black turns to white, yellow turns to blue, and green turns to purple) where the images intersect.
- **Shadow Map.** The bottom image is seen through a shadow of the top image.
- **Magic Combine.** Combines the top and bottom images based on luminance values.

You can change your compositing method at any time, until a floating

FIGURE 9.12 *Clockwise from the top left, the six compositing methods:* ***Default***, ***Gel***, ***Colorize***, ***Reverse-Out***, ***Shadow Map***, *and* ***Magic Combine***.

selection is dropped. Each time you change your compositing method, the new method replaces the old one.

MASKING

There are a number of new masking tools included in X2.

Generate Mask

X2 automatically generates masks for floating selections. Select the item to be masked, then choose **Generate Mask...** from the Edit menu. The masking options on the **Floating Selection** menu provide controls for how an item is masked.

Masking Brushes

Masking brushes give you another option for masking floating selections. Rather than mask an entire selection, as with the **Generate Mask** command, Masking brushes allow you to mask parts of a floating selection using brush strokes.

Masking brushes are available from a separate Brush library. Click on the **Library** button on the extended Brush palette, and choose **Masking Brushes** from the dialog box. Click **OK**, and the Masking brush icon is displayed. If you find yourself frequently using the Masking brushes, use the Brush Mover to add it to the standard brush library.

The new Masking brushes are:

- Masking Airbrush
- Masking Chalk
- Big Masking Pen
- Masking Pen

Figure 9.13 shows sample strokes from each Masking brush.

Customizing Masking Brushes

You may customize Masking brushes using the standard brush customizing techniques covered in Chapter 4. Fractal Design Corporation has also added five new masking methods to the **Methods** pop-up menu:

- Flat Mask Cover
- Soft Mask Cover
- Grainy Hard Mask Cover
- Grainy Edge Flat Mask Cover
- Grainy Soft Mask Cover

These methods follow the same conventions as the methods for standard brushes (see Chapter 4), except they

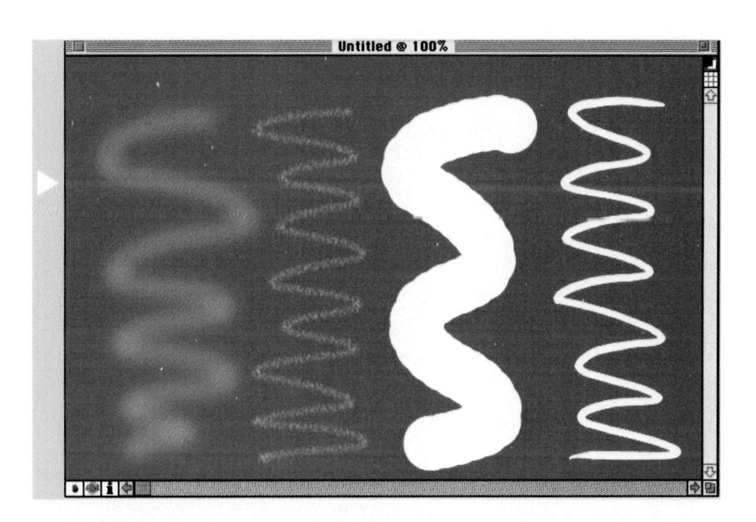

FIGURE 9.13
From left to right, strokes from the ***Masking Airbrush****, the* ***Masking Chalk****, the* ***Big Masking Pen****, and the* ***Masking Pen*** *brush variants.*

are denoted by the word "Mask." For example, the **Grainy Hard Mask Cover** method provides strokes that react to paper texture, have hard edges, and hide underlying brush strokes. All **Masking** methods use the **Cover** method, which means they hide underlying strokes.

COLOR FEATURES

PainterX2 provides you with two important color features: color sets and cartoon cel fills.

COLOR SETS

Color sets are designed to provide greater color consistency throughout a given project, including an annotation feature that informs you of a color's name. To access the default Color Set palette shown in Figure 9.14, select **Color Set** from the Windows menu.

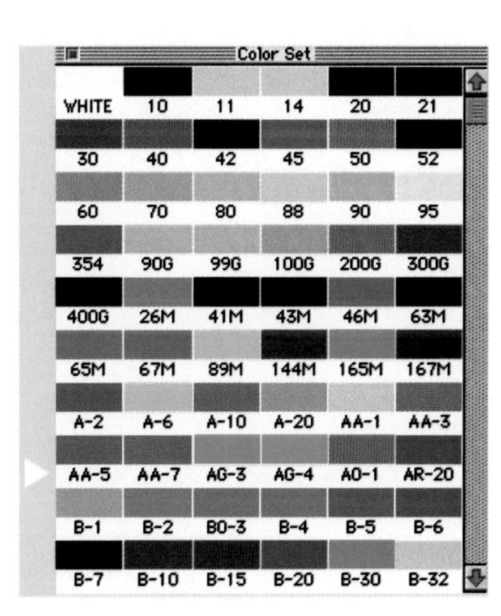

FIGURE 9.14
The default Color Set palette.

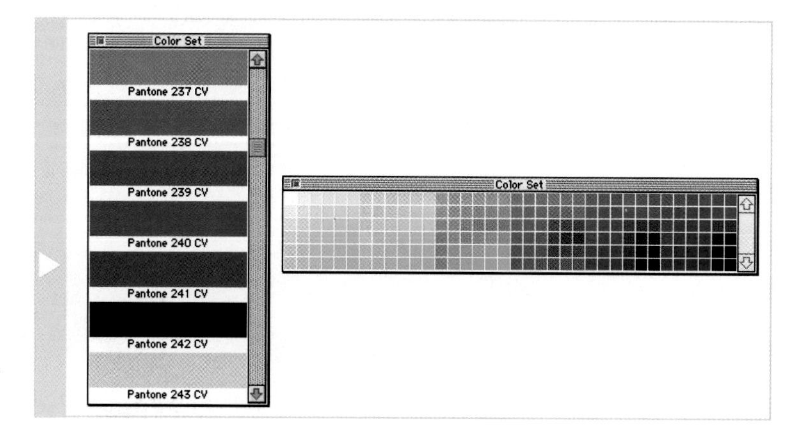

FIGURE 9.15 *The* PMS *(left) and* RGB *(right) color sets.*

To open an existing color set, select **Open Color Set...** from the Options menu. Select the set you want to open, and click **OK**. Figure 9.15 shows the PMS and RGB color sets.

You can create a new color set based on the colors in an existing image. Make sure the image is open, and select Digitize Color from the Options menu. Click on a color in your image you want to add to the set, and the color is displayed in the dialog box, as in Figure 9.16.

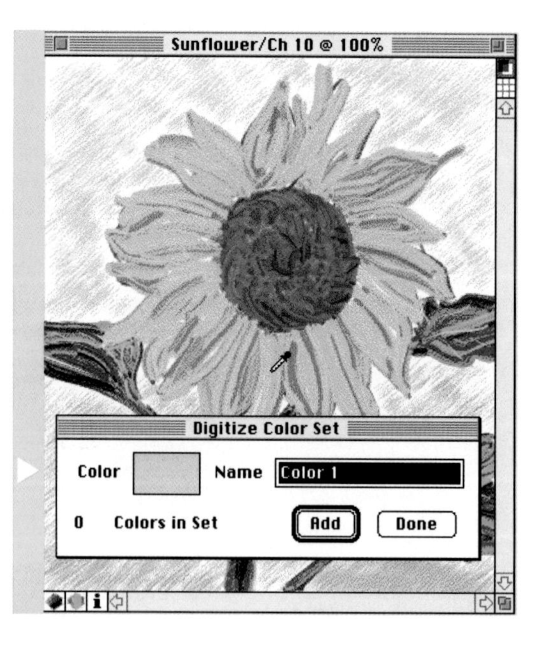

FIGURE 9.16 *The Digitize Color Set dialog box with a selected color.*

Type in the name of your color, and click **Add**. When you are finished adding all of the colors you want, click **Done**, and enter the name for your new color set, and click **Save**. You'll

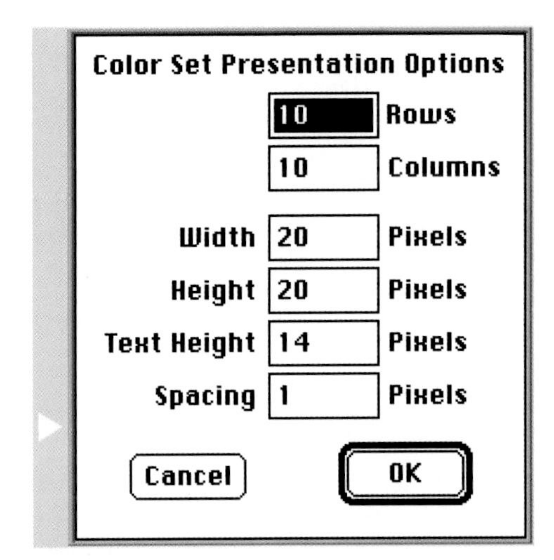

FIGURE 9.17
The Color Set Presentation Options dialog box.

see the Color Set Presentation Options dialog box shown in Figure 9.17.

Enter the number of rows and columns for the set, as well as the width and height for each color patch. Click **OK**, and you're done. Figure 9.18 shows a new color set created from the image on screen.

Annotating Colors

The Annotation feature labels your image based on the names in a PMS or custom color set. Annotations "float" over your image and can be saved in files using Painter's native RIFF format.

Select **Annotate...** from the Options menu. Click on the color you want to annotate, and drag your cursor off the color. Release the cursor, and the annotated name is displayed. When

FIGURE 9.18
Our new color set.

FIGURE 9.19

Annotating an image.

you are through annotating, Click **Done**. Figure 9.19. shows an image being annotated.

Use the **Annotations** selection on the Options menu to toggle annotations on and off.

CARTOON CEL FILLS

Cartoon cel fills allow you to fill an area enclosed by line art. You must draw your outlines with the **Scratchboard** tool in black for this feature to work. Choose **Generate Mask...**from the Edit menu, make sure **Image Luminance** is selected from the

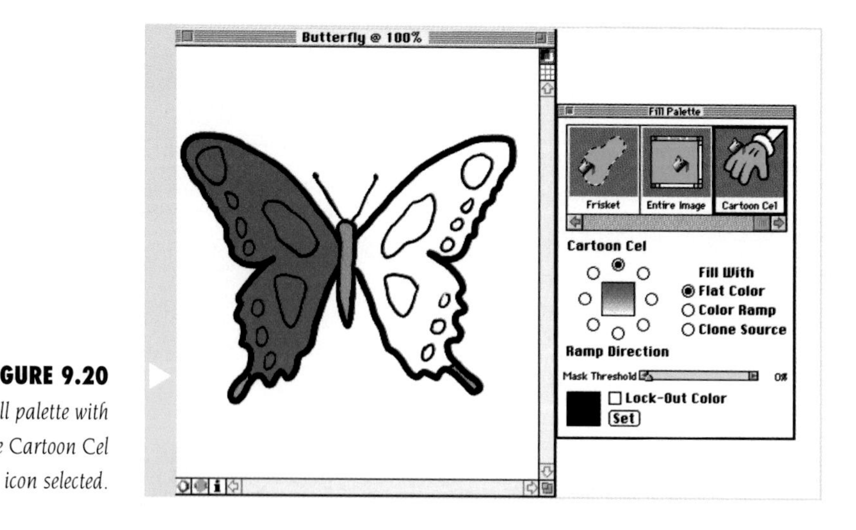

FIGURE 9.20

The Fill palette with the Cartoon Cel icon selected.

Using pop-up menu, and click **OK**. This creates a mask protecting your outlines.

Select the **Fill** tool, then open the Fill palette and select the new Cartoon Cel icon.

Use the **Fill** tool and the Color palette to add colors inside your outlines.

If you are drawing outlines that are not completely closed, the color will leak out. To avoid this, turn on the frisket, and use any masking brush to plug the leak.

There are two more new options on the Fill palette:

- **Mask Threshold** lets you protect non-black lines by giving them a more solid mask. There is no set formula for making this work, so you'll have to play with it a bit.

- **Lockout Color** prevents a particular color from being painted over. On the Color palette, select the color you want to lock out, then click the **Set** button. The default is black (to work with Cartoon Cel fills), but you can change it at any time.

PRACTICE SESSION

1. Paint a flower, select it with the **Frisket Knife** tool, and make it a floating selection by clicking on it with the **Floating Selection** tool.

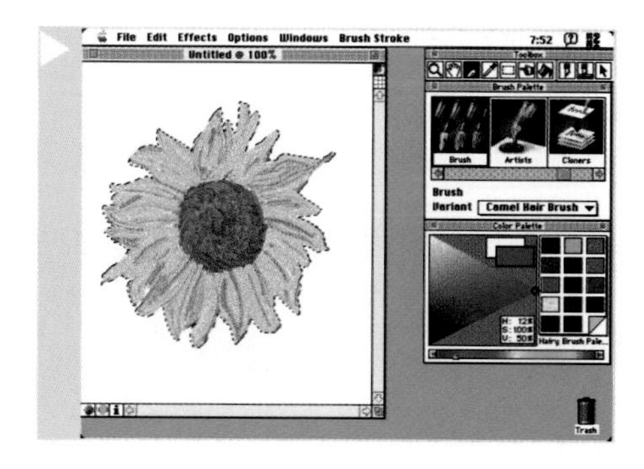

2. With the flower selected, hold down the **Option** key and drag the image onto the Portfolio palette. Next, select the **Earth** floating selection that comes on the default Portfolio and drag it into your document. Center it over the flower, and keep it selected.

3. Select **Scale** from the **Orientation** cascading menu under the Effects menu, and use the control handles to scale the earth image to fit into the middle of the flower.

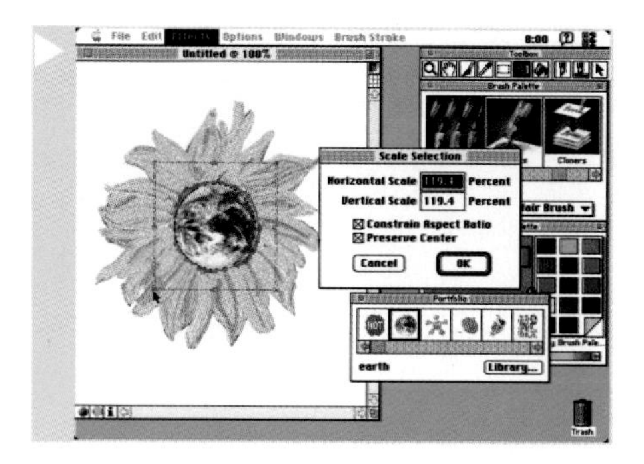

PRACTICE SESSION CONTINUED

4. Open the Floating Selection palette, and double-click on the earth label in the Item List. From the Item Attributes dialog box, select **Magic Combine** and click **OK**.

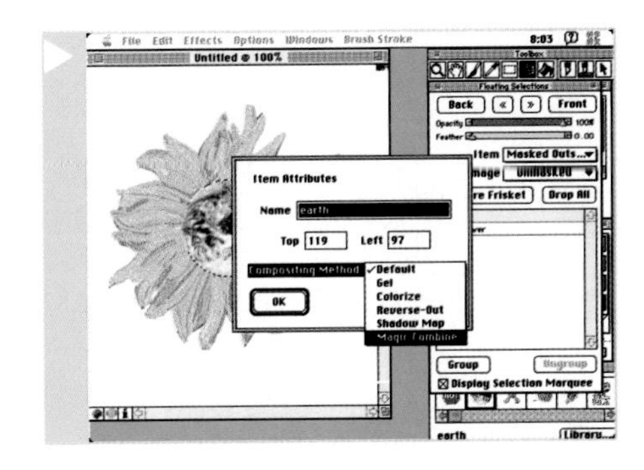

5. From the Portfolio palette, select the copy of the flower you placed there in Step 2. Center it directly over the existing flower, double-click on its name in the item list, and select **Reverse-Out** in the Item Attributes dialog box. Click **OK** and your image is reversed.

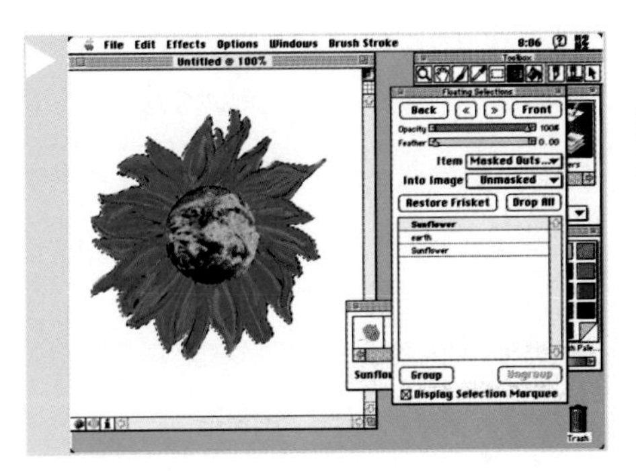

6. Open the Paper palette, and select an interesting texture, like Acid Etch or Wriggles. Select **Generate Mask...** from the Edit menu, and make sure **Paper Texture** is selected in the Using menu. Click **OK**, and turn on your frisket.

PRACTICE SESSION CONTINUED

7. Paint over the entire image, reverse the frisket, and paint again with a contrasting color. Shut off your frisket, and you're done. For an interesting effect, try dropping all of your floating selections before reversing the frisket and painting on your second background color.

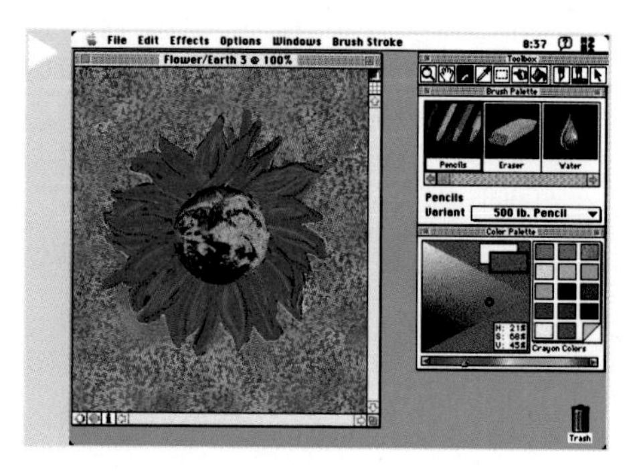

Recording Sessions and Resizing Images

CHAPTER 10

Painter can literally record your brush strokes and special effects to be saved for playback at a later time.

If you've ever created a drawing at 72 pixels per inch, the sized it up to, say, 300 pixels per inch, you may have been disappointed in the blurry, imprecise results. However, if you record the lower-resolution session, then play your brush strokes back at a higher resolution, your problem is solved! Painter re-creates your image at the higher resolution, complete with rescaling your brushes, paper textures, masks, and many effects.

Recording is very helpful if you're creating an image with repeated brush strokes. Simply record the stroke or strokes, then play back the session.

This feature is also very handy for teaching or demonstrating. Instead of re-creating your examples, record them the first time, and play them back *ad infinitum*.

This feature works just like tape recording. Start the recording, stop it when you're done, then play it back when needed. It's really that simple. (Are we surprised?)

RECORDING AND PLAYING BACK INDIVIDUAL BRUSH STROKES

This feature is great if you have multiple strokes to apply, and want to take advantage of the electronic medium you are using. Just let Painter do it for you.

You must have a file opened to record a brush stroke.

Select **Record Stroke** from the **Brush Stroke** menu, shown in Figure 10.1.

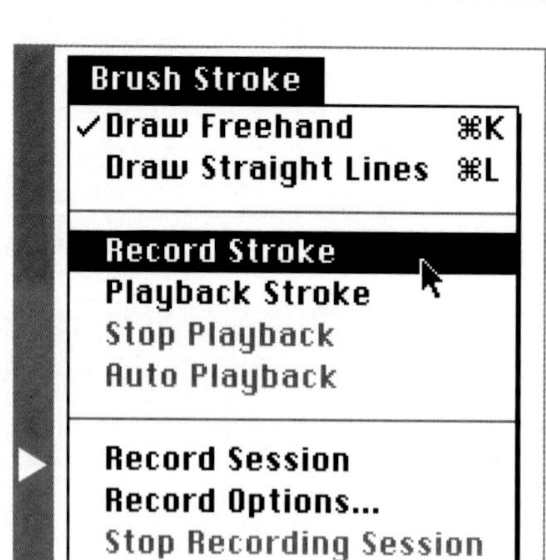

FIGURE 10.1 *Selecting Record Stroke from the Brush Stroke menu.*

Make any brush stroke you want, and the stroke is automatically recorded.

STROKE PLAYBACK

To playback the stroke, select **Play-**

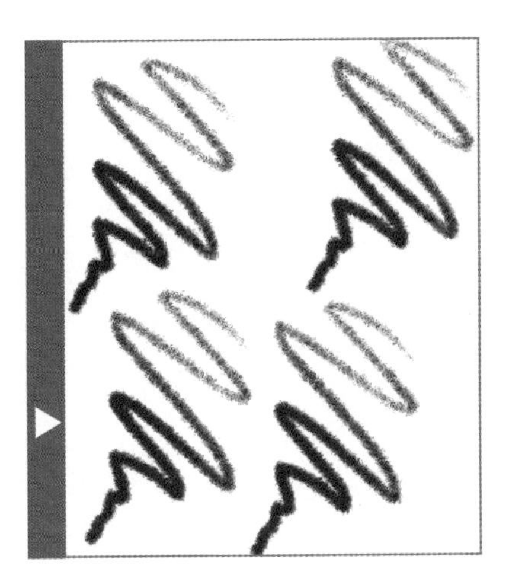

FIGURE 10.2
Playing back a recorded brush stroke.

Artist Pastel Chalk variant in blue, then change your selected variant to the **Feather Tip Airbrush** variant using green, your recorded stroke changes accordingly. Figure 10.3 shows the recorded stroke played back using different brush variants and colors.

back Stroke from the **Brush Stroke** menu, then click where you want the stroke to appear in your image. The stroke replays each time you click, as in Figure 10.2.

When you are through playing back your stroke, stop the playback feature by selecting **Stop Playback** from the **Brush Stroke** menu.

The color and brush variant of a recorded stroke changes according to the currently selected variant and the current color on the Color palette. For example, if you record a stroke using the

PLAYBACK WITHIN FRISKETS AND SELECTIONS

You can confine your stroke playback to a frisket selection or standard selection. When you do this, strokes are automatically applied using a random pattern.

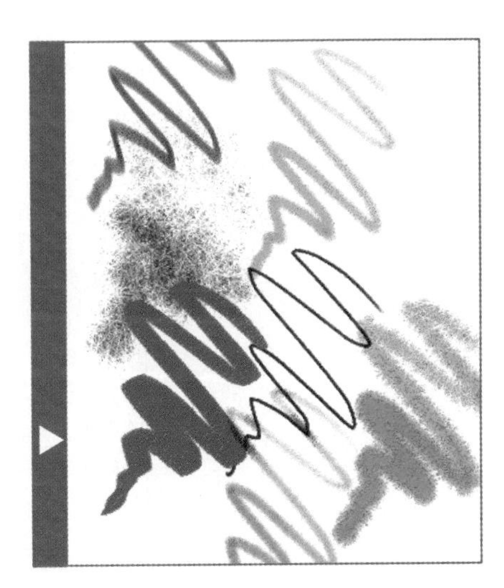

FIGURE 10.3
Playing back the stroke using different variants and colors.

Select the area to which you want to apply random strokes. Then choose **Auto Playback** from the **Brush Stroke** menu. When the selection is filled to your satisfaction, as in Figure 10.4, click once, and the playback stops.

If you make your selection using the **Selection** tool, strokes may sometimes extend beyond the selected area, as in the left side of Figure 10.5. If you don't want this to happen, make your selection using the Frisket Knife tool, as in the right side of Figure 10.5.

RECORDING AN ENTIRE SESSION

There are quite a few reasons to record an entire work session. Some are:

- For playback at a higher resolution.
- To reuse techniques in other projects.
- To have a record for teaching or demonstrating.
- To have a record of how you created an effect.

RECORD OPTIONS

Select **Record Options...** from the **Brush Stroke** menu. The Record Options dialog box, shown in Figure 10.6, is displayed.

If you *check* **Record Initial State**, the session is recorded intact, including the brush variants, colors, and paper textures used during the session. The currently

FIGURE 10.4
Filling a frisket selection using Auto Playback.

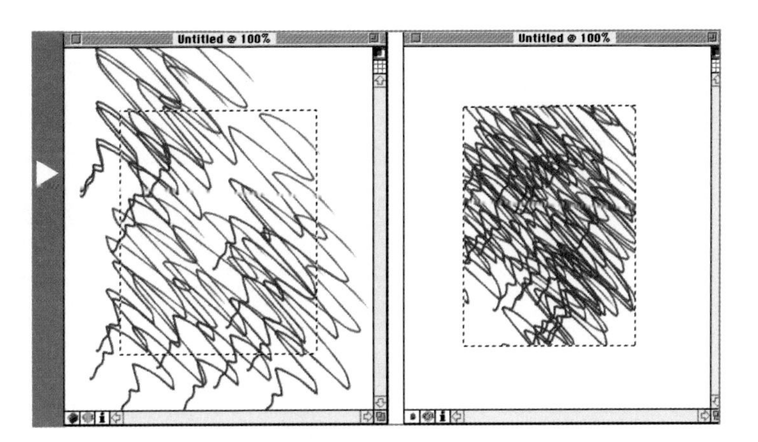

FIGURE 10.5
Strokes may extend beyond a selection made with the ***Selection*** *tool (left). To avoid this, use the* ***Frisket Knife*** *tool (right).*

selected brush variant, color, and paper texture do not affect the playback.

If you *uncheck* **Record Initial State**, the playback is dependent on the currently selected brush variant, color, and paper texture.

RECORDING A SESSION

Choose **Record Session...** from the **Brush Stroke** menu, and begin making your brush strokes. Change variants, colors, and textures, and add all of the special effects you want—Painter keeps track of them. When you are through with your session, select **Stop Recording Session** from the **Brush Stroke** menu.

Enter a session title in the Name the Session dialog box that is displayed, and click **OK**. Your session is now added to the current library. There is no limit to the number of sessions you can record.

SESSION PLAYBACK

When you are ready to playback your session, select **Playback Session...** from the **Brush Stroke** menu. The dialog box shown in Figure 10.7 lists all of the sessions you have recorded.

Select the session to playback, then click **Playback**. Painter replays your session.

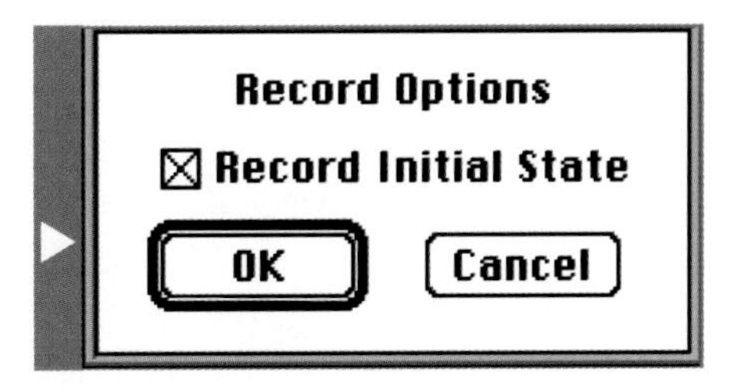

FIGURE 10.6
The Record Options dialog box.

If you want to cancel a session while it is in progress, press **Command+.** (the period).

PLAYBACK AT A NEW RESOLUTION

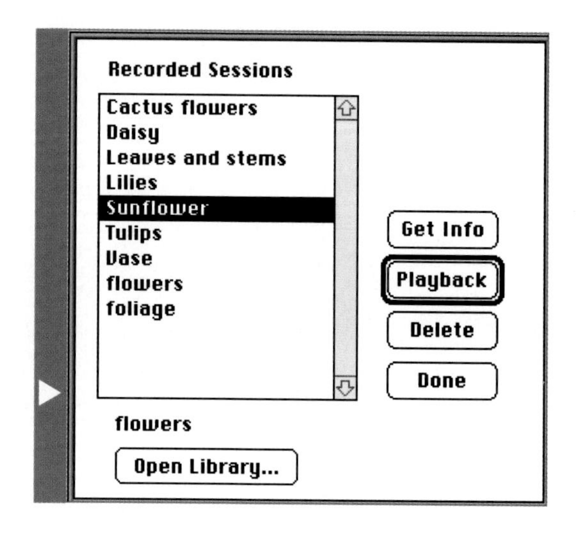

FIGURE 10.7 *The Recorded Sessions dialog box.*

You may record at one resolution, then playback at another, but you must follow a specific set of steps for it to work properly.

Recording

Open a new image file, and choose **Select All** from the file menu. Believe it or not, next you choose **Deselect All** from the **File** menu. Record and save your session as usual.

Playback

Open a new image file with a different resolution. However, make sure the dimensions of the file are the same as the recorded session.

Choose **Select All** from the **File** menu, then **Automatic Playback** from the **Brush Stroke** menu. Your session is replayed in the selected area.

CREATING LIBRARIES OF SESSIONS

As with many of Painter's features, you can create libraries of recorded sessions, organized in any way that suits your working habits.

NEW LIBRARIES

To start a new library, select **Playback Session...** from the **Brush Stroke** menu. The Recorded Sessions dialog box, shown earlier in Figure 10.7, is displayed.

Click **Open Library...**, and the standard Apple file open dialog box is displayed. Click on **New**, and enter a

FIGURE 10.8
The Create File dialog box for creating a new library.

name for the new library in the Create File dialog box shown in Figure 10.8, and click on **Save**.

OPENING A LIBRARY

From the Recorded Sessions dialog box, click on **Open Library...**, and from the file open dialog box select the library you want to open. Click **OK**. You may now select and playback any session saved in that library.

EDITING LIBRARIES

You may append, move, and delete entire libraries or library contents using the **Session Mover**. Select **Session Mover...** from the **Movers** cascading menu under the **Options** menu. The **Session Mover**, shown in Figure 10.9, is displayed.

Edit and append your libraries as required, and click on **Quit** when you are through.

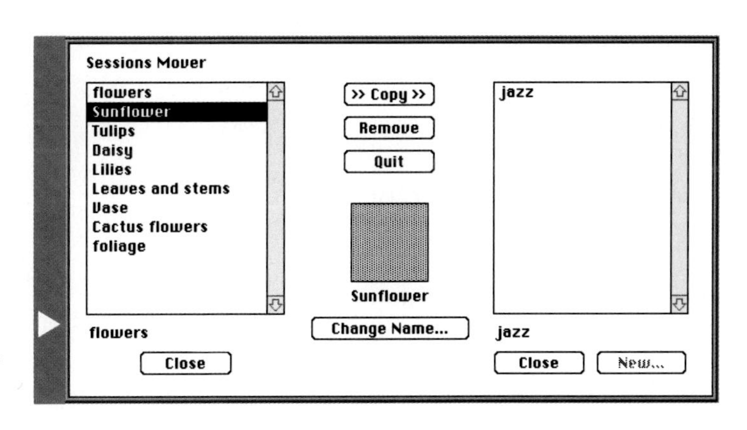

FIGURE 10.9
The Session Mover dialog box.

PRACTICE SESSION

1. Select **Record Options** from the **Brush Stroke** menu, and make sure the **Record Initial State** option is checked. Since we are going to record a session at one resolution, then re-create it at a higher resolution, open a new file (350 pixels by 400 pixels) at 72 pixels per inch.

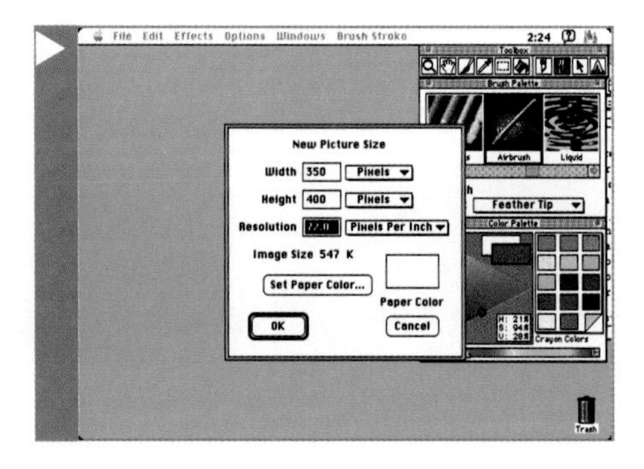

2. Choose **Select All** from the **Edit** menu, then immediately choose **Deselect All** from the **Edit** menu.

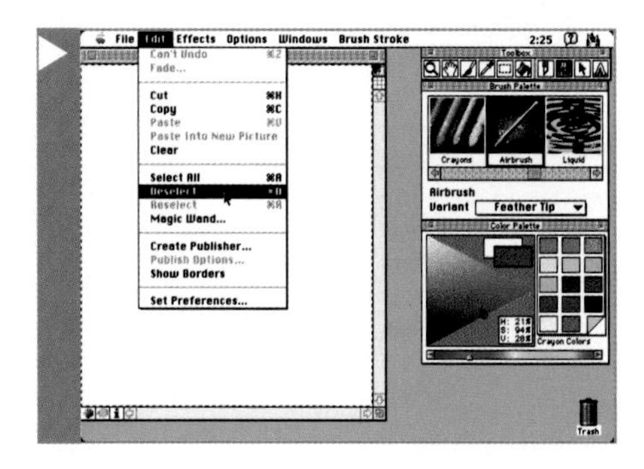

3. Select **Record Session** from the **Brush Stroke** menu, then begin painting a sunflower. Use a variety of colors, brushes, textures, and effects. If you use multicolored strokes, make sure you create them manually. If you select them from the Impressionist color squares, they will playback as monochromatics.

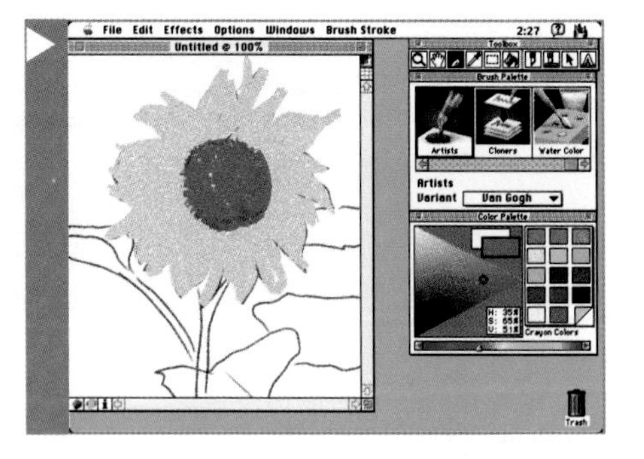

PRACTICE SESSION CONTINUED

4. When you are through with your painting, select **Stop Recording Session** from the **Brush Stroke** menu, name your session **Sunflower**, and click **OK**. Create a new document with the same dimensions (350 pixels by 400 pixels), but at a higher resolution of 300 pixels per inch.

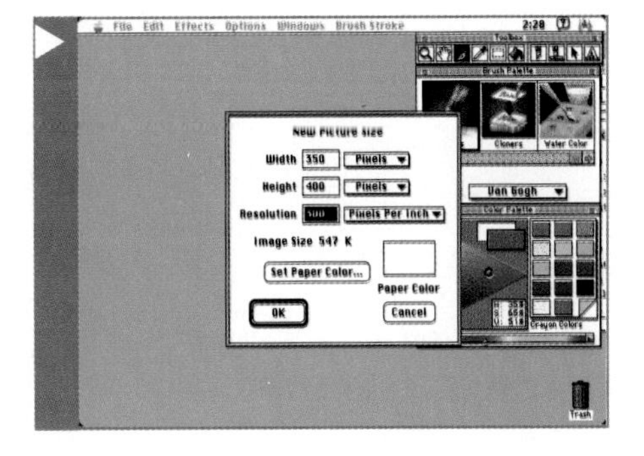

5. Choose **Select All** from the **Edit** menu, then immediately choose **Automatic Playback** from the **Brush Stroke** menu. Select the **Sunflower** session you just created, and watch it playback at a higher resolution.

Outputting Your Art

Painting courtesy Dennis Orlando.

CHAPTER 11

Well, this is it. You've learned almost everything there is to know about creating artwork in Painter. Now all you need to do is output your work.

Your selection of output is as important as your artwork. If you don't produce final copy that does justice to your work, your work isn't going to have the impact it should.

You have a variety of options for output, and the technology is now growing to a point where you can even output your art directly to watercolor paper or canvas! (See the last section of this chapter for some incredible options.)

Painter supports any PostScript or QuickDraw device. Many of the better options involve expensive equipment, but most metropolitan areas have service bureaus that provide access to these high-end machines at per piece costs (you may also use non-local service bureaus via overnight shipping or high-speed modem).

We'll cover most of your options, but please check with your service bureau or the manual for your printing device for specific instructions on file type and page setup requirements.

COLOR MONITOR CALIBRATION

A key issue with any digital art is monitor calibration. Your artwork is created on a monitor and most likely will not provide a completely accurate color match with your output. Light reflecting off a printed medium and off a computer monitor are perceived differently by the human eye. There are a number of color calibration devices available if color accuracy is an important issue for you. Most artists, however, are quite satisfied with proofing their work to a color printer, rather than calibrating their monitors every week.

EXPORTING FILES

Painter files are created and saved using the RGB color model. To place illustrations in many page layout programs, you *must use* CMYK files. While Painter can't convert your files to CMYK, you may open Painter files in most color retouching or photo editing programs (such as ColorStudio, Digital Darkroom, or Photoshop) and convert them there.

Decide which file format works best with the program into which you'll be importing Painter files, and select that format from the Save As... dialog

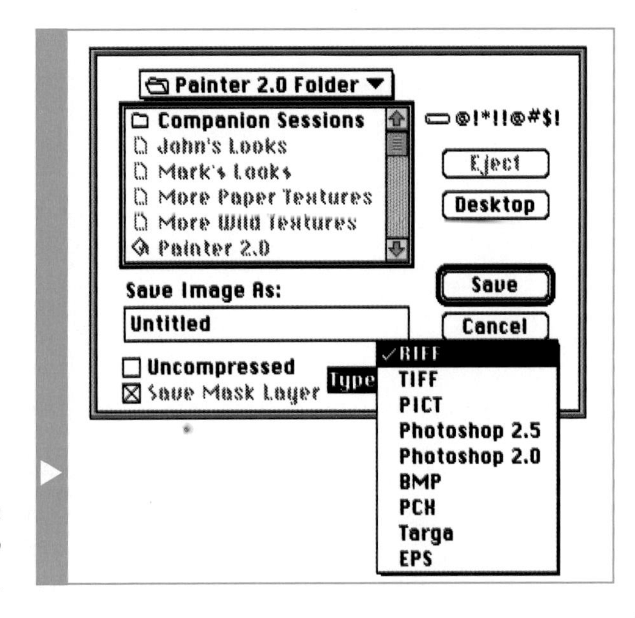

FIGURE 11.1
*The Save As... dialog box with exporting options on the pop-up **Type** menu.*

box. Select **Save As...** from the **File** menu, and you'll see the dialog box in Figure 11.1. Select an exporting option from the **Type** pop-up menu, enter a file name in the **Save Image As** field, and click **OK**.

Your exporting options are:

- **RIFF** (Raster image file format). This is the default option. Select the RIFF format to toggle the **Uncompressed** option. To save file space, always leave the **Uncompressed** option unchecked.

- **TIFF** (Tagged image file format). A versatile graphics format that stores a map specifying the location and color associated with each pixel. TIFF is supported by IBM-compatible and NeXT systems.

- **PICT.** Collections of QuickDraw routines needed to create an image. It is the main format used by the Macintosh clipboard.

- **Photoshop** (version 2.0 or 2.5). The native file format for Adobe Photoshop files. Photoshop files are always full 24-bit color.

- **BMP.** Bitmap files are the main format used by the Microsoft Windows (IBM-compatible computers) clipboard.

- **PCX** (Picture exchange). A format used by many scanners and paint-style programs.
- **Targa.** A file format used by high-end, PC-based paint programs. Targa files can have 8, 16, or 32 bits per pixel.
- **EPS** (Encapsulated PostScript). Painter's EPS files conform to the EPS-DCS 5-file format, used for desktop color separation. Please note that files saved in this format *cannot be reopened* by Painter. If you want to be able to reopen a file saved in this format, save it in another format (with another name) *before* saving it as an EPS file.

Selecting **EPS** opens the EPS Save As Options dialog box, shown in Figure 11.2.

- *Hex (ASCII) Picture Data*. Select this option for programs, such as PageMaker, that require it.
- *Suppress Dot Gain*. This option enables Painter's dot gain adjustment.
- *Suppress Screen Angles*. This option enables Painter's screen angle adjustment.
- *Clip Path Frisket*. Select this option to save only the portion of an image inside a frisket. A frisket must be active for this option to be enabled.
- *Use Page Setup Settings*. This option disables Painter's default printer settings: 133 lpi, standard screen angles, and 16 percent dot gain.
- *Spot Type*. Select a dot,

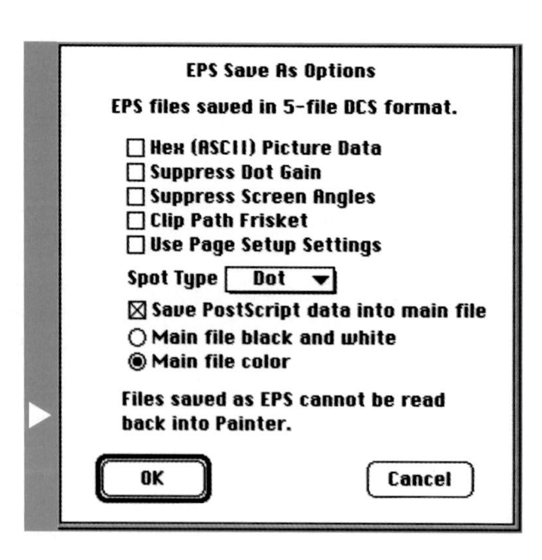

FIGURE 11.2 *The EPS Save As Options dialog box.*

line, ellipse, or custom shape for your halftone screen grid. The **Custom** option lets you create your own shape using a PostScript command. You must know the PostScript language to do this.

- *Save PostScript data into main file.* This option saves a printable preview of your EPS document. When this option is selected, the radio buttons for color or black-and-white previews are enabled.

PAGE SETUP OPTIONS

In addition to the file type, you may select from a number of page setup options for your images. To access these options, select **Page Setup** from the **File** menu. You'll see the dialog box shown in Figure 11.3.

Paper Type, **Printer Effects**, and **Orientation** are relatively self-explanatory and are found as page setup options in most Macintosh programs. **Printer/Press Dot Gain** adjusts the size of halftone dots according to the requirements of your print shop.

Monitor Gamma refers to the brightness of your monitor. Unless you're using a monitor calibration device or have a monitor that has other gamma requirements, you're pretty safe with the default setting. **Spot Type** determines the shape of your halftone dots.

Use the fields in the **Halftone Screens** area to change the settings for the grid of dots printed when using

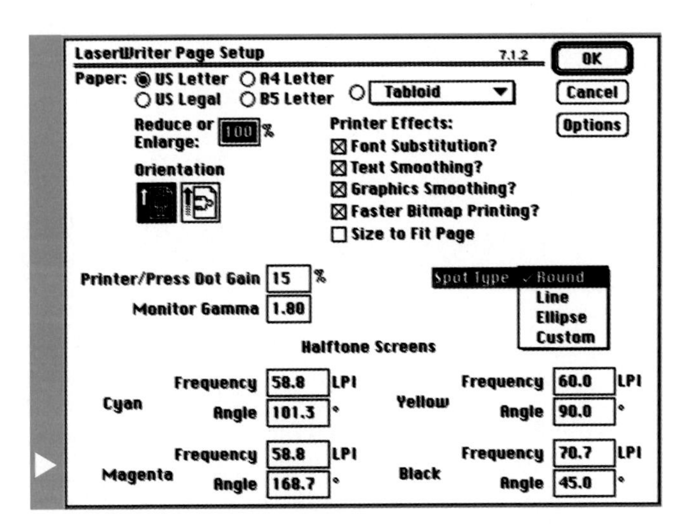

FIGURE 11.3

The Page Setup dialog box.

halftone screens (**Frequency**), or the angle at which the screens lay on your image (**Angle**). These settings may be adjusted for all four colors in the CMYK process.

IMAGE RESIZING AND RESOLUTION

Before outputting an image, you may want to change its dimensions (often called *resizing*) or resolution (often called *resampling*) to fit your output device. When outputting your work, the relationship between the image size and its resolution is very important.

Resolution refers to the numbers of *pixels per inch* (ppi) displayed on your monitor, or the number of *dots per inch* (dpi) used in the printing process. Most monitors have a resolution of about 72 ppi, typical laser printers have a resolution of 300 dpi and can go as high as 600 dpi, imagesetters can have resolutions of 1,200 dpi to more than 5,000 dpi, and most color printers usually range from 260 dpi up past 300 dpi.

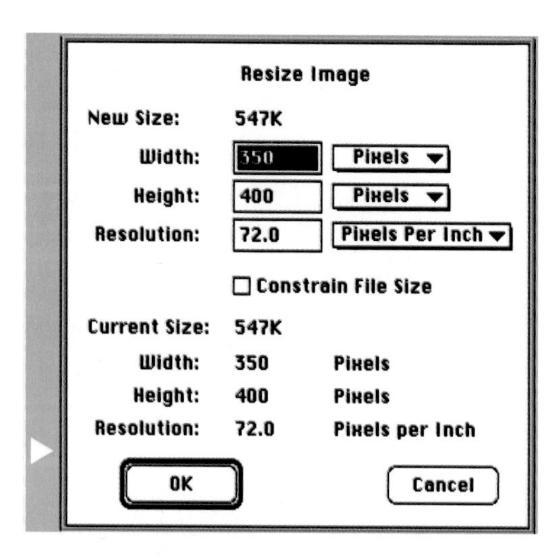

FIGURE 11.4 *The Resize dialog box.*

We'll say it again: *Read the device user manual or contact your service bureau to determine the exact resolution requirements.*

Select **Resize...** from the **File** menu to access the Resize dialog box shown in Figure 11.4.

The lower half of the box provides you with current information about your document, including its dimensions and resolution. The current size refers to the amount of RAM your image takes up, not to the amount of hard disk space it uses.

To resize your image, enter new values in the **Width** and **Height** fields. Change the resolution of an image using the **Resolution** field. Use the pop-up menus next to these fields to change the units of measurement for your image. Click on the **Constrain File**

Size box to keep your document from taking up any additional memory.

When you have resized your image, click **OK** to accept your changes.

You can also find out your image size and resolution by clicking on the **i** in the lower left of your document window (next to the frisket icons). The pop-up box, shown in Figure 11.5, also shows how your image fits on the page size selected in the Page Setup dialog box.

When increasing the resolution of an image by large leaps and bounds, you may occasionally get fuzzier results than you would like. To avoid this, use the record and playback method for increasing image resolution, discussed in Chapter 10.

PRINTING

Once you have determined the size, resolution, and page setup options for your image, select **Print** from the **File** menu to open the Print dialog box, shown in Figure 11.6.

Most of this dialog box follows standard Apple LaserWriter printing conventions, and are relatively self-explanatory.

The four bottom options allow you to select from the four printing methods supported by Painter.

- **Color QuickDraw.** Use this option for printers that use QuickDraw (color or black-and-white), such as many ink jet printers. Dot gain and halftone screen options do not apply to QuickDraw printers.
- **Color PostScript.** Check this option if you use a PostScript printer (most color laser printers, thermal wax printers, imagesetters, and dye-sublimation printers). Dot gain and halftone screen settings apply.

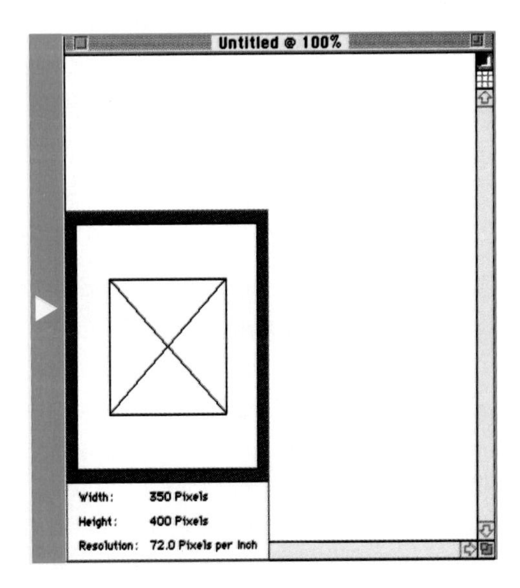

FIGURE 11.5 *Clicking on the **i** in the lower left of your document window displays image size, resolution, and placement.*

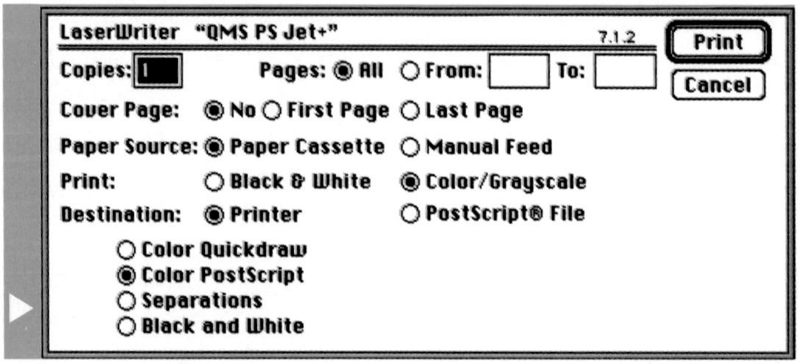

LaserWriter "QMS PS Jet+" 7.1.2
Print
Cancel
Copies: 1 Pages: All From: To:
Cover Page: No First Page Last Page
Paper Source: Paper Cassette Manual Feed
Print: Black & White Color/Grayscale
Destination: Printer PostScript® File
Color Quickdraw
Color PostScript
Separations
Black and White

FIGURE 11.6

The Print dialog box.

- **Separations.** Use this option if you want to print color separations (usually done on an imagesetter) directly from Painter. If you are using your own device, please check your documentation for specific page setup settings. If you are using a service bureau, please contact it for specific instructions before outputting files. This will save them a lot of aggravation due to incorrect settings, and will eliminate unnecessary delays.
- **Black and White.** This option applies to users of black-and-white laser printers.

When you have made your selections, click **OK** to begin printing.

OUTPUT OPTIONS

There is a large assortment of printer types available on the market today, some of which are affordable, and others that are generally more cost-effective if used through a service bureau. You'll have to carefully weigh your needs with cost considerations: black-and-white PostScript laser printers and ink jet color printers start at under $1,000, and go up to several thousand dollars; color laser copier systems begin around $60,000; used imagesetters begin at around $10,000, new ones at $70,000; thermal wax printers range from a couple of thousand dollars to more than $10,000; dye sublimation printers begin where thermal wax printers leave off; and Vutek systems (use to print directly onto gessoed canvas) begin at $500,000 (no, that's not a typo).

We'll briefly cover some of the options available, but due to a technology that changes faster than the phases of the moon, we haven't been able to cover it all.

We recommend reading the following section, contacting some printer companies for more information (*always* ask for print samples), and, most important, talk to other people in your field to get first-hand feedback on the advantages and disadvantages of a particular device that interest you.

LASER PRINTERS

Laser printers operate in a similar fashion to photocopy machines: A laser passes over a negatively charged drum, which then attracts negatively charged toner and is rolled over positively charged paper. The paper then passes through a heated roller to adhere the toner to the paper. (*Hint*: This means if you get toner on your clothing or carpeting, you can wash it off with *cold* water. If you use hot water, the toner will adhere to the textile just as fiercely as if it were a piece of paper.)

Laser printers are available for black-and-white as well as color printing. Laser printers are not continuous tone printers. To print grays or colors, they use a screen, and depending on the resolution of the screen, you'll likely notice the dots.

COLOR LASER COPIERS AS PRINTERS

A number of companies are now using color copiers, via a special raster image processor (RIP), to provide color output. The most prominent copier in this field is the Canon CLC using a Fiery RIP. This technology provides continuous tone images (like a photograph, not using visible dots), and allows a little latitude in your selection of paper. Thicker paper and highly textured paper may produce questionable results. Depending on the copier, your paper size will range from standard letter size to legal- or tabloid-size paper.

A color laser copier produces very vivid, sometimes fluorescent, colors. If you are using one as a proofing device for an image that will be reproduced using process printing, keep in mind that process printing will not produce the same vivid results. The closest you can get to accurately reproducing some of these colors will be to print additional PMS colors over the process prints.

If you are simply using the color copier to produce limited edition prints, and are not interested in accurate color proofs, this is an excellent choice, although somewhat cost-prohibitive. Color laser prints are available from some service bureaus, but are not as common as other types of color prints (such as Iris prints) that provide better color proofing for process color printing.

THERMAL WAX TRANSFER PRINTERS

Thermal wax transfer printers work more like dot matrix printers than like laser printers. But instead of pins pressing against a ribbon, they press melted wax onto a page, and they are much quieter.

Most thermal wax printers provide 300 dpi, non-continuous prints, with good color coverage. Although not entirely color accurate, they are generally pretty good proofing devices, especially considering that they are affordable enough for many of us to own. This is a good option for artists who do not have large corporate coffers to dig into, do not have large trust funds to tap, or have not (yet) won the lottery.

DYE-SUBLIMATION PRINTERS

Dye-sublimation printers work in a similar fashion to the thermal wax transfer method, except they provide continuous-tone color coverage. Rather than heat wax and transfer it directly onto the paper, dye-sublimation heats ink, which then turns into gas. The gas is sprayed onto the paper, and returns to its solid form. Cool. It looks great too.

Results from a dye-sublimation printer provide photographic-quality results (sometimes even better than photographs), particularly on smooth, glossy paper. A number of printers work well with a variety of mediums, including watercolor paper.

Probably the most famous of this type is the Iris printer. Most major service bureaus provide Iris prints. Most dye-sublimation prints, particularly Iris prints, are excellent proofing tools.

The catch: Beginning at $10,000 with a per page print cost of as much as $5, dye-sublimation technology is prohibitively expensive for most artists and companies to own.

INK JET PRINTERS

Ink jet printers use little nozzles to squirt ink onto your paper. The more expensive the ink jet printer, the more sophisticated a method it uses to squirt ink.

You get continuous-tone images, but usually with a lower resolution than dye sublimation printers (as low as 180 dpi), and you have to wait for the ink to dry. Some models may experience clogging of their nozzles and may require special paper. They are generally *very* quiet machines.

There is good news: Color ink jet printers can be had for less than $700, or can run up to $5,000. The lower-end ink jet printers are slower, provide less accurate color proofing, and have a lower resolution, but you don't have to mortgage the farm to own one.

IMAGESETTERS

Imagesetters provide high resolution (1,200 dpi to 3,600 dpi) resin-coated (RC) paper or film to make plates for commercial process printing. They are frequently known by their brand names, including Linotronic, Varityper, or Agfa. At a price of $50-70,000 new, most of us will never own one, nor will we want to.

PRINTING DIRECTLY TO CANVAS

We've saved the best for last. There is one source we know of that will print your image directly onto gessoed canvas, using continuous-tone acrylic paint, at almost any size you could possibly need.

The 16-foot printer was originally designed for the outdoor (billboard) industry to provide continuous-tone 14 feet by 48 feet prints directly onto vinyl. The technology is manufactured and patented by Vutek (Meredith, New Hampshire—information on their agent is listed at the end of this section, they do not handle orders directly).

The company also makes a smaller 8-foot machine that is currently being used to transfer Painter images to canvas. The width of the canvas they stock is 5 feet, so they suggest paintings be kept at a maximum width of 4 feet, to allow extra canvas for stretching on frames. Since the canvas is on a roll, length is almost no issue. In fact, Richard Noble, who handles orders for the process, suggests paintings be no smaller than 6 feet in length, since that's the size at which the process really begins to shine. (He suggests Iris prints for smaller images.)

The ink is acrylic-based and sprays through four CMYK jets simultaneously. Since it was designed for the outdoor industry, the ink is extremely stable when exposed to sunlight, and is excellent for archival pieces. You also have the option of applying a glossy overcoat, or even manually reworking a painting, and the output is sturdy enough to be stretched. Figure 11.7 shows Richard Noble with one of his paintings that has been transfered to canvas and then stretched on a frame.

Substrates in stock include pre-gessoed, acid-free, cotton canvas, as well as some paper stocks.

According to Richard, images processed via this technology are 18 dpi. Yes, we said 18 dpi, not 180 dpi, not 1,800 dpi. (For the outdoor industry, the standard is 6 dpi—they have just pushed the envelope here to provide higher quality for fine art output.) We don't exactly understand that one, but we hear the results are incredible.

The low dpi requirement allows file sizes to remain relatively small: a 3-foot square Iris print at 150 dpi can easily run over 80Mb. At 300 dpi, the same file can easily run over 300Mb. A 5-foot painting at 18 dpi can run less than 5Mb; people have actually sent files that fit on floppy diskettes.

The process supports any file type that can be read by Photoshop, and can handle images from either Macintosh or PC platforms. Images can be sent either on SyQuest cartridges or floppy diskettes, 18 dpi, with the dimensions you want for the final output.

Since this sounds too good to be real, we'll hit you with the best part: Prints are affordable. There's a setup charge of $35, $30 shipping and handling, and a charge of $12 per square foot. This includes stock canvas or paper; special-order substrates are more. Actual print time runs an hour or two, but order turnaround takes two to four weeks. At $500,000, owning the technology is really out of reach, but at least the prints are affordable.

To order or receive more information, contact Richard Noble, Noble & Company, 899 Forest Lane, Alamo, CA 94507, phone 510-838-5524, fax 510-838-5561. Richard is the only authorized agent for the process worldwide.

FIGURE 11.7
Richard Noble and one of his paintings that has been printed on canvas, then stretched on a frame. Painting and photograph © Richard Noble.

Section II

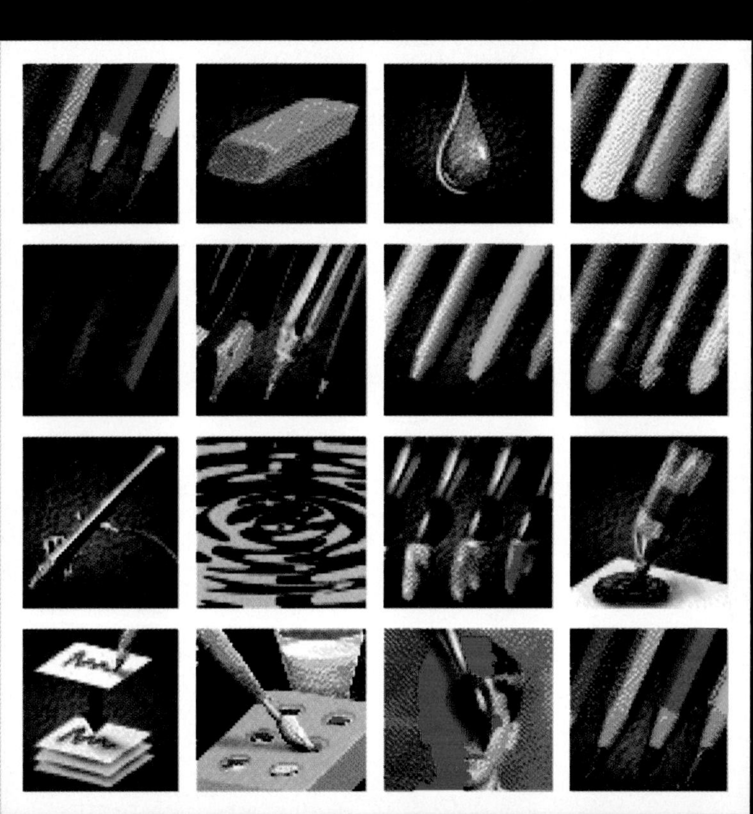

Dennis Orlando

CHAIR WITH TULIP TREE FLOWERS

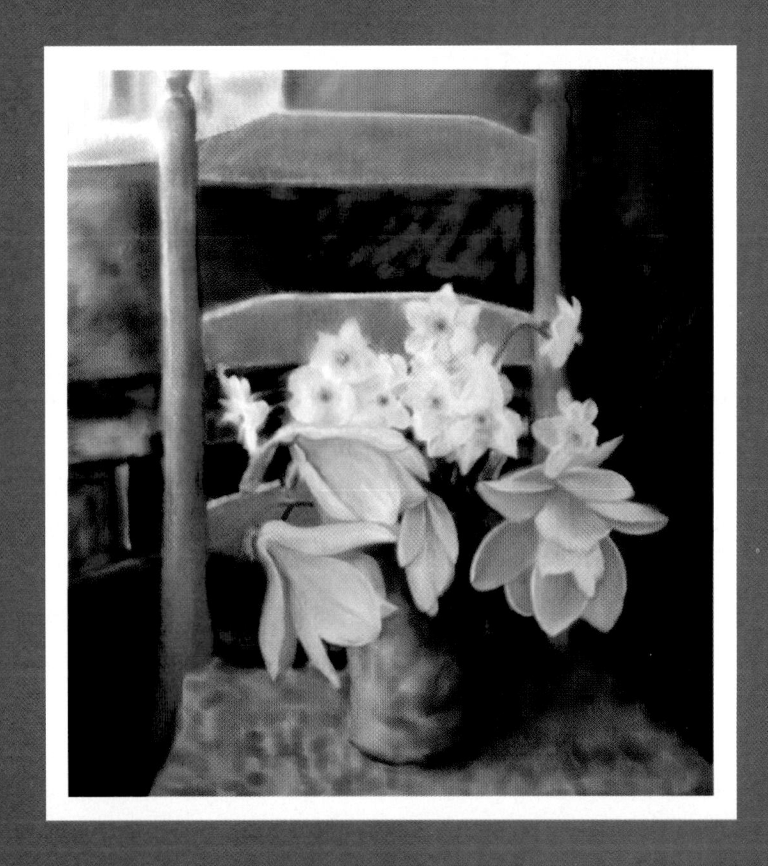

CHAPTER 12

ARTIST PROFILE

Traditionally trained at the Hussian School of Art in Philadelphia, Pennsylvania, and Bucks County College in Newtown, Pennsylvania, Dennis is an award-winning commercial graphic designer, creative director, and fine artist. He has spent more than 20 years working with water colors, markers, pastels, oils, and pen and ink. He is currently the creative director for K.I. Lipton Marketing Communications in Doylestown, Pennsylvania.

In 1989, Dennis was instrumental in setting up one of the first Macintosh-based advertising agencies in the Philadelphia area, and helped convince artists, printers, color separators, and clients that a new era was dawning.

Dennis' digital studies of Cézanne, Monet, and Picasso have convinced many that capabilities now exist for an artist to create masterpieces electronically. His digital paintings are stored on disk and magnetic cartridges and will soon be available on CDs.

Digital paintings produced by Dennis have been exhibited at computer shows in Los Angeles, San Francisco, Boston, and Philadelphia, and he plans to participate in upcoming gallery shows with both traditional and digital artists. He is currently experimenting with multimedia applications for his art, and will be conducting a series of workshops for faculty and students at Drexel University in Philadelphia.

To create his digital paintings, Dennis uses a Macintosh IIci with 20Mb of RAM, a 20-inch SuperMac color monitor with a 24-bit video card, Fractal Design Painter and X2 software, a Wacom ArtZ drawing tablet with a wireless stylus, and an EFI Fiery RIP connected to a Canon CLC 300 color laser printer .

ON USING PAINTER

I had been working on the computer doing electronic design and photo retouching in commercial applications. My fine arts work was always done traditionally. Slowly, I was losing the ability to work in those mediums because I was losing space, plus the mess and wet paint. I had eased off of fine arts work, which was upsetting to me.

I had been working in Photoshop. I was familiar with some of the digital capabilities, but it just did not have a natural feel to it. I was wondering if there was anything else out there when I came across an article in a magazine that featured Painter. I figured if the article was even half true, I could once again do any fine arts work in a way that is convenient and comfortable for me. I had worked with earlier programs like Pixel Paint *and* MacDraw, *but they were toys and they only scratched the surface of what can be done.*

For the first few paintings I did, I took masters' works like Picasso *and* Monet, *because I wanted to see if I could do fine art studies directly from the masters' work and how effective they could be. A lot of traditionally based artists were trained from the masters' works by studying the compositions and techniques, and I tried to do this by using the computer.*

One of the earliest I tried was Picasso's still life, Pitcher with Apples. *I did that with a mouse. It was magical. It was like nothing I had ever experienced before in my life. The reaction and interaction I had with this painting—I found myself starting paintings at* 9 PM *and working until the next morning, even when I had to go to work the next day. I couldn't believe the kind of connection that was occurring between me and the machine. It's just absolutely amazing: the reaction and interaction between the tools and the medium—the feedback from the monitor was almost hypnotic—I got hooked. I decided to invest in a drawing tablet and a stylus and I just found I took to them immediately. Again, I noticed an enormous amount of control. I have continued to grow with it. Even after almost two years, I feel like I have only scratched the surface of what is possible with this application.*

CHAIR WITH TULIP TREE FLOWERS

A springtime dinner invitation at a friend's home was an occasion to bring fresh cut flowers. Dennis set up the flowers and vase on a chair outside against a wall, and photographed it. The still life photo was filed away for reference material over 14 years ago and remained untouched. Last year, he had some spare time to paint and reviewed his old collection of reference photos. He came across the photo of the Chair with Tulip Tree Flowers and thought it would be a beautiful subject to paint.

STEP-BY-STEP

1. Dennis set up the Painter file to the dimensions he wanted to use. As he usually does, he pulled up a medium canvas texture, then penciled in a drawing with Painter's **Pencil** tool. He never thinks of a painting as complete until he signs it, but he likes to begin with elements placed in composition the way he wants it.

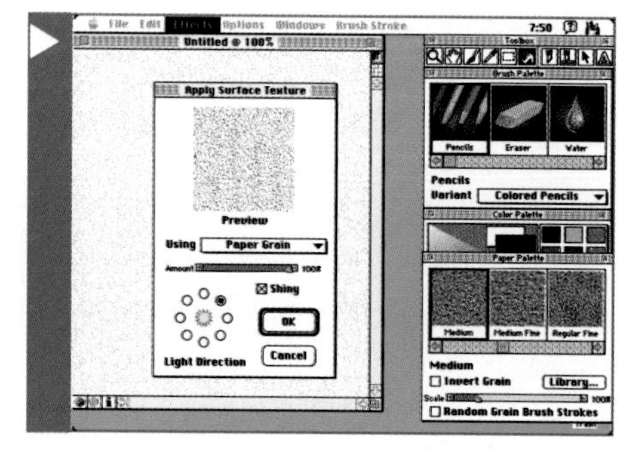

2. Next, he selected Painter's **Pastel** tool and began drawing with flat, broad strokes, blocking in most of the larger areas. This established the flowers, chair, vase, wall, and other details. Dennis then started to work in areas of light and dark, also using pastels. This set up contrast ranges for the painting, and continued to let him redefine his painting. He changed to the **Total Oil Brush Liquid** tool and set the brush range into an almost impressionistic color palette, allowing him to introduce more color and contrast into the painting. Rather than focusing on a particular element, he began to work over the entire painting, almost in a circular motion. He added variations of color to the existing tonal values to break up larger blocks of

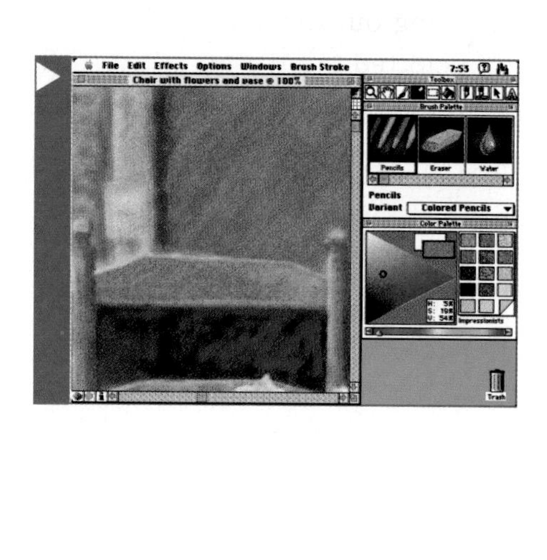

STEP-BY-STEP CONTINUED

color and make them more active. Dennis continued to work back and forth over the painting, developing areas until the painting started to come to life.

3. Continuing with the **Liquid Brush**, Dennis flowed color onto some areas—like the flower petals, the vase, and the wood on the wall—to bring out those areas. He then selected the **Water** tool to help blend some of the tones back into each other. He says this technique uses a kind of pulling back and forth—pulling color out in some areas, then blending them back in other areas. He sometimes returned to the **Pastel** tool for the way it picks up the texture of the canvas.

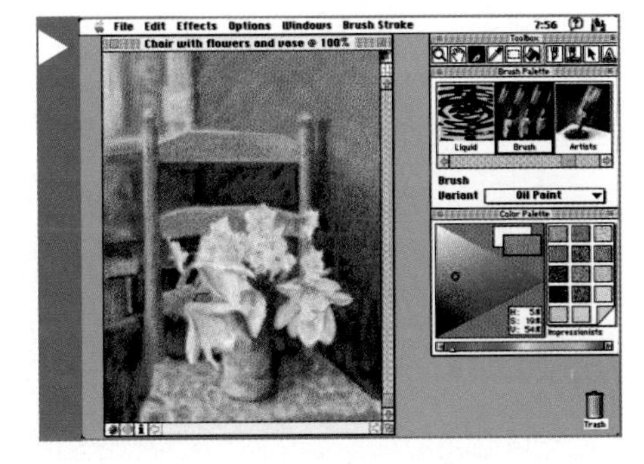

4. Dennis applied the shaft of light coming in from the left corner using Painter's **Lighting Controls**. Since the light source was already established, he simply used this tool to accentuate it and create a more dramatic effect. Once the light shaft was added, Dennis accentuated and blended it to refine the computer-generated effect.

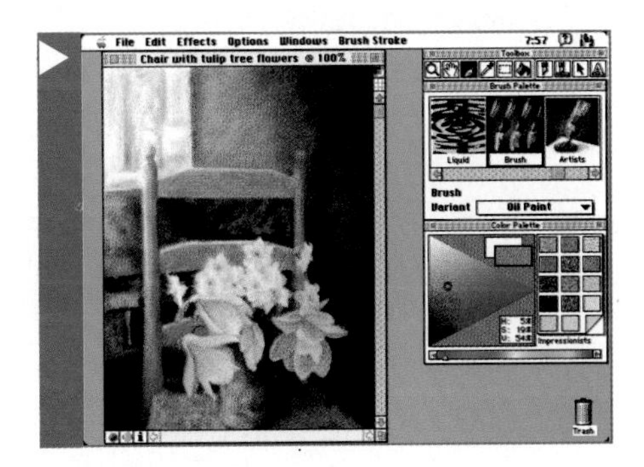

PORTFOLIO

All of Dennis' digital paintings are done traditionally, by eye-to-hand. He usually starts with a rough pencil/pastel sketch to set up the composition on the screen, and the painting evolves from there. No photography was scanned or manipulated to create any of these images.

ORCHARD AT PONTOISE, *an original digital painting inspired by the paintings of Camille Pissarro and Paul Cézanne. Dennis used the new* ***Growth Brush with Trees and Leaves*** *to create the foliage and sky.*

MONET'S GARDEN PATH, *a digital fine art study of Claude Monet's* Garden Path at Giverny, *was done with the* ***Growth Brush*** *and* ***Pastel*** *tools to create a variety of plants and flowers worked over a canvas texture.*

PORTFOLIO CONTINUED

DOCK WITH COLORFUL BOATS, *an original digital painting, inspired by a 20-year-old photograph taken in New England, supplied by a friend. Dennis fell in love with the composition and the random color of the boats and had to paint it.*

STILL LIFE WITH FRUIT BASKET, *an original digital painting inspired by Paul Cézanne. Dennis penciled out the composition for this painting, then painted with the* **Pastel**, **Liquid**, *and* **Water** *tools using his own impressionistic color palette to help capture the Cézanne style and brush work.*

PORTFOLIO CONTINUED

PITCHER WITH APPLES, *is Dennis' study of Picasso's still life, which illustrates the level of painting that can be done even with a basic mouse.*

Ayse Ulay

RECYCLING

CHAPTER 13

ARTIST PROFILE

Ayse received a BA in graphic design from the Academy of Fine Arts in Istanbul, Turkey, and a BFA in illustration from the Art Center College of Design. She was a freelance artist until 1990, when she formed Ulay & Ulay Communications, a partnership with her husband, a graphic designer. Ulay & Ulay provides illustration and design services, with Ayse managing the illustration and her husband handling the graphic design work.

Ayse uses a Macintosh Quadra 700 with 20Mb of RAM, a 2 gigabyte hard drive, a 12" x 12" Wacom tablet and pressure sensitive stylus, a Microtek color scanner, a GCC ColorTone dye-sublimation printer, and a SyQuest drive.

ON USING PAINTER

When I decided to make my transition to computers in 1988, I was not particularly taken in with the available drawing programs. Traditionally, I work with pastels. It's a unique medium that reacts to surfaces. Fluid lines are major elements in my style. The vector drawing programs lack the immediacy of drawing along with the textures, and filters used in the raster drawing programs add a superficial dimension, rather than creating a life-like texture. Most importantly, I feel that they conceal the individuality of the artist.

When Painter came along, I was very impressed with the limitless combination of mediums. All of these ingredients allow the artist to find a unique touch with the mediums of their choice. I like its synchronization with my traditional skills—they are not obsolete in this case. Painter enables me to concentrate on the drawing itself without the distraction of the technical aspects, or insufficiencies existing in most drawing programs.

RECYCLING

Recycling is the first image Ayse created with Painter when she began using it in 1992. The assignment was for Great Western Bank to accompany a newsletter on a recycling program that the bank had started.

The published version of the image was rendered in black and white with charcoal. The figure was excluded from the final version since the client felt it was not necessary because their involvement with recycling was indirect.

Ayse used her original sketch to explore Painter's capabilities and create a portfolio piece to show skeptical clients both traditionally rendered and computer-generated versions of the same image.

STEP-BY-STEP

1. Ayse frequently begins a project by creating a manual pencil sketch on paper. Then she scans and opens it in Painter, using it as a guide for the **Tracing Paper** feature. She has created Custom Brush settings that are used for all of her illustrations. She ended up with eight variants of the **Artist Pastel** tool, and divided them into thin and thick smooth lines with soft cover and grainy thin and thick lines with grainy hard cover using rough paper texture. She also created four sets of fills: light fills with less concentration and penetration, and opaque fills that provide more coverage using the soft cover method. The same set of fills were repeated using the Grainy Hard Cover method to make it react to the surface texture. The **Brush Size** slider was adjusted to various thicknesses for the eight custom brushes.

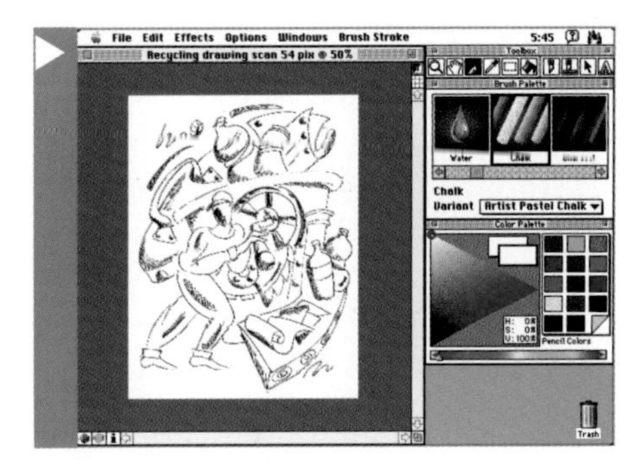

2. Ayse usually creates a **Custom Color Palette** for each piece before she begins. She starts working over her scanned image by placing outlines. Next, she turns off the **Tracing Paper** function and adds the fills without the distraction of the scanned image in the back-

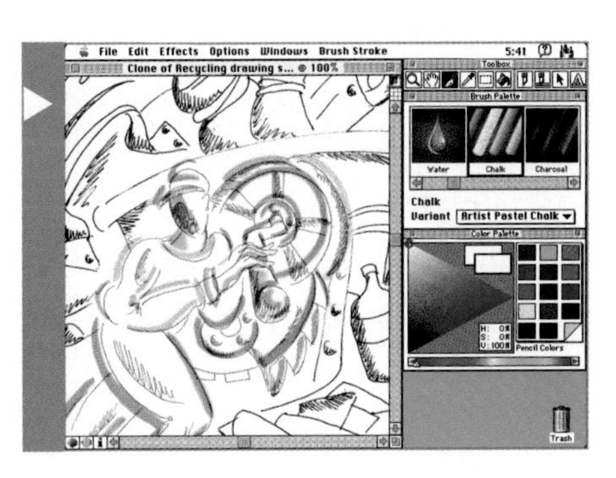

STEP-BY-STEP CONTINUED

ground. In some areas between color fills, she prefers to let the paper show through. Ayse uses the **Ultrafine Bleach** tool to feather the edges of the objects if she feels more paper needs to show through where she added fills.

3. To complete an illustration, she adds accent lines to balance the overall color and to give it a more dynamic sense of movement. When she is satisfied with the results, she outputs her work either from a dye-sublimation printer or a Canon color copier with a Fiery RIP.

4. Ayse saves her work as RIFF files while she is creating an illustration because RIFF files take up less disk space than TIFF files. Then, when an illustration is complete, she saves it in a TIFF format. If an illustration is destined for print, she imports the artwork into Photoshop to convert it from Painter's RGB format to CMYK for four-color output. In addition to the high-resolution final TIFF file, Ayse also provides designers with a low resolution file so they can work with a smaller graphics file to compose their pages.

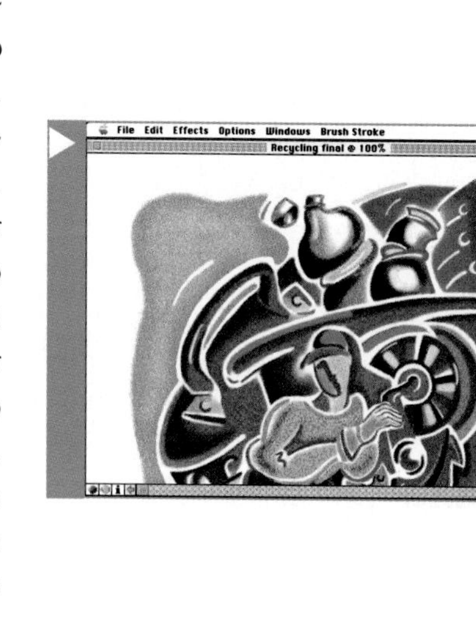

PORTFOLIO

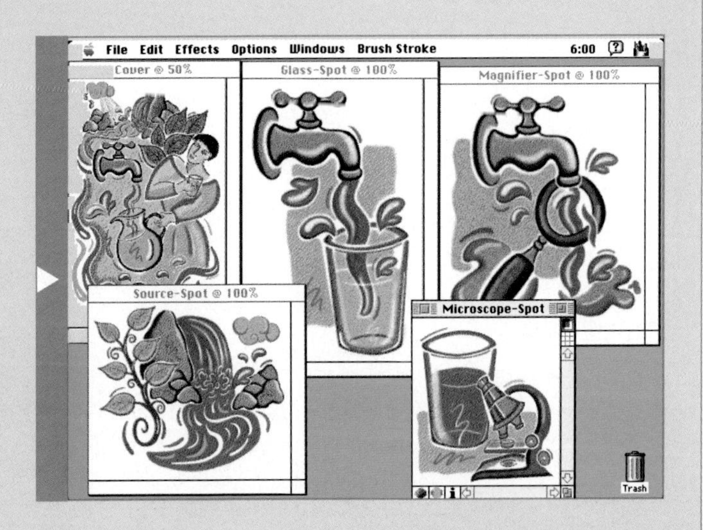

CITY OF SANTA MONICA *is a series of illustrations created for the City of Santa Monica, California.*

PERFECT WEDDING *is an illustration used for packaging for Perfect Wedding (wedding planning software).*

PORTFOLIO CONTINUED

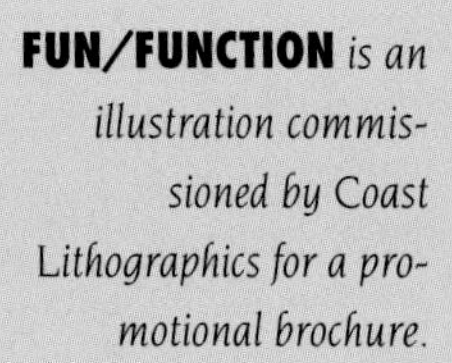

FUN/FUNCTION *is an illustration commissioned by Coast Lithographics for a promotional brochure.*

SITTING FIGURE *is an unpublished promotional piece.*

Gary Clark

WHAT A DAY FOR A DAYDREAM

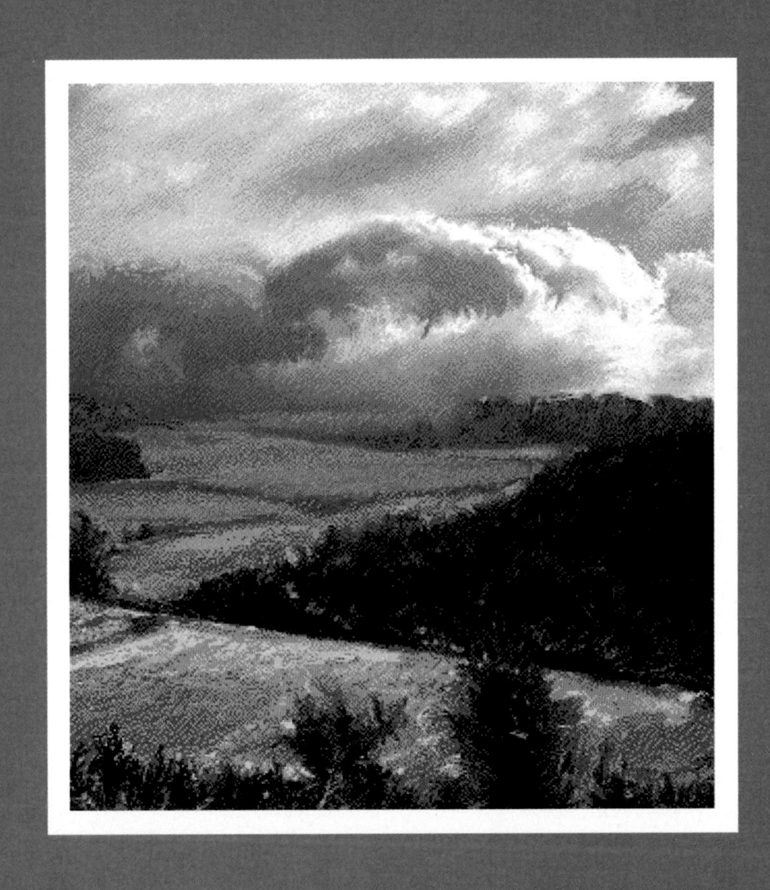

CHAPTER 14

ARTIST PROFILE

Gary is a professional artist, and has been a professor at Bloomsburg University in Bloomsburg, Pennsylvania for 22 years, teaching computer graphics, drawing, and design. He has a BFA in graphic design, an MA in sculpture, and a Pennsylvania teaching certification. Gary is self-taught on the computer and has been creating computer art for about eight years.

Gary is represented by Alber Galleries, Haverford, Pennsylvania. His recent exhibitions include a solo exhibition at the Russell Rotunda in the United States Senate Office Building (Washington, D.C.), a two-person exhibition at the Haas Gallery of Art (Bloomsburg, Pennsylvania), the Larson Biennial Drawing Competition (Clarksville, Tennessee), and the Spring International Art Competition and Exhibition (Miami, Florida).

Gary creates his artwork using a Quadra 950 with 24Mb RAM, a 400Mb built-in hard drive and a 1-gigabyte external hard drive, a Wacom 12" x 18" graphics tablet, a 21" Apple color monitor with a RasterOps 224XLTV video board and a DayStar graphics accelerator, SyQuest 44Mb cartridge drive, a QMS 100-30i ColorScript thermal wax printer (in-house), and an LFR Laser Graphic slide maker (in-house). Gary uses a service bureau for Iris prints or photographic prints via 4" x 5" transparencies.

THE FUTURE

Gary is working on a project with Dr. Helmut Doll of the Department of Mathematics and Computer Science of Bloomsburg University. The official title of the project is "Fractal Landscape Generation, as Mathematics and as Art" and is funded by the Pennsylvania State System of Higher Education Faculty Professional Development Council.

Dr. Doll is writing computer programs that will image fractal landforms and allow them to then enhance the resulting images with such attributes as light and shadow, texture, transparency, and point of view. When they have created visually significant forms, the forms will be rendered. Gary will then use the rendered three-dimensional landscapes as source material in new artwork and used with other programs such as Painter, Photoshop, and Alias Sketch. If the project is successful, the art will be framed and exhibited on the Bloomsburg Universitites campus, and possibly elsewhere.

ON USING PAINTER

I first discovered Painter in a magazine review and then found a colleague at another university who had it on his machine, so I had a chance to play with it. It was just wonderful. It was an analogy to the natural materials I was used to and the interface was pretty straightforward, so it was natural to use. I use natural media now only to enhance what I do with the computer. Sometimes I'll make some studies with inks or dyes or paints, and I may scan those in and use them as part of the work. Or sometimes I'll use them underneath as a template and pull pieces up with the Cloning function.

I show my work, I sell my work. I've been showing nationally and internationally in a mix of traditional and computer art shows. I'm finding that traditional art shows have a lot of trouble finding where to include electronic art. My art might make it into a show as a drawing, as a photograph, or even as a print. I find it depends on the show prospectus how I'll enter the work. I'll even find myself calling to find out what their preferences are in terms of which category the work might fit into. One of my pieces was given a Purchase Award at a the Larsen National Drawing Biannual at Austin Peay State University in Clarksville, Tennessee. It was the only computer drawing at the show.

I'm finding you'll have to read the perspective very carefully and have some alternatives for output—I may have the work printed as a photograph and again as an Iris print. Then, depending on the show, pick the one that seems more suitable. At one show in Oregon, I won a prize and there were lots of favorable comments on the work, but the biggest comment was "Can you tell me what an Iris print is?"

I feel the public has the misconception that the computer makes the work and that you make thousands of prints, but nobody questions someone who makes a silk screen or an etching. So there's this idea that electronic art is infinite and that the computer creates them. I hope one of the things that I've helped to do is to change people's vision of what computer art is. The more people who see electronic art, the more it breaks their misconception that computer art is blocky or the computer creates the art.

WHAT A DAY FOR A DAYDREAM

Gary painted this piece as a more traditional landscape than what he generally creates. It differs from much of his other work in that it is a more naturalistic, painterly, softer kind of landscape.

STEP-BY-STEP

1. Gary started with still video captures using an RC570 Canon still video camera. The land was taken from a piece of landscape he shot as he was driving along one spring day. Using Painter, he combined the shot with a sky from another sequence taken one autumn day. He then worked with Painter's **Chalk** and **Distorto** tools.

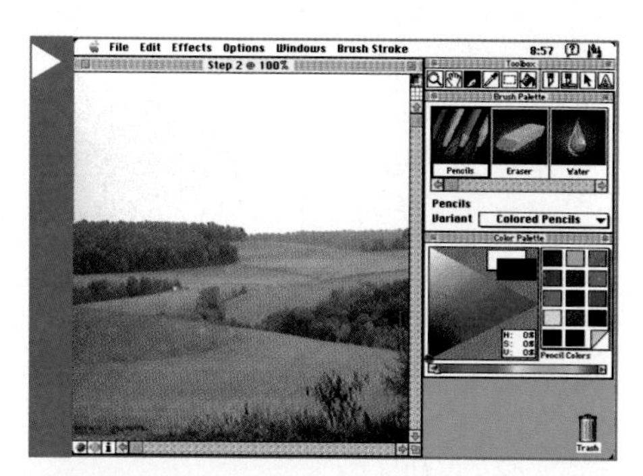

2. Because the land and sky were from different seasons, the colors had no reference to each other, so Gary brought the contrast down by removing the color until he had a gray image. He made the image into a gray template using Painter's **Tracing Paper** feature.

3. Then he started to block in large areas of color so each part of the image became a shape, giving it general shapes and a general overview of color. After that, he started building some subtle textures using Kai's Power Tools. He began filling in more color, texture, and detail using Painter's **Oil Paint** tools for some more texture and color, in particular, to lay color on top of shapes in the foreground; the **Scratchboard** tool was used to

STEP-BY-STEP CONTINUED

add detail and texture (especially on the edges); the **Water Droplet** tool was used to add subtlety to the edges; and the **Coarse Distorto** tool was used to move paint around. Gary continued to use these tools until he completed the process of building up layers of color and texture.

4. Gary created the deckled edge on the image by using a combination of a textured brush the same color as the background and the **Coarse Distorto** tool.

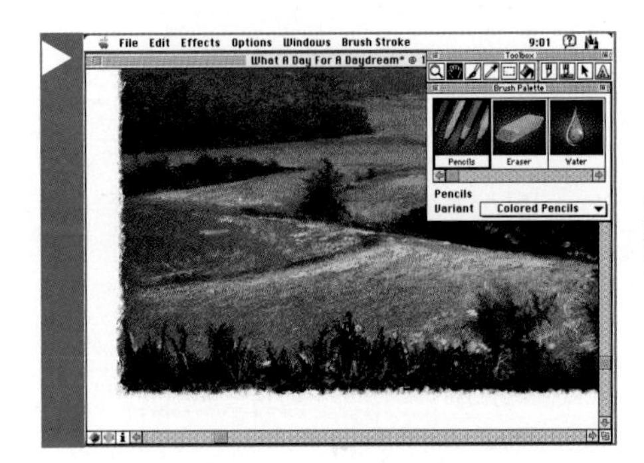

5. To complete the project, he sized the work, proofed it on the QMS printer, then made some color changes. When he was satisfied with the results, he shipped the image to a service bureau to output an Iris print on Arches paper. He had this image generated with a large border so it would have the feeling of a watercolor.

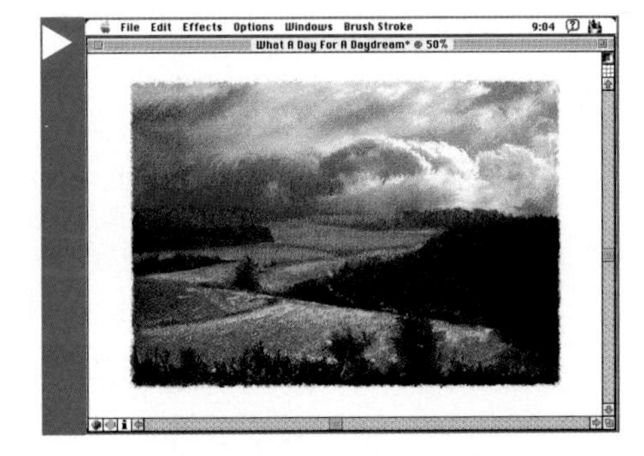

PORTFOLIO

Most of Gary's art is created by using a combination of Painter and Photoshop. The landscape forms are generated using fractal mathematics, and are pieced in and colored in Painter using a variety of tools (Gary's favorites being the **Pastels**, **Distorto**, and **Watercolor** tools). He used the **Cloner** feature to modify the basic look of some of his pieces, and Kai's Power Tools for textures and gradients. His skies are shot with an RC570 Canon still video camera and then are composited in Painter. Each piece is different, and his method of working and selecting the final output is based on reactions to the ongoing process, his original idea, and how the final output is to be viewed. Gary believes that experience and experimenting are important, and he never finishes a work session without making many new discoveries.

LET'S CALL IT A NIGHT

PORTFOLIO CONTINUED

NORM AND FORM

TREE OF LIFE

PORTFOLIO CONTINUED

EVERY DOGMA HAS ITS DAY

EVERYTHING THAT MOVES CAN BE MEASURED

Kathleen Blavatt

MACINTOUCH COVER ART

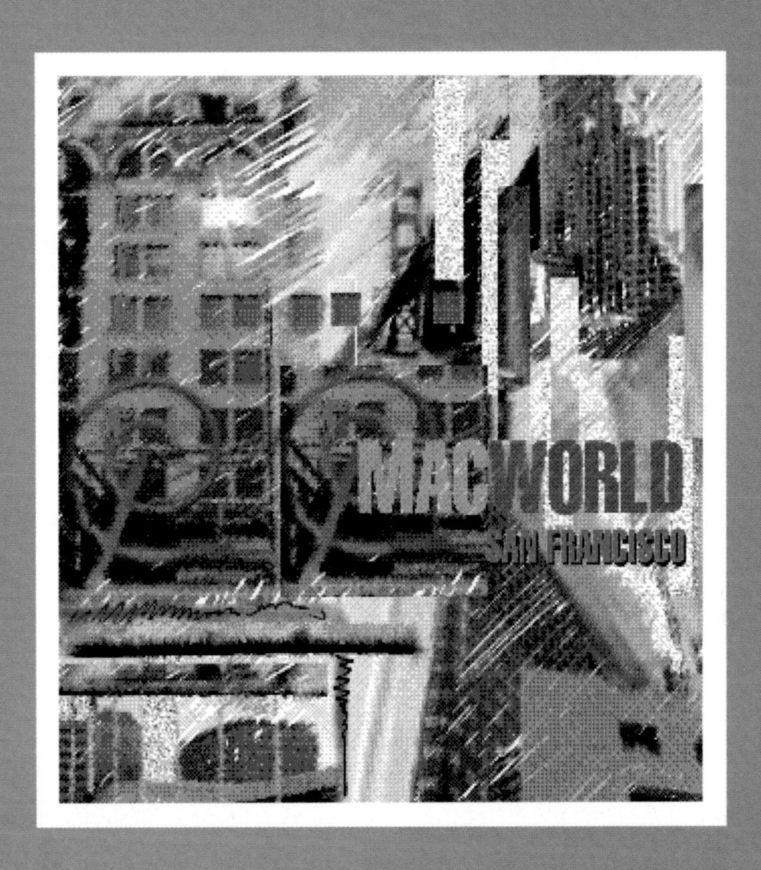

CHAPTER 15

ARTIST PROFILE

Kathleen's work includes teaching fine art to developmentally disabled adults at St. Madeline Sophie's Center. She also teaches traditional and electronic graphic arts at Platt College in San Diego, and provides private tutoring on the computer.

As an illustrator and designer, she illustrates book supplements, designs presentation materials, and produces publications for a variety of educational programs for the San Diego Unified School District. Kathleen also runs a design studio where she provides art direction, graphics, and illustration for advertising, publications, and promotions.

Kathleen was the art director for *Macintouch* (formerly *Resource*), the magazine of the San Diego Macintosh User Group, and currently writes a monthly art column for the magazine. Since 1992, she has demonstrated pressure-sensitive drawing tablets for Wacom at MacWorld, SIG Graph, Seybold, and other computer exhibitions. Kathleen has degrees in fine arts and graphic communications.

Kathleen uses a Quadra 950 with 24Mb RAM and a 1 gigabyte hard drive, an Apple 14" monitor, a LeCie color scanner, a Wacom graphics tablet, a SyQuest cartridge drive, a Fargo Primera color printer, and an Apple NTX laser printer.

ON USING PAINTER

When I was the Art Director for the San Diego Mac Users Group, I would review programs for the Mac. I reviewed Painter at the same time I reviewed the Wacom tablet.

I fell in love with it the minute I tried it. I was so impressed when the paint can came in the mail. The title of my article was: "I Had Died and Gone to Artists' Heaven."

I've always enjoyed my Mac, but now I feel like a real artist again. Not since I earned my degree in fine arts have I had so much fun just doing art for art's sake, and yet I've thought of hundreds of ways I can incorporate this technology into commercial art.

MACWORLD SAN FRANCISCO

Kathleen produced this image for the cover of *Macintouch*. The image was used to promote the feature review article on the MacWorld computer trade show in San Francisco. She was born in the Bay Area and has always thought of San Francisco as a vibrant city. She wanted to convey that vibrancy through this piece, as well as trying to show the effects of using different tools in Painter and to create a montage look.

STEP-BY-STEP

1. Kathleen began by scanning photos she took while previously in San Francisco. The grayscale scans were individually cleaned up in Photoshop, then assembled as a collage in one large Photoshop document. When assembling the montage, she left white or ragged edges around some of the buildings to give it a more hand-drawn look. She imported the document into Painter, and recreated it using the **Chalk Cloner Paintbrush** tool.

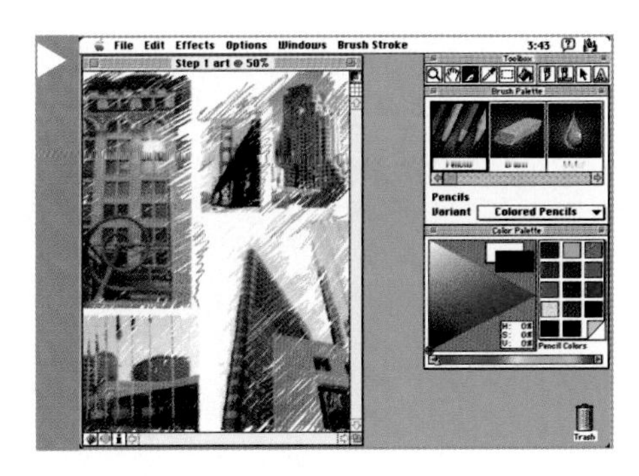

2. Using a Wacom pressure sensitive tablet, she applied drawn and painted elements. She further refined the painting by moving, deleting, and manipulating it with friskets. In some of the rectangular areas, she deleted the existing image to get a white surface, then added paper textures. Kathleen wanted to show *Macintouch* readers the range of effects that can be achieved with Painter, so she used as many tools as possible.

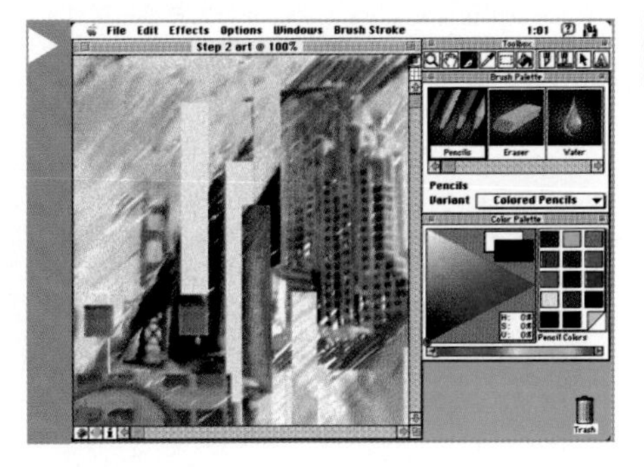

3. Kathleen saved the Painter document in Photoshop format, then brought it into Photoshop where she applied type and converted the image to CMYK for four-color process printing.

PORTFOLIO

TREES *was created by using* **Pastel** *tools refined by* **Water** *tools.*

WOMAN ON RUG *was created by using* **Paintbrush**, **Airbrush**, **Pencil**, **Marker**, **Chalk**, **Paper Texture**, *and* **Water** *tools.*

PORTFOLIO CONTINUED

GOLDEN MONKEYS *was created by using* **Pencil**, **Airbrush**, **Hairy Brush**, **Water**, and **Bleach Eraser** *tools.*

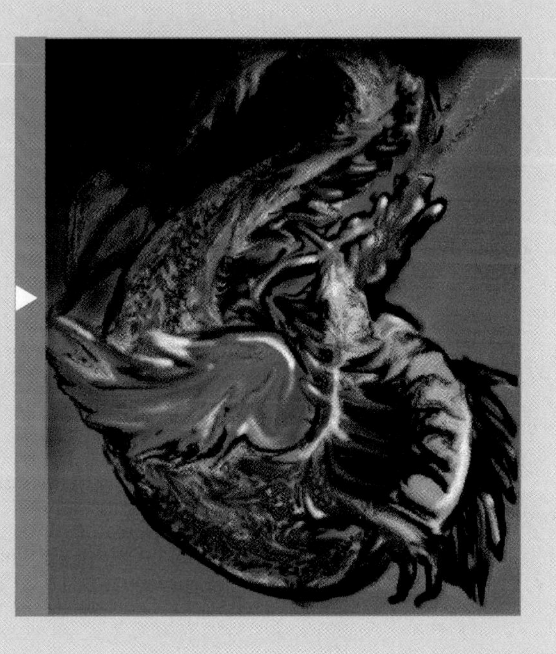

DRAGON *was created by using* **Chalk**, **Serat**, **Airbrush**, **Bleach Eraser**, *and* **Pixel Dust Pen** *tools, and* **Liquid Distorto** *was used to pull out shapes.*

ST. MADELINE SOPHIE'S CENTER

Kathleen teaches painting and drawing to developmentally disabled adults at St. Madeline Sophie's Center in El Cajon, California. The center provides value-centered education that respects the dignity and development of the whole person. One hundred and fifty developmentally disabled adults, are given vocational training so they may reach their full potential as active contributors to society.

The two St. Madeline Sophie's students featured here, Mark and Kristina, have developed their own style and take great pride in their work.

MARK RIMLAND

Mark Rimland was born with autism in San Diego in 1956, when relatively little was known about his disability. This inspired his father, Dr. Bernard Rimland, to establish the Autism Research Institute. Dr. Rimland, an international autism authority, served as a consultant on the movie "Rainman."

Mark is becoming a career artist. Because of his autism, he has a very efficient way of blocking out distractions, and can focus intently on his work for long periods of time.

Mark has worked on the computer since mid-1991. An advantage to his work is that he has no fear or apprehension about computers. Mark's first lesson involved learning the computer tools, type, drawing abstracts, and simple cartoons. He advanced to drawing in more realistic styles, gained more control over the mouse, and learned SuperPaint and FreeHand. He then began working in Painter using a Wacom tablet.

Mark is developing a national reputation. His art was displayed in the Reagan Library, and Wells Fargo Bank hired him to draw their Christmas cards. There is a ready market for his original works and prints. Mark was one of four featured artists in an art show for autistic adults held in Palo Alto, California. He has won many awards and has been a featured artist in several magazines and newspapers.

ST. MADELINE SOPHIE'S CENTER CONTINUED

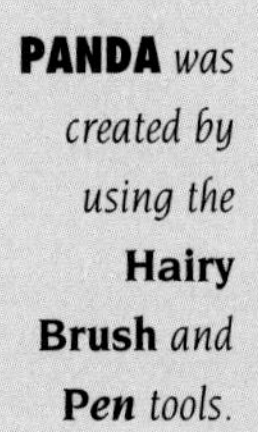

PANDA *was created by using the* **Hairy Brush** *and* **Pen** *tools.*

DOLPHIN *was drawn with the* **Airbrush**, **Chalk**, *and* **Water** *tools.*

KRISTINA WOODRUFF

Kristina Woodruff is an accomplished artist and an autistic savant. Her artwork has been used on many postcards, shown in art exhibits, sold, and has won numerous awards.

Kristina, like Mark, has the ability to focus intensely on her work. She is very passionate about her art, and is enthusiastic about the computer. She'll easily turn out two or three drawings in a two-hour session. Kristina enjoys learning new techniques, and working on the computer is second nature to her.

TEMPLE *was created by using the* **Chalk** *tool for the foreground and the* **Airbrush** *tool for the sky.*

TROLLEY *is a published note card painted with the* **Pencil**, **Chalk**, **Pen**, **Marker**, *and* **Water** *tools.*

John Derry

THE WALL

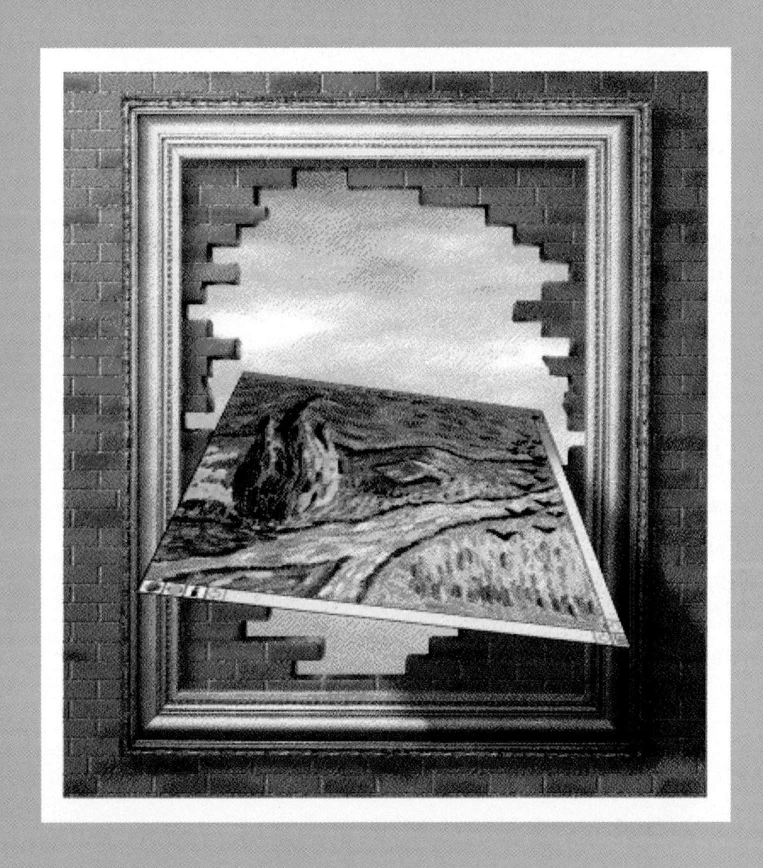

CHAPTER 16

ARTIST PROFILE

John became particularly interested in mixed media work while acquiring a BFA in painting and drawing and an MFA in painting. In 1983, he became fascinated with the computer and immediately got involved with computer graphics. It was the next natural step for him since it tied into the path he was on, both in terms of mixed media and technical overhead. John previously spent a lot of time studying photography and hand stone lithography—two areas that require a certain degree of technical knowledge before anything could be created. Although the computer also has a certain degree of technical overhead, he was not daunted by it.

John uses a Macintosh Quadra 800 with a SuperMac Thunder 24 video card, a Daystar 128 QuadronCache card, a Wacom 6" x 8" graphics tablet, and 3M Rainbow proofs or Xerox color copier proofs to create his digital art.

ON USING PAINTER

I originally worked with Time Arts, *known in the* DOS *world for an application called* Lumena. *I was basically a demo artist for them, but with my background I had a real command of traditional art tools, so I was really instrumental in getting the company to think about the concept of traditional tools—like brushes and pencils and chalk. I was an early proponent there of attempting to simulate traditional tools on the computer. Then* Time Arts *created* Oasis, *the first application on the* Mac *that significantly showed the use of pressure with a pressure sensitive tablet. During this time, Mark Zimmer and Tom Hedges started working on* Painter. *One thing lead to another, and I quickly realized the future was going to be with* Fractal Design, *so I moved on to work on* Painter.

I am Vice President of Creative Design, *involved in a number of activities—from how the products look in print to actual product development.*

THE WALL

The Wall was created in September and October of 1993 for an art show Fractal Design Corp. held at the Seybold Show (San Francisco, California). John was trying to come up with a theme for the show, and he arrived at the phrase "against the wall" to refer to the idea that computer-generated art was being hung on walls instead of being viewed on monitors. The initial idea was to use a brick wall, and he then decided to add a Magrite-like concept of removing bricks to see sky behind it. He thought that an art-related element was needed, so John located an image of a picture frame to signify fine art. He then added an image to the frame that related to computer-generated art.

STEP-BY-STEP

1. The first half of the illustration involved creating the illusion of a brick wall. John began by laying down a brick red background color. Next, in a separate image, he created the beginnings of mortar joints by using Painter's **Snap To Grid** feature to make a set of black lines in a staggered grid. To produce an irregular joint line, he used the **Expression** palette to set the Width Control of the **Scratchboard** tool to Random. Using this as an underlying template for the brick texture, John selected the **Tracing Paper** feature so he could see the image. With the bricks as a reference, he added the random variations of the brick red color with the **Spatter Airbrush** tool. To give the surface additional roughness as well as uniformity, John selected the **Mountain** texture using the **Apply Surface Texture** feature.

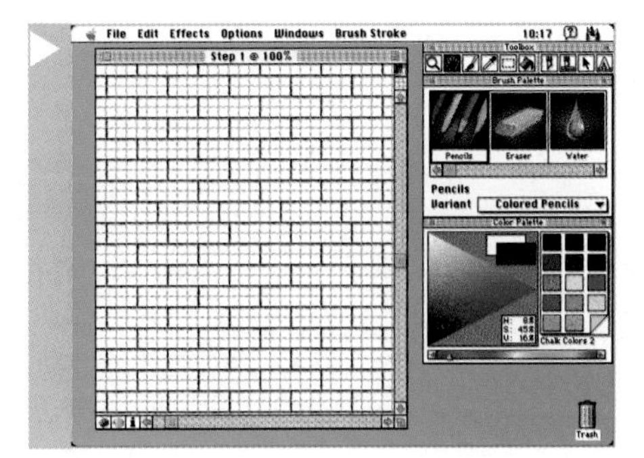

STEP-BY-STEP CONTINUED

2. To apply the mortar joints, John generated a mask using the black mortar grid to create the mask channel in the frisket layer. Then he went in using X2 to copy the whole panel and floated it over the colored brick texture by using **Item: Masked Inside** on the Floating palette. This made only the mortar joints visible. Using the **Fill** command in the active floating mortar element, he colored the mortar element black to create the shadow side of the brick work. He registered the brick work and the shadowed mortar joints together. To create the illusion of highlights, John duplicated the shadow floating selection, filled it with a lighter color, and offset it from the shadow element. Next, he used **Apply Lighting** to create the effect of a light source positioned at the upper-left corner of the wall. The final result is a highlight and shadow effect that simulates a light source from the upper left.

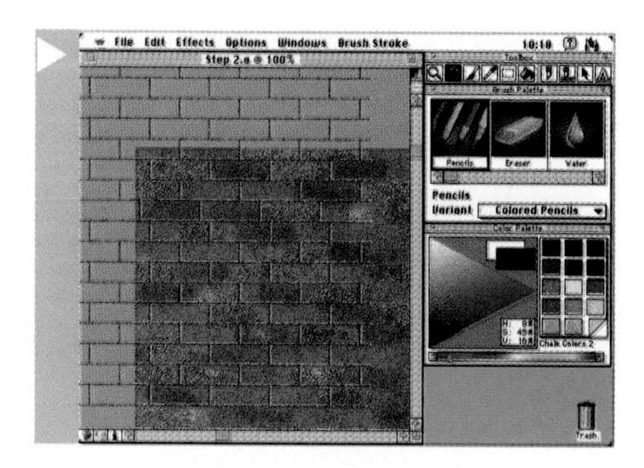

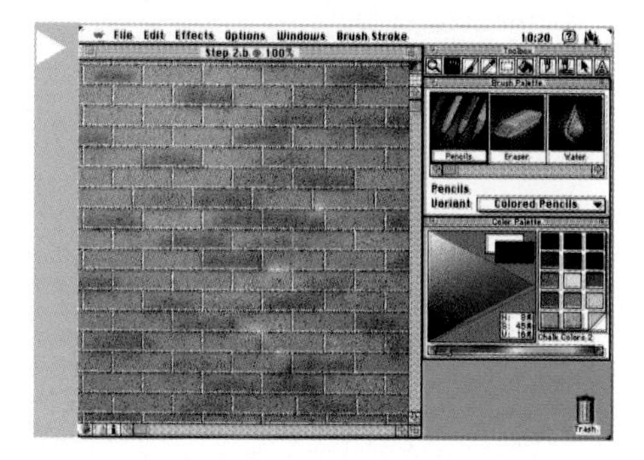

3. Next, John wanted to punch a hole in the wall. To do this, he had to temporarily drop the wall element. To cut the hole in the wall, John used a **Frisket Knife**

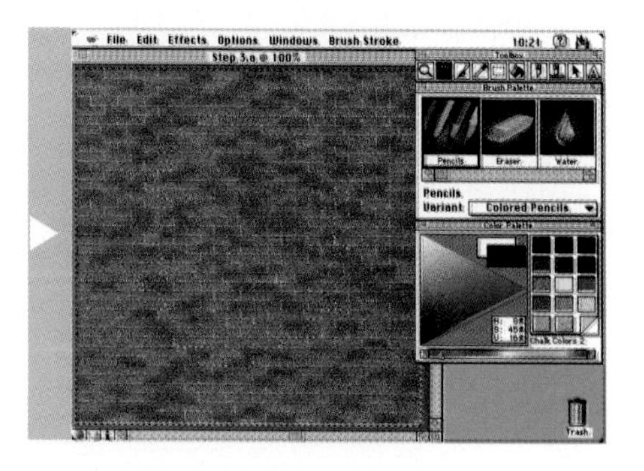

STEP-BY-STEP CONTINUED

Straight Edge tool to cut around some of the mortar joints of the brick to make a zig-zag hole. He created a larger frisket outline around the entire wall, and generated an inner-hole element by converting the zig-zag hole into a negative frisket. When he was done, he made it back into a floating element using **Item: Mask Outside** on the Floating Items palette.

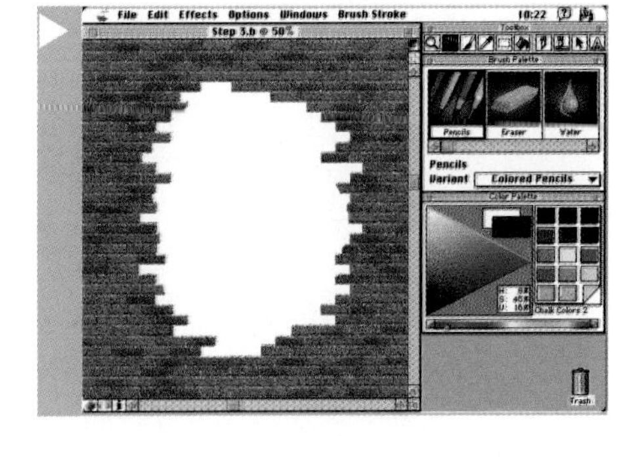

4. To make the hole in the wall visible, John had to create a convincing blue sky. First, he created a gradation beginning with a lighter cyan at the horizon, up to an intense cerulean blue at the top. To do this, he used the Foreground and Background colors, and created a gradation using the **Fill** tool. Then John put in naturalistic clouds. He selected **Clouds** from the Patterns in the Nature library. To eliminate any artificiality, he stretched it horizontally, which reduces the appearance of the artist's hand. John generated this as another floating element, about the same size as the brick wall.

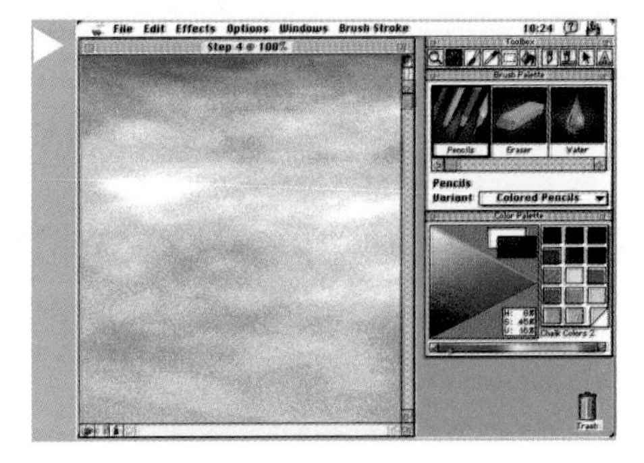

STEP-BY-STEP CONTINUED

5. Using the layering of X2, he added the sky as the backmost element. He discovered there was no depth or three dimensionality to the bricks at the edges of the hole. He generated a special element to create the depth of the bricks as an additional element and applied texture, light, and shadow.

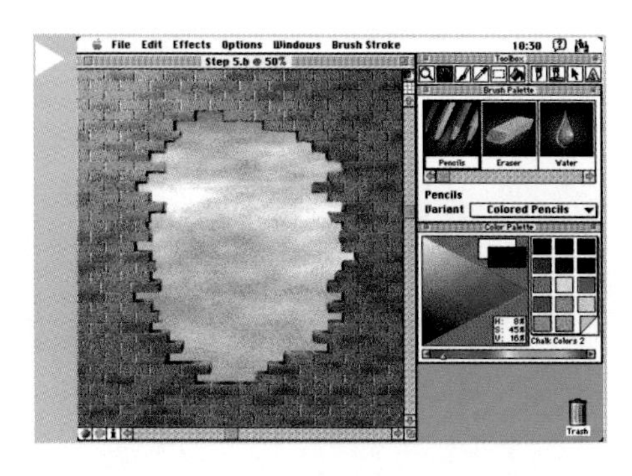

6. The picture frame was added next. John found an image containing a gilded painting frame and scanned it into Painter. He selected it with the **Frisket Knife Straight Edge** tool and then floated it with the **Floating Item** tool. To give it a sense of reality, he copied the cut-out frame, filled it with black, then used X2's Floating Item palette's **Opacity** and **Feathering** controls to get the right look of a shadow, and floated it behind the frame. He positioned it with respect to the apparent light source in the upper left.

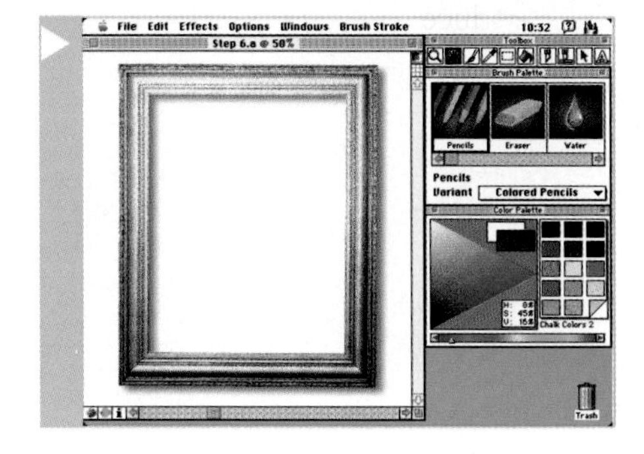

7. John then inserted the Painter-generated piece of artwork coming through the wall, to create the illusion that it was this element that punched the hole in the wall. For this artwork, he selected existing

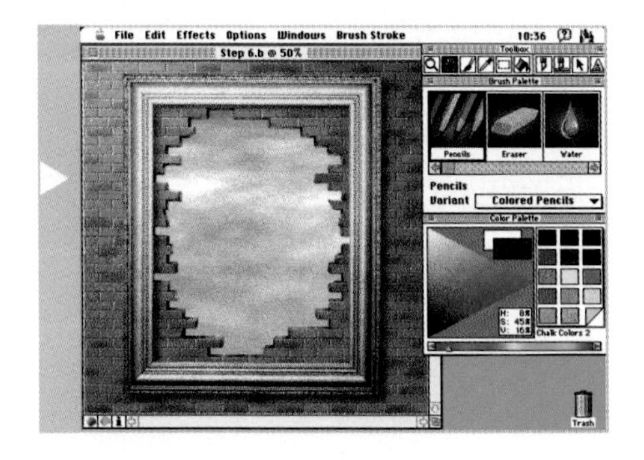

STEP-BY-STEP CONTINUED

art by Fractal Design Corp. President Mark Zimmer. To associate the image with the computer, he opened it in Painter, then used a screen capture utility to capture the image along with the title and scroll bars. He then added the illusion of perspective using the **Distort** command, taking the corners and repositioning them to produce a three-dimensional look with a one-point perspective.

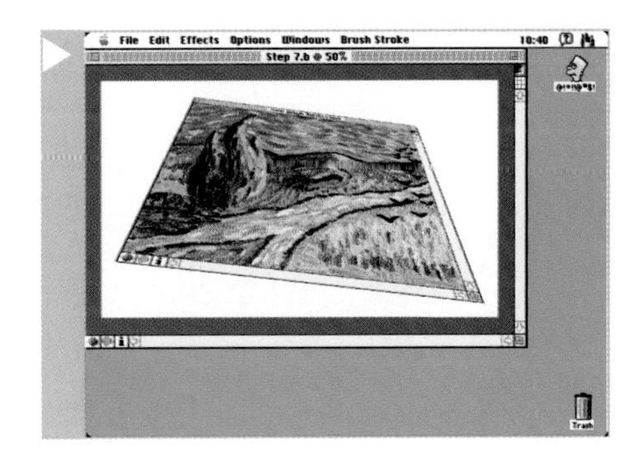

8. Then John added shadows to produce the illusion that the painting was a part of the wall scene. The Lower shadow is a trapezoidal shape that falls on the wall. The upper shadow is on the backmost portion of the painting that is protruding through the wall. First, he dropped the wall and sky elements to create a single base layer. Then he created destination marks with the **Straight Edge Frisket** tool to protect all areas except the wall surface. Next, John created a couple of large shapes filled with black, floated them, and adjusted their opacity to create positionable transparent shadow elements. These were composed

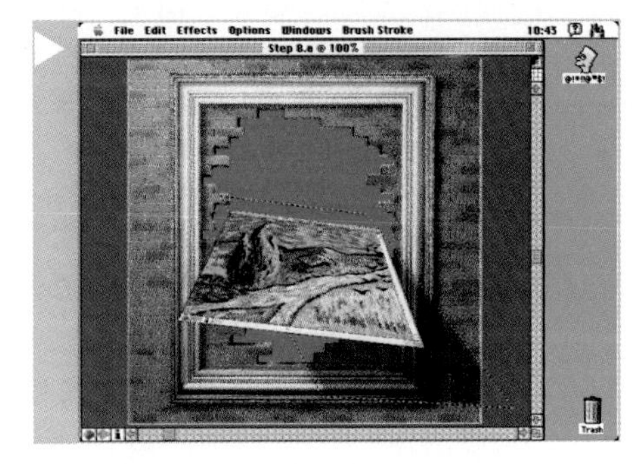

STEP-BY-STEP CONTINUED

together with the destination masks by setting the **Into Image** control in the Floating Items palette to **Masked Inside**. John gave the upper-shadow element a density gradation with the **Masking Airbrush** by airbrushing with white (which represents zero percent density) along the bottom of the painting's shadow element.

9. Finally, John dropped all of the elements, and saved it as a five-file EPS file in X2 so it could be accepted in QuarkXPress and laid out in its final poster format.

PORTFOLIO

PAINTER 2.0 ADVERTISEMENT. *This was artwork for the print advertisement used for the launch of Painter 2.0. John and Fractal Design Corporation president, Mark Zimmer, came up with the concept of "So Hot, So Cool" as a description of Painter 2.0's features. From that concept came the burning ice cube sticker that was included in each paint can. The style borrows from the local design aesthetic of the surfboard and skateboard manufacturers for both the sticker and the advertisement. The main object of this illustration was to show off as many of Painter 2.0's features as possible, so techniques like textures, lighting, marbling, glass distortion, and text manipulation all make an appearance.*

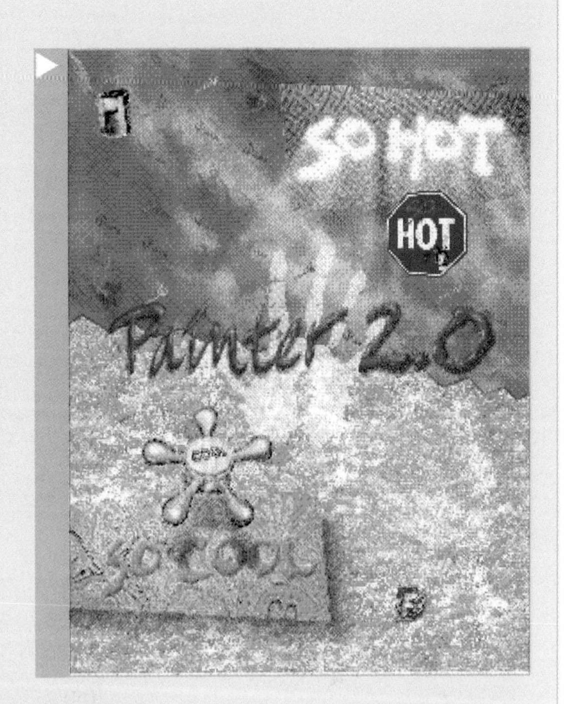

LUSH STREAM 2. *This painting was created as a demonstration of Painter's* ***Trees and Leaves Brush Looks*** *feature. John likes to say that* ***Trees and Leaves*** *let you paint with nature. He wanted to go beyond having to paint each individual leaf and twig in a nature scene.*

PORTFOLIO CONTINUED

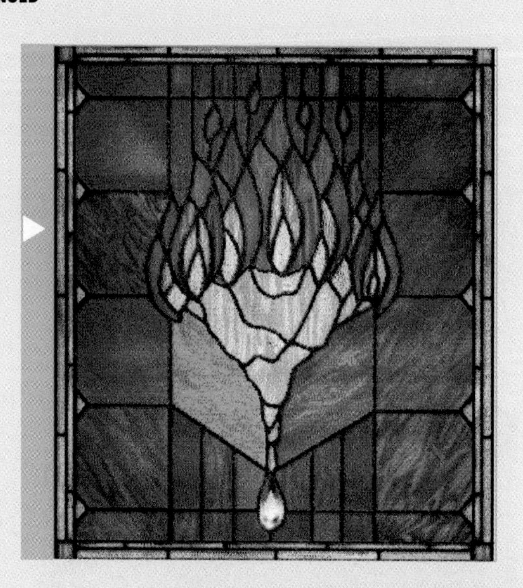

STAINED GLASS. *John thought it would be interesting to cast Painter 2.0's visual metaphor of "So Hot, So Cool" in an iconic fashion. Painter's* **Glass Distortion** *feature was perfect for creating this illusion of a stained-glass surface.*

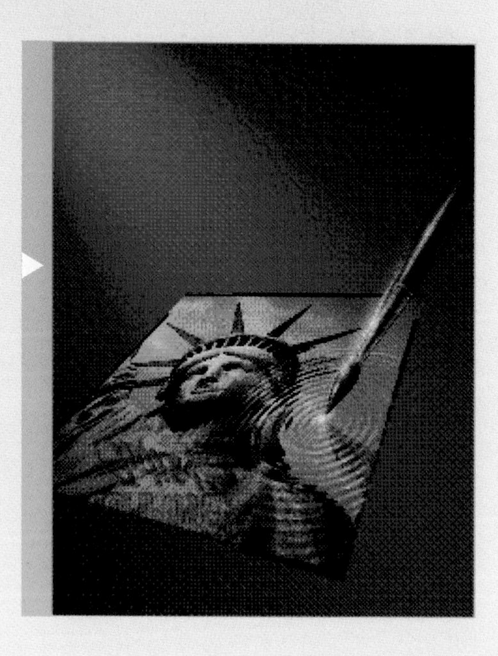

COVER, COMPUTER ARTIST MAGAZINE. *This magazine cover originated in a conversation with Bruce Sanders, Computer Artist magazine's art director. John made a comment that Painter's* **Liquid** *tools let him dip a brush into a photograph. Bruce said, "That's the cover!" John said, "More easily said than done," but you can judge the results for yourself.*

Kerry Gavin

SOLO BASSIST

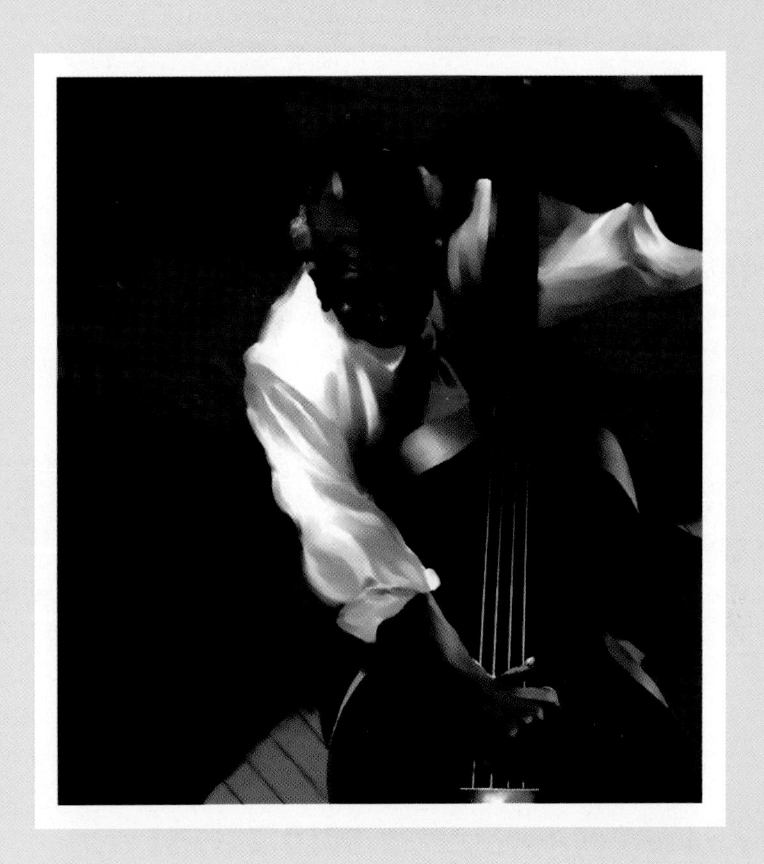

CHAPTER 17

ARTIST PROFILE

Kerry graduated from Pratt Institute in 1974 with a BFA in printmaking and a minor in education.

He is a publications designer and editorial illustrator, with clients that include *The Washington Post*, *Ladies Home Journal*, *MacUser*, *Psychology Today*, *Glamour*, and *Woman's Day*.

Kerry uses a Macintosh Centris 650, a RasterOps 20T Multiscan monitor with a Paint Board Turbo video card, a 12" x 12" CalComp graphics tablet, a LaserWriter Select 360 printer for black-and-white proofs, and Iris color prints from a service bureau to create his digital paintings.

ON USING PAINTER

I've been using the computer in design for the last two and a half years, mostly using QuarkXPress. *For whatever reason, I just didn't want to make the jump to computer illustration. Up to then, I used primarily watercolor and pen and ink. In the last four years I shifted from traditional watercolor to adding airbrushing. Very recently—the last eight months—I began illustrating on the computer. The very first program I really tried working with was* Painter. *I read about it in a couple of publications, and it sounded like it was maybe a little more intuitive than some of the more techie-oriented programs, so I sent away for a sample disk.*

I played around with it a little bit and really liked it because it was more intuitive. I really responded to that. I worked with it for a few months, and in that time developed a dozen or so images, including Solo Bassist. *I then began to use* Adobe Illustrator. *Now I'm using* Illustrator *mostly for income-producing work, and* Painter *for more personal work. I've made a total transition from traditional work to the computer in the last eight months.*

I find that Adobe Illustrator *is object oriented—it uses shapes and forms—while* Painter *is very drawing oriented. So I sit down and draw and paint, which is something I haven't done in 20 years. It's a really different process. I feel that* Adobe Illustrator *draws on my design background, while* Painter *draws on my painting and drawing background.*

SOLO BASSIST

Solo Bassist is closely related to a lot of other images Kerry has created recently: He is also a musician, and has been influenced by that.

STEP-BY-STEP

1. Kerry began *Solo Bassist* in about as traditional a way as possible—he picked up a #2 pencil and sketched out his composition. However, he did that using a Calcomp tablet and Painter's **2B Pencil** tool. Kerry worked with his image until he was satisfied with it. Next, Kerry sketched some broad areas in color using the pastels—mostly purples and blues—to lay down the colors and tones he wanted to use for overall effect.

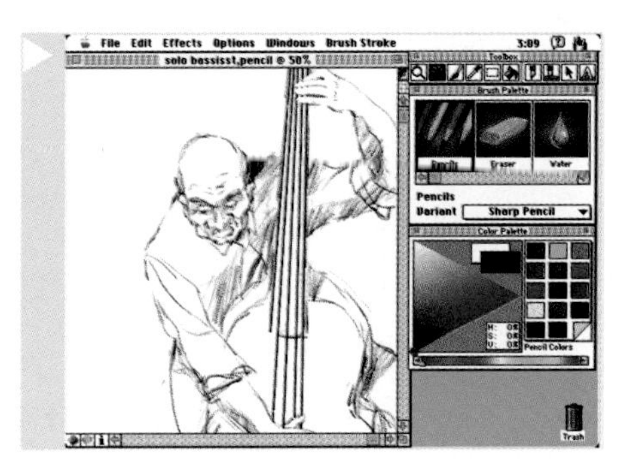

2. The broad strokes of pastels in the background also helped Kerry develop the sense of light and mood that are so important to this piece. He approached Painter's **Pastel** tools almost as oil pastels, creating a smeary effect by smudging them with water. Kerry refined his image by cutting a frisket to the bass player and the bass. Then he started further defining the background.

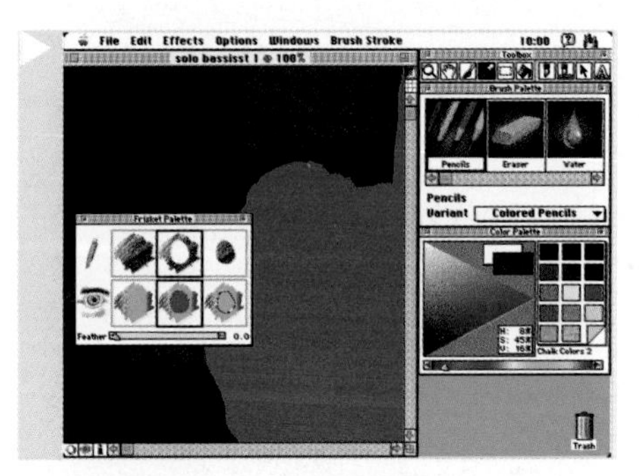

3. Once the background was more completely laid out, he reversed the frisket so the background was protected, and then he developed the image of the bass player.

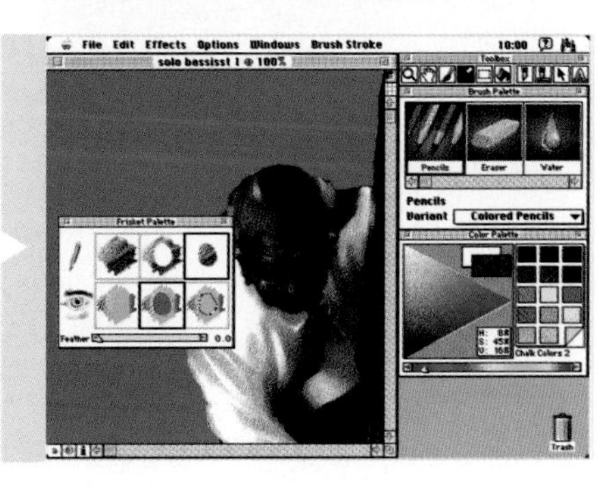

STEP-BY-STEP CONTINUED

4. After refining the bass player, Kerry frisketed out all but the bass, focusing on how the wood reflects the light. He used the **Straight Line** tool to give a very sharp look to the strings. He does not know of any traditional way he could have achieved that effect.

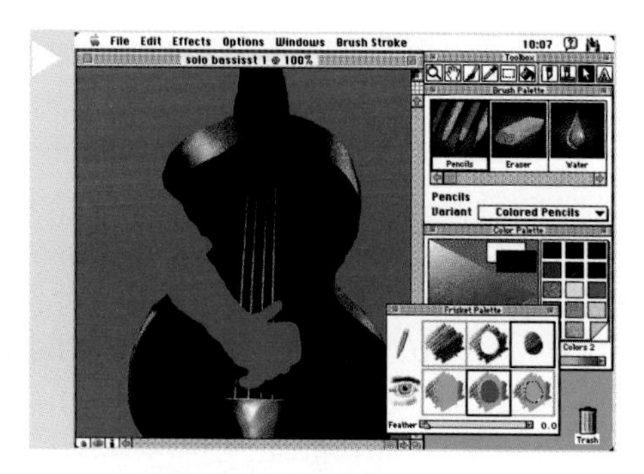

5. Kerry returned to the background by reversing the frisket again to add elements and details to the darkened room—the table, glasses, etc. To finish the piece, he used the filter to intensify the color. He then played with the three elements (background, bass player, and bass) independently until he created a denser, richer color than he had originally started out with.

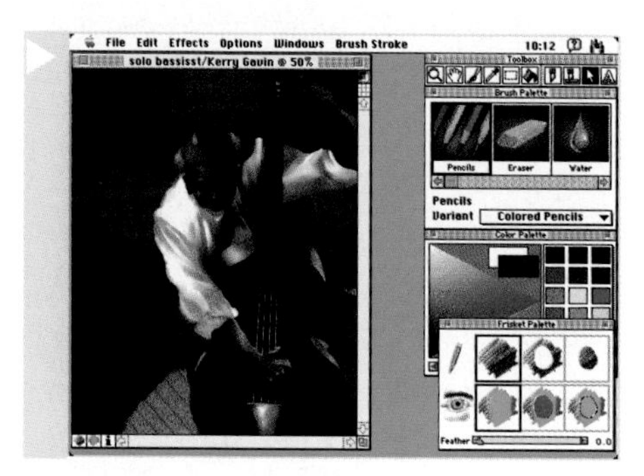

PORTFOLIO

It has been 20 years since Kerry sat down and painted, and he is surprised that he waited until he had a computer to do it. But since he has started to use Painter, he wants to sit down and paint strictly for enjoyment. Kerry says Painter is very intuitive, yet he doesn't know how many of its features could be re-created traditionally (for example, the ability to work with pastels by laying down friskets).

FOOTBALL

GUITAR PLAYER

Susan LeVan

RED FOX

CHAPTER 18

ARTIST PROFILE

Susan has an MFA in printmaking, and began her career doing editorial illustrations using traditional methods. Her husband and business partner, Ernest Barbee, is an architect and exhibit designer who has been working with Macs since 1984. One-and-a-half years ago they began looking for a way to work together, and the computer seemed to be a logical connection, so they formed LeVan/Barbee Studio.

Susan uses a Macintosh Quadra 700 with 20 RAM, a 20" SuperMac display with a SuperMac Thunder Light graphics card, a 10" x 13" SD510c Wacom graphics tablet, and a Techtronics Phaser II SDX (in-house) or Iris prints (service bureau) to output her artwork.

ON USING PAINTER

In the Fall of 1992, we went to pick up some new computer equipment. The salesman was talking about tablets and how much he didn't like them. The minute he described it, I said "I have to try this thing." I sat down at a computer, and the program that was open happened to be Painter. I did a few quick little cartoony sketches, and I turned to Ernie and said, "I have to have this." We bought the program and tablet on the spot.

Two things were going on: All of my work, both fine art and illustrative art, are in mixed media. It became obvious that with this particular program, and other digital methods, you could mix all kinds of media that you can't mix in the real world. You can put down a swath of watercolor and cut through it with a scratchboard tool, erase it with an eraser, then paint over it with oil paint. It also seemed to be the answer to our finding a way to work together. Before the tablet and Painter, manipulating the mouse just didn't work for me.

There are so many possibilities with this program, technically, that it is good to start out doing what you know. Do not get caught up in the technical tricks. Explore it like any painting tool. Then, as you feel comfortable, start adding the extra textures and little gizmos you want. It is like any other tool, and needs to be driven by the artists' concepts of work they want to do, rather than by the technology.

THE RED FOX

Susan drew the Red Fox about two or three months after she bought Painter. It was part of an experimental series used to explore Painter's capabilities. The illustration was completed in an hour or two, and she still uses it as a portfolio piece.

STEP-BY-STEP

1. Susan began *Red Fox* with a green crayon, using the default **Crayon** tool, and drew a quick cartoon fox.

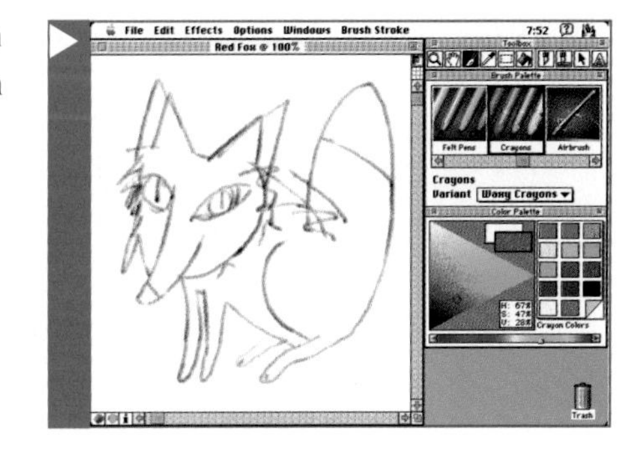

2. She then began filling in color with the **Bucket** tool. Susan selected red for the fox, yellow for behind the fox, and a greenish-gray for underneath the fox. She also used **Bucket** tool to add gold for the eyes.

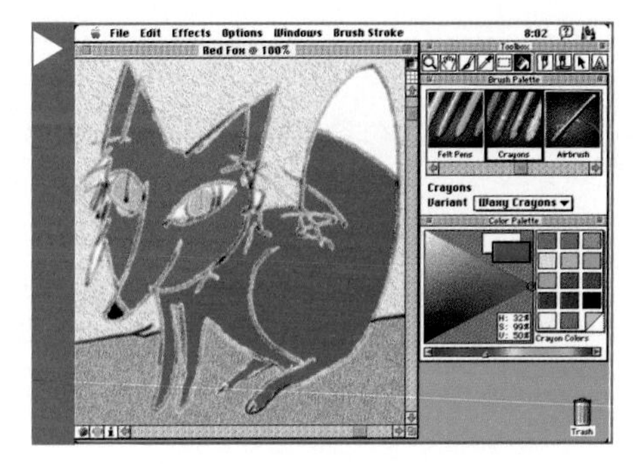

3. Next she chose the **Airbrush** tool to add some orange-red and white colors to the piece. On the feet, tail, and nose, she used the **Airbrush** tool to place some black.

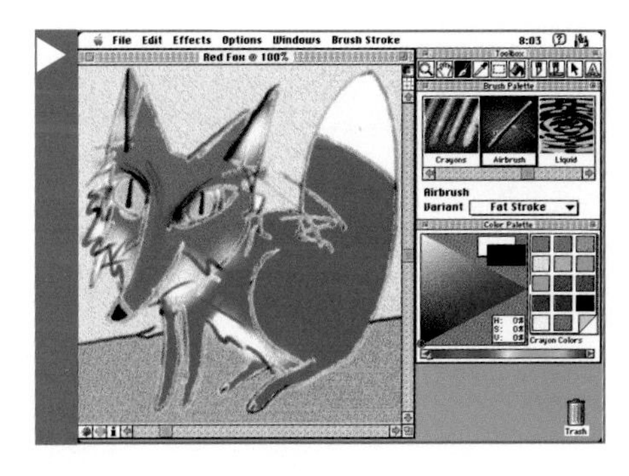

STEP-BY-STEP CONTINUED

4. Using the **Felt Marker** tool, she added some red marks and some black marks around the ears. She also used this tool to write the name "Red Fox" in the lower corner.

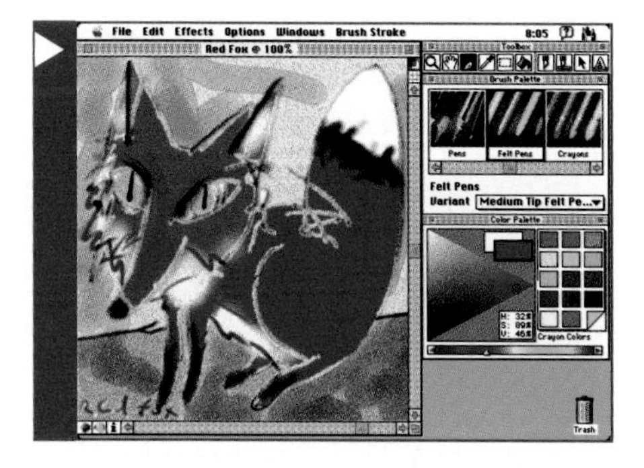

5. Next, Susan returned to the **Airbrush** tool, using some black and blue in various parts of the illustration. The **Watercolor** tool was then used to place a transparent orange throughout the image. To finish the illustration, Susan selected the **Scratchboard** tool to draw the finishing touches, such as the little white hairs in the ears.

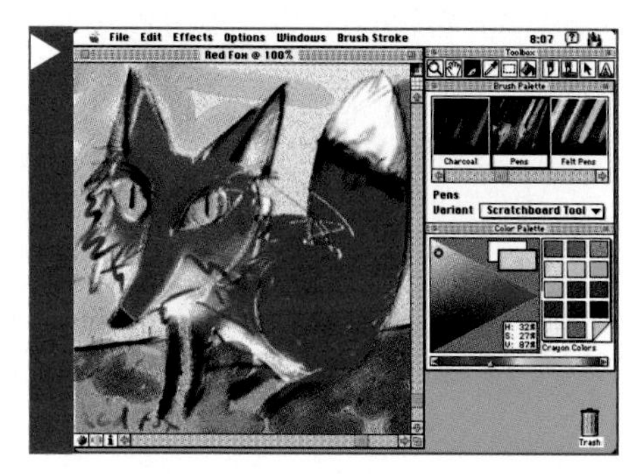

PORTFOLIO

Susan now does all of her work with Painter. She uses X2, including animation and interactive, as well as traditional print media.

One of the things she likes about Painter is that it is completely intuitive and you don't have to be a computer genius to use it: you just have to start working with it—pick up the tool and use it—which is very appealing to artists. She says, "It really is magic. It is like painting with light—the color is very intense. It is pretty amazing."

SHE SITS BY THE WINDOW *was created using a* **2B Pencil**, **Airbrush**, **Simple Water**, **Medium Felt Tip Pen**, **Scratchboard**, *and* **Fill** *tools.*

DREAM ROOM *is a promotional piece drawn with the* **Scratchboard** *tool with several colors on black paper. Additional details were added with the* **Artist Pastel Chalk** *tool along with the* **Airbrush** *and* **Simple Water** *tools on different paper textures.*

PORTFOLIO CONTINUED

PONY *is a promotional piece created with the* **Watercolor** *tool and* **Basic Paper Textures***, along with the* **Simple Water Brush***,* **Scratchboard***, and* **Medium Felt Tip Pen** *tools.*

ARM CHAIR *is a promotional piece drawn with the* **Artist Pastel Chalk***,* **Simple Water***, and* **Smooth Ink Pen** *tools.*

Extensions and Third-Party Software

APPENDIX A

This appendix includes short reviews and descriptions of extensions and third-party software that may be used in conjunction with Painter. Retail prices suggested by the manufacturer are included, but if you shop around you'll probably be able to save some money.

SPECIAL EFFECTS

ADDDEPTH

This is an instant perspective application that allows users to create 3D graphics in line art and type. It offers full support for Type 1 fonts, Adobe Illustrator, TrueType fonts,and Aldus FreeHand.

System requirements: Any color-capable Macintosh, 4Mb of RAM, and System 6.0.5 or later. *Suggested retail price*: $175.

Ray Dream, Inc., 1804 N. Shoreline Blvd., Mountain View, CA 94043. Phone: 415-960-0765, fax: 415-960-1198.

EFFECTS SPECIALIST 2.0

This is a font styling program capable of transforming fonts into display type. The program has 120 unique special effects that work with any font in a system, and can output to virtually any device. There is full color support, import/export capabilities, compatability with painting and drawing programs, desktop publishing, and word processing programs.

System requirements: Macintosh Plus or later, 1Mb of RAM. *Suggested retail price*: $179.95.

Postcraft International, Inc., 27811 Avenue Hopkins, Suite 6, Valencia, CA. 91355. Phone: 805-257-1797, fax: 805-257-1759.

INFINI-D

An animation package that creates photorealistic images and animation. Anything can be animated with the unique visual animation sequencer including lights, objects, surfaces, and cameras. It completely integrates modeling, rendering, and animation.

System requirements: Macintosh II family, 4Mb of RAM, 8- or 24-bit color, System 6.0.5 or later. *Suggested retail price*: $895.

Specular International, PO Box 888, Amherst, MA 01004. Phone: 413-549-7600, fax: 413-549-1531.

KAI'S POWER TOOLS

A filter plug-in for Painter, Photoshop and others. It has real-time previews, channel operation apply nodes, works with 500 colors at one time, and preset viewing.

System requirements: Macintosh System 7, at least 4Mb RAM and 4Mb hard drive, color display. *Suggested retail price*: $199.

HSC Software, 1661 Lincoln Blvd, Suite 101, Santa Monica, CA 90404. Phone: 310-392-8441, fax: 310-392-6015.

MORPH

This program smoothly transforms one image into another (*morphing*). Graphics can be generated from Macintosh compatable painting and drawing programs, and digitized or scanned images.

System requirements: Macintosh LC or larger, System 6.0 or later. *Suggested retail price*: $149.

Gryphon Software Corp., 7220 Trade Street, Suite 120, San Diego, CA 92121. Phone: 619-536-8815, fax: 619-536-8932.

PAINTERX2

This is an extension to Painter that simplifies photo compositing and has new tools for working with color. Multiple floating selections may be moved, layered, scaled, distorted, skewed, and saved as RIFF format. Any image can be automatically turned into a frisket.

System requirements: Any Macintosh (except Plus, Classic, and SE), 4Mb of RAM, hard disk, 8-bit color (24-bit color recommended), System 6.0.5 or later, Painter 2.0, 32-bit QuickDraw, Floating Point Unit (FPU) required for some effects. *Suggested retail price*: $149.

Fractal Design Corp., 335 Spreckles Drive, Aptos, CA 95003. Phone: 800-647-7443, fax: 408-688-8836.

PIXAR TYPESTRY 1.1 (PIXAR)

This software turns TrueType and Type 1 fonts into three-dimensional images. Fonts are converted into objects that can be rotated, scaled uniformly or non-uniformly, extruded, blurred, patterned, shadowed, and embossed, among other special effects.

System requirements: Macintosh II, 8M of RAM, math coprocessor, 32-bit QuickDraw, MultiFinder, System 6.0.5 or later.

Pixar, 1001 W. Cutting Blvd., Richmond, CA 94804. Phone: 510-236-4000, fax: 510-236-0388.

RAY DREAM DESIGNER 2.0

This is a three-dimensional modeling and rendering application that produces full color photorealistic 3-D artwork. This program is capable of handling the complexities of 3-D. It automatically creates lighting, shadows, transparency, reflections, and perspective.

System requirements: Any color-capable Macintosh with a math coprocessor, 5Mb of RAM, a hard drive, 8- or 24-bit video board recommended, 32-bit QuickDraw 1.2 or later, and System 6.0.5 or later. *Suggested retail price*: $299.

Ray Dream Inc., 1804 N. Shoreline Blvd., Mountain View, CA 94043. Phone: 415-960-0765, fax: 415-960-1198.

SHOWPLACE 2.0

Users can create realistic, high-impact, three-dimensional graphics with this program. Objects can be viewed from different angles, arranged in different scenes, and set lights, all without learning complex rendering and modeling technologies. *Suggested retail price*: $695.

Pixar, 1001 W. Cutting Blvd., Richmond, CA 94804. Phone: 510-236-4000, fax: 510-236-0388.

STRATA VISION 3D 2.6

This is a computer illustration program that creates photorealistic, three-dimensional modeling, scene composition, rendering, and animation. There are unlimited light sources of varying types. Transparency, refraction, shadows, transparent shadows, image mapping, texture mapping, and smooth shading are just a few of the rendering options available. This program is also compatable with QuickTime technology.

System requirements: Macintosh II family or LC with Floating Point Unit (FPU), 4Mb of RAM, hard disk,32-bit color QuickDraw, System 6.0.3 or later.

Strata Inc., Two W. Saint George Blvd., Suite 2100, St. George, UT 84770. Phone: 800-628-5218, fax: 801-628-9756.

COLOR EDITING AND PROCESSING

CIS COLORACCESS

This is a color separation software that imitates the capabilities of drum scanners. Users can achieve high quality color reproduction, tonal compression, color accuracy, and sharpening. ColorAccess works with any image save in Photoshop file format, which means it can be used with desktop scanners.

System requirements: Macintosh II, 5Mb of RAM, hard disk drive, System 6.0.5 or later, CIS 3515 or CIS 4520 RS recommended.

PixelCraft, A Xerox Co., 130 Doolittle Drive, San Leonardo, CA 94577. Phone: 510-562-2480, fax: 510-562-6451.

FRACTAL DESIGN COLORSTUDIO

This is color illustration software that offers professional quality image assembly. You can create original images, retouch images, and assemble montages. It supports PMS, CMYK, and HSV color systems. A Photoshop plug-in assures instant access to scanners, other input/ouput devices, filters, and effects. Output capabilities include, PostScript and QuickDraw printers, and high-resolution imagesetters.

System requirements: Macintosh LC, II, or Quadra, 4Mb of RAM, hard disk drive, 8-bit color video card, 32-bit QuickDraw.

Fractal Design Corp., 335 Spreckles Drive, Aptos, CA 95003. Phone: 800-647-7443, fax: 408-688-8836.

ALDUS DIGITAL DARKROOM

This is an image processing program that works like a darkroom to enhance and compose scanned images, such as photos. Some of the features included are automatic image manipulation, detailed retouching, AutoTrace, unique selection tools, and image enhancement.

System requirements: Macintosh Plus or larger, 1Mb of RAM, hard disk drive recommended, System 6.0.4 or later. *Suggested retail price*: $395.

Aldus Corp., 9770 Carrol Center Road, San Diego, CA 92126. Phone: 619-695-6956, fax: 619-695-7902.

KODAK COLORSENSE COLOR MANAGER

This program simplifies color balance for the entire system. The colors seen on the monitor will match the colors on the original scanned photographs, transparencies, or Photo CD as well as the ouput from a printer. Included is a hardware tool that calibrates the monitor for consistent screen display over time and a scanner target for scanner calibration. *Suggested retail price*: $499.

Eastman Kodak Co., Digital Pictorial Hard Copy & Printer Products Division, 343 State Street, Rochester, NY 14650. Phone: 800-242-2424, or 800-465-6523 in Canada.

ADOBE PHOTOSHOP

This is a photo design and production tool that allows creation of original images using advanced painting funtions. It features a wide selection of painting and editing tools, custom tools and brushes, special effects, textures, and patterns. A number of image types is supported including grayscale, RGB, HSL, and CMYK. There is tremendous color control over display colors.

System requirements: Macintosh SE or larger, including portables. *Suggested retail price*: $895.

Adobe Systems, Inc., 1585 Charleston Road, PO Box 7900 Mountain View, CA 94039. Phone: 415-961-4400, or 800-833-6687.

POSTERWORKS

This program can generate point-of-purchase displays, posters, tradeshow exhibits, theatrical backdrops, and billboards. There are many unique controls including tools to configure layout size, vary panel size, gap between panels, overlay and printer calibration. A complete library of predesigned templates is included.

System requirements: Macintosh II or larger, 2Mb of RAM, 20Mb hard disk drive, System 6.0.3. or later.

S. H. Pierce & Co., One Kendall Square, Suite 323 Building 600, Cambridge, MA 02139. Phone: 617-338-2222, fax: 617-338-2223.

BACKGROUNDS AND TEXTURES

ATMOSPHERES BACKGROUND SYSTEMS

This program provides full-page color and grayscale background images, plus Watermark—a special effects software tool. Watermark allows the user to change image color intensity (ghosting) to permit text placement over the background artwork. Backgrounds are high resolution to provide output of professional quality on laser printers, imagesetters, four-color printing, 35mm transparencies, and on screen.

System requirements: Macintosh Plus or larger, hard disk drive with 1Mb free, SuperDrive, System 6.0.7 or later. *Suggested retail price*: $129.

TechPool Studios, 1463 Warrensville Center Road, Cleveland, OH 44121. Phone: 800-777-8930, fax: 216-382-1915.

FOLIO 1 PRINT PRO CD

This is a collection of 100 photographic backgrounds and textures for graphic design. They are in categorized under the headings of Abstract, Fabric, Food, Marble, Masonry, Metal, Nature, Novelties, Paper, and Wood. There is unlimited editing.

System requirements: Macintosh SE/30, LC, II, or Quadra, CD-ROM drive. *Suggested retail price*: $499.95.

D'pix, Inc., 414 W. Fourth Avenue, Columbus, OH 43201. Phone: 800-238-3749, fax: 6914-294-0002.

FOUNTAIN VIEW 3.0

This is an assemblage of 104 gradient screens (*fountains*) and a utility program that allows the user to create new fountains. Each fountain may be viewed in relation to other page elements, then positioned, sized, and selected to change its shape. A fountain modifier is included allowing users to create new fountains of any halftone and screen angle.

System requirements: Macintosh Plus or larger. *Suggested retail price*: $75.

Isis Imaging Corp., 3400 Inverness Street, Vancouver, BC, Canada V5V4V5. Phone: 604-873-8878.

IMAGECELS CD-ROM

This is a library collection of 1,150 royalty-free photorealistic high-resolution texture maps, full screen backgrounds, and images. Included are 14 common file formats.

System requirements: Macintosh II, 2Mb of RAM, hard disk drive, CD-ROM drive. *Suggested retail price*: $495.

IMAGETECTS, 7200 Bollinger Road, San Jose, CA 95129. Phone: 408-252-5487, fax: 408-252-7409.

PIXAR ONE TWENTY EIGHT

This program creates graphic visual effects that can be integrated with any 128 TIFF formatted digital texture in design, video, and multimedia applications. There is a library of unique high quality textures that can be tiled for high-resolution images. *Suggested retail price*: $198.

Pixar, 1001 W. Cutting Blvd., Richmond, CA 94804. Phone: 510-236-4000, fax: 510-236-0388.

POWER BACKGROUNDS

This program features high-tech PICT files in 35mm color slide backgrounds. A manual is included with pyschological effects of color and complete indexes and illustrations of design and color combinations.

System requirements: Macintosh Plus or larger. *Suggested retail price*: $97.50.

California Clip Art, 1750 California Street, Corona, CA 92719. Phone: 909-272-1747, fax: 909-272-3979.

STRATASHAPES

This is a collection of three-dimensional objects for creating photorealistic images and animation in StrataVision. The library is comprised of predefined 3D geometry and real life material attributes. Some of the library shapes are Lighting, Furniture, and Starter.

System requirements: Macintosh II family or LC with floating point unit (FPU), hard disk drive, StrataVision 3d. *Suggested retail price*: $179.

Strata Inc., Two W. Saint George Blvd., Suite 2100, St. George, UT 84770. Phone: 800-628-5218, fax: 801-628-9756.

STRATATEXTURES

This is an assemblage of surface and solid textures in libraries that allow the user to apply predefined attributes to three-dimensional objects. The libraries include wood textures, stone textures, metal textures, tile textures, brick textures, off-beat textures, solid textures, and starter textures. These libraries impart greater flexibilty when creating photorealistic illustrations by increasing the available surface options.

System requirements: Macintosh II family or LC with floating point unit (FPU), hard disk drive, StrataVision 3d. *Suggested retail price*: $139.

Strata Inc., Two W. Saint George Blvd., Suite 2100, St. George, UT 84770. Phone: 800-628-5218, fax: 801-628-9756.

VISUALS

This extension consists of specialized libraries that contain wallpaper, stone, interior, still life, and flooring. The visuals are created with seamless edges. This allows for perfect mapping in three-dimensional render programs and three-dimensional text programs. Included is a manual with individual specs on each texture and hints on how to apply them.

System requirements: Macintosh II or larger. *Suggested retail price*: $50 to $70.

Visual Imagineers, 748 N. Highway 67, Florissant, MO 63031. Phone: 314-838-2653.

WRAPTURES ONE AND TWO

These are CD-ROM libraries of seamless tileable textures. Wraptures One includes a wide range of image categories, such as architecture, astronomy, earth and moon, botanical, natural elements, gumbo, and others. A utility called Browser, is included on the disk, and allows the user to scan the textures and copy them to the hard drive.

System requirements: Macintosh LC or larger, CD-ROM drive. *Suggested retail price*: $129.

Form and Function, Dist by Educorp, 7434 Trade Street, San Diego, CA 92121. Phone: 800-843-9497, fax: 619-536-2345.

IMAGING UTILITIES

ALDUS FETCH

This is a mulituser, mixed-media database that allows users to catalog, browse, and retrieve images, animations, and sound files. Without opening the source application, each image and movie can be viewed, and the sound files can be heard. All file formats are supported and can be stored and retrieved from anywhere on a network.

System requirements: Macintosh Classic, SE/30 or larger, 4Mb of RAM, (5Mb recommended), hard disk drive, System 6.0.7 or later. *Suggested retail price*: $295.

Aldus Corp., 411 First Avenue South, Suite 200, Seattle, WA 98104. Phone: 206-622-5500.

DEBABELIZER

This program can be used by anyone who creates or uses graphics, by providing automated graphics processing and translation. It is a compliment to paint, drawing, or image editing software. A set of functions enhances the ability to process graphics. When used with its internal scripting function, graphics are automatically edited, manipulated, and translated.

System requirements: Macintosh Plus or larger, hard disk drive, system 6.0.7 or later. *Suggested retail price*: $299.

Equilibrium, 475 Gate Five Road, Sausalito, CA 94965. Phone: 800-524-8651, fax: 415-332-4433.

ENHANCE 2.0

This is an image analysis and enhancement application with a combination of sophisticated paint, filter, and retouching tools that manipulate grayscale images. Users can open and edit mulitiple files larger than available memory. To protect against unwanted mistakes and for greater flexibilty, multiple undos are available. High-speed image filters to improve brightness and contrast levels, and enhanced image features that perform special effects are provided.

System requirements: Macintosh SE/30 or larger, 2Mb of RAM, hard disk drive, System 6.0.5 or later, 32-bit Color QuickDraw. *Suggested retail price*: $375.

MicroFrontier, Inc., 3401 101st Street, Suite E, Des Moines, IA 50322. Phone: 515-270-8109, fax: 515-278-6828.

FASTEDDIE 2.0

This program compresses and converts 24-bit images without the loss of image quality. Bitmapped and low-resolution grayscale images can be converted to high quality grayscale images through proprietary sampling routines. The converted files can be imported into page layout, manipulation applications, or used in applications that read and write standard file formats.

System requirements: Macintosh II or Quadra, 4Mb of RAM, hard disk drive, color monitor, System 6.0.5 or later. *Suggested retail price*: $169.

LizardTech, PO Box 2129, Santa Fe, NM 87504. Phone: 505-989-7117, fax: 505-989-9292.

IMPRESSIT

This program provides compression and decompression of grayscale images. Image preview window, thumbnail, snapshot, virtual memory, and Adobe Photoshop plug-in are all included. If automatic image compression is selected, images are compressed when they are saved to the hard disk. The compression process is transparent to the user when this is executed.

System requirements: Macintosh II family. *Suggested retail price*: $159.

Radius Inc., 1710 Fortune Drive, San Jose, CA 95131. Phone: 800-227-2795, fax: 408-434-6437.

JAG II

This program is used for resolution boosting and to eliminate the jaggies (stair-stepped edges) on digital images and animation. Performs on paint images, scans, animation, 3-D illustrations, multimedia, and bit-mapped images. Most Macintosh file formats are supported.

System requirements: Macintosh color capable, 2Mb of RAM, hard disk drive, 8- or 24-bit video board recommended, System 6.0.5 or later. *Suggested retail price*: $115.

Ray Dream Inc., 1804 N. Shoreline Blvd., Mountain View, CA 94043. Phone: 415-960-0765, fax: 415-960-1198.

KODAK COLORSQUEEZE

This is image compression software. PICT and 24-bit TIFF files can be compresssed and reconstructed to their original size when needed. Thumbnails of compressed files can be viewed quickly on the monitor. There is a preview option that allows the user to see a series of images before selecting one to uncompress.

System requirements: Macintosh II family, System 6.03 or later. *Suggested retail price*: $179.

Eastman Kodak Co., Personal Printer Products, 343 State Street, Rochester, NY 14650. Phone: 800-233-1650 or 800-233-1647 in New York.

MULTI-AD SEARCH 2.0

This is an image cataloging and retrieval system. Users can open or search multiple catalogs and print text lists or catalogs. Many Macintosh file formats are supported.

System requirements: Macintosh Plus or larger, 2Mb of RAM, System 6.0.3 or later. *Suggested retail price*: $249.

Multi-Ad Services, Inc., 1720 W. Detweiller Drive, Peoria, IL 61615. Phone: 309-692-1530.

OFOTO 2.0

This is scanning software that scans photographs and line art. Autoscan straightens, crops, eliminates moire patterns, and ensures precision line art. Adaptive Calibration matches the scanned image to the original image, automatically.

System requirements: Macintosh Plus or larger, 1Mb of RAM, hard disk drive, System 6.0.7 or later. *Suggested retail price*: $395.

Light Source, Inc., 17 E. Sir Francis Drake Blvd., Larkspur, CA 94939. Phone: 415-461-8000, fax: 415-461-8011.

Command Key Shortcuts

APPENDIX B

PAINTER

Application Memory Information:	
Memory Information Window	**Shift+I**
Apply Surface Texture	**Command+/**
Bring to front	**Command+Click on any palette**
Brush Behavior Window	**Command+5**
Brush Looks	**Command+-**
Brush Palette	**Command+2**
Brush Size Window	**Command+4**
Brush Stroke Designer	**Command+8**
Brush Stroke: Draw Freehand	**Command+K**
Brush Stroke: Draw Straight Lines	**Command+L**
Cloning: Sets Clone source	**Control+Click on image**
Color Palette	**Command+3**
Color Palette:	
To fill with new color in a color square	**Option+Click in color square**
Distort Command: Enables rotation	**Command+Click on corner handles**
Edit: Cut	**Command+C**
Edit: Deselect	**Command+D**
Edit: Paste	**Command+V**
Edit: Reselect	**Command+R**
Edit: Select All	**Command+A**
Effects: Fill	**Command+F**
Expression Palette	**Command+7**
Eyedropper Access: Enable eyedropper	**Command+Brush tool, Selection, or Paintbucket**

File: New	**Command+N**
File: Open	**Command+O**
Fill Palette	**Command+O**
Frisket Knife: Add to frisket	**Command+Click and Drag**
Frisket Knife: Creates variable width friskets based on stroke	**Control+Click and Drag**
Frisket Knife: Curve-shape and existing frisket edge	**Shift+Draw within 16 pixels of existing frisket**
Frisket Knife: Subtract from frisket	**Command+Option+Click and Drag**
Frisket Knife: Toggle Frisket Knife between curve shaping and relaxing	**Shift+T**
Frisket Palette	**Command+9**
Frisket Pointer Tool: Adds or removes from active friskets	**Shift while selecting friskets**
Frisket Pointer Tool: Constrains aspect ratio	**Shift+Pointer at corner handles**
Frisket Pointer Tool: Enables Rotate	**Command+Pointer at corner handles**
Full Screen Mode on or off	**Command+M**
Grid Overlay	**Command+G**
Hide or unhide Palette	**Command+H**
Imported Masks: Use in floating selection as masks	**Shift+M**
Magic Wand: Adds current selection	**Shift+Click and Drag**
Options: Dry	**Command+Y**
Options: Grid Overlay	**Command+G**

Options: Tracing Paper	**Command+T**
Paintbucket Tool: Build color set for contiguous fill	**Click and Drag**
Paper Palette	**Command+6**
Paper Palette: Converts ColorStudio Fill Pattern Library into Painter Paper Textures	**Option+Click on Library Button**
Selection Marquee: Adjust size of current rectangle	**Shift+Click and Drag**
Space Naciagtion: Enables Zoom out	**Spacebar+Command+Option**
Space Navigation: Enable Zoom in	**Spacebar+Command**
Space Navigation: Move floating selections and friskets in one pixel increments	**Arrow Keys**
Straight Lines Brushes: Constrain lines at 45 degree angles	**Shift+Click and Drag**
Straight-Edge Frisket Knife: Constrain lines at 45 degree angles	**Shift+ Click and Drag**
Toolbox	**Command+1**
Tracing Paper	**Command+T**
Wet layer Diffusion: Diffuse currently selected area (Wet Layer must be active)	**Shift+D**
Zoom Factor: Zoom down when another tool is selected	**Option+Command+Spacebar**
Zoom Factor: Zoom up when another tool is selected	**Command+Spacebar**
Zoom out	**Option+Command+Spacebar**

PAINTERX2

Abort a fill	**Command+-**
Adds an item to the group	**Shift+click**
Edit: Copy	**Command+C**
Edit: Select All	**Command+A**
Edit: Undo	**Command+Z**
Effects: Fill	**Command+F**
Options: Annotations	**Command+-'**
Window: Portfolio	**Command+]**
Windows: Color Set	**Command+=**
Windows: Fill palette	**Command+0**
Windows: Floating Selection	**Command+**
Windows: Frisket Palette	**Command+9**

Glossary

alpha channel

A 32-bit color system used to mask areas for transparencies, overlays, and special effects.

bitmap

A graphic image represented by individual dot (pixels) laid out on a grid.

camera-ready copy

Graphics, illustration, text, etc. in its final form ready to be photographed for reproduction.

chromalin

Translucent color photographic film, sometimes called a *transparency* or a *chrome*.

clone

An exact copy of an image. When using a cloned image, the source document must remain on screen.

CMYK color

A color model using cyan (C), magenta (M), yellow (Y), and black (K) as the basic inks to form different colors. It is generally used for color separations.

color key

A method developed by the 3M Company that shows progressive color breakdown. The resulting proofs are useful for checking registration, size, and blemished. Color keys are not a good method for checking actual color.

comp

Abbreviation for composition layout. A mock-up of a design to be used by the client or designer.

concentration

Intensity and saturation of paint.

continuous tone

A unscreened photograph or illustration containing gradient tones from black to white.

cyan

A greenish-blue color used in process color printing.

desktop publishing

Using computers to produce high-quality text and graphics output to be sent to commercial printers. The common abbreviation is DTP.

dot gain

A defect in printing when temperature, ink, and paper type cause an increase in the size of each drop of ink.

double-burning

A process by which two images are imposed on each other for the purpose of creating one image.

DPI

(*dots per inch*) A printer resolution measurement.

dye transfer

A continuous-tone print produced from a transparency.

dye-sublimation print

A color printing method that uses dye, instead of ink, to produce continuous color that approaches photographic quality.

EPS

(encapsulated PostScript) A high-resolution graphic format that allows you to manipulate and preview your image on screen.

feathering

Blending the edges of an object in an irregular way.

FPO

Placing of art work "for position only" and not for reproducing.

halftone

A continuous image made by a screen that causes the image to be broken into various sized dots. Smaller dots produce lighter areas, and larger dots produce darker areas.

HSV

(*Hue, Saturation, and Value*) A color model that relates to the way the human eye perceives color. Painter uses HSV as the model for its color palette because this color-wheel-based system is most familiar to artists.

hue

The property of a particular color relating to its frequency, or wavelength of light.

ink-jet printing

As paper moves through the printer, rows of minute jets squirt ink to form an image.

LPI

(*lines per inch*) A resolution measurement for halftone screens.

luminance

The amount of light radiated by a monitor.

magenta

A bluish-red color used in process color printing.

masking

Blocking out part of an image to deselect it, to get rid of unwanted details, or to add to it.

mechanical

Camera-ready art that has been physically put together by cut-and-paste methods.

multimedia

Information from several sources using graphics, text, audio, and full-motion video.

pen tablet

A graphics drawing tablet used for sketching, drawing, and painting in conjunction with drawing or painting software.

penetration

The degree to which paint permeates into paper.

pixel

Short for picture element. The smallest element or dot that can be seen on a computer screen.

plates

The actual thin sheet of metal or plastic on a printing press containing the image to be printed. When it is inked, it produces the printed master.

PMS

(*Pantone Matching System*) A worldwide system of standardized ink colors used to specify and check color.

PostScript

A computer language used to describe images and type for laser printers and other output devices developed and trademarked by Adobe Systems, Inc.

prepress

The complete preparation of camera-ready materials up to printing.

process color

Also called *four-color process*. Mixing the four standard printing color inks (see CMYK) to create images.

A transparency is made for each individual color, and the color effect is created by overlapping the four transparent ink colors.

RAM

(*random access memory*) The amount of space your computer provides to temporarily store information. RAM space is considered volatile, as anything stored in it is erased when your computer is turned off.

resample

Changing the resolution of an image.

RGB color

Typically used to create transmitted colors, and the method used by color monitors and color televisions. RGB shows colors by using clusters of red, green, and blue phosphors, often referred to as *pixels*.

RIP

(*raster image processor*) Prepares data for an output device, usually a printer.

saturation

The extent to which a color is comprised of a selected hue, rather than a combination of hue and white, as in the difference between red (a heavily saturated color) and pink (a less saturated color).

scanning

Converting line are, photographs, text, or graphics from paper to a bitmapped image for manipulation and placement on a computer.

spot color

Color applied only to a specific area. At the time of color separation, the spot color is assigned its own plate.

stripping

The physical placement of photographs, illustrations, text, graphics, and color areas in preparation to making a plate.

stylus

A pressure-sensitive pen-like instrument the enables you to control the rate of flow from a tool in a drawing or painting program.

targa file

A file format most common in higher-end PC-based paint systems.

thermal wax printing

A medium-resolution printing process that transfers paraffin-based pigments onto paper.

TIFF

(*tagged image file format*) A versatile graphics format, developed by Aldus Corp. and Microsoft Corp., that stores a map that specifies the location and color of each pixel.

transparency

Color translucent photographic film, sometimes called a *chrome* or *chromalin*.

trapping

An overlapping technique that allows for misregistration of the color plate to prevent gaps in color.

value

The degree of lightness or darkness in a color.

Index

C

D

E

F

G

K

L

M

N

O

P

Q

R

S

T

U

V

W

INSTALLING THE PAINTER DEMO

Before you start, copy the contents of the enclosed disks into a folder on your hard drive. The disks contain the Painter Demo, Painter Settings, Paper Textures, Painter Brushes, Painter Friskets and sessions recorded in Painter. Run the Painter Demo by double-clicking on its icon.

Please note that this demo version of Painter does not print or save your files, nor will it record a session.

Please refer to the contents of this book for instructions on how to create a new document, open existing documents, and how to use Painter's vast palette of features. Use the Painter Demo and the step-by-step practice sessions offered in the book to get the most out of your introduction to Painter.